This book is dedicated to my mother
and my wife, Nancy, without whose
indulgence such a project would be
simply unthinkable.

THE BREWER'S COMPANION™

A source-book for the small-scale brewer.

WRITTEN & DESIGNED BY

RANDY MOSHER, H.B.

ILLUSTRATED BY

CHARLES FINKEL AND RANDY MOSHER

TRADE-MARK
ALEPHENALIA
PUBLICATIONS

Seattle, Washington, USA · 1995

Published in the United States by Alephenalia Publications. Printed in Hong Kong. Distributed by Alephenalia Publications, 140 Lakeside Avenue, Suite 300, Seattle, WA 98122-6538.

Direct all inquiries to the above address.

ACKNOWLEDGEMENTS

The author wishes to thank the many people who made this book possible: my original SpangMo brewing partner, Ray Spangler; Bill Siebel and the rest of the folks at Siebel Institute of Technology; Dr. George Fix; Dr. Karl Markl of Anheuser Busch; Maryanne Gruber of Briess Malting; all the Beer Geeks of the Chicago Beer Society for their enthusiasm and support; Charles and Rose Ann Finkel, Thomas E. Leavitt, Ian McAllister, Michael Thompson, Fal Allen, and all the other folks at Liberty Malt, Pike Place Brewery, and Merchant du Vin; and the countless unnamed brewers who, since the dawn of civilization, have pursued their art with wisdom and diligence.

The Brewer's Companion
By Randy Mosher
Designed by Randy Mosher
Illustrations by Charles Finkel and Randy Mosher

ISBN 0-9640410-1-4

Printed in Hong Kong

FOREWORD

BY CHARLES FINKEL

IT IS ESTIMATED that almost one percent of the American population brew beer. Estimated, because unlike league bowling or even model airplane building, the roots of making beer are planted in antiestablishment terrain. Like activities between consenting adults for which the government passes nonenforceable laws, no one registers as a homebrewer. It is curious that such an ancient and traditional craft received its greatest impetus when prohibition was passed in 1919. The Volstead Act made the manufacture and sale of beer illegal in the United States. The government gave the serious beer drinker little choice and the number of homebrew shops grew like the yeast they sold. Few people, including the Feds, were convinced that the material these brew shops sold was for any purpose other than homebrewing, in spite of the myriad cookbooks detailing other uses of malt extract and adding such warnings as, "Caution, please don't add yeast and sugar to this malt extract or an alcoholic beverage could result." Repeal of the so-called "Noble Experiment" in 1933 did little to slow the ferment. In spite of the availability of legal beer, the government had, in effect, taught the American brewer that homebrewing was either very cheap, very good, or both, and the movement continued to gain momentum. There was hardly a burp, forty-six years later, when President Jimmy Carter, a teetotaller himself, signed a bill making homebrewing legal. Coincidentally, the President's brother embarrassed the whole country, and beer enthusiasts in particular, with his infamy as a beer drinker. He even licensed breweries to produce a mass-marketed swill called Billy Beer.

People often tell the story of Grandpa's homebrew blowing up in the closet. They talk about its legendary kick, but seldom do they boast about its adherence to a traditional brewing style. Let's face it, until the last few years, Grandpa had few good role models when it came to making beer. For the forty years after prohibition, almost every commercial brewer in America made light lager, full of adjuncts, with little taste.

Recently, a beer renaissance has given American beer drinkers something to stout about. Today, retailers in most parts of the country offer excellent examples of each of the classic brewing styles. Many of the finest and most famous ales and lagers of England, Germany, Belgium, and the Czech Republic are now available in the United States. More than 300 local microbreweries and brewpubs, most of them founded by homebrewers gone amok, add to the excitement.

Like some of the most delicious breads, which are baked at home, many of the best beers are homebrewed. As commercial examples of Oatmeal and Imperial Stout, Brown and Pale Ale, Barley Wine and Porter, Trappist Ale and Lambic beer, White and Weizen, smoked beer, and a host of beers brewed to traditional recipes becomes more available, homebrewers are increasingly challenged. One of the finest beers I have ever tasted was, appropriately, called Nirvana and was brewed by Randy Mosher, H.B. (Home Brewer), the author of this book. The delicate and satisfying beer was a real surprise since it was seasoned with chanterelle mushrooms in addition to hops. It was the perfect complement to poached salmon. Like many of the top homebrewers, Randy is guided by tradition, but not hamstrung by it.

Randy is a very exceptional brewer and an even better teacher. Randy does a superb job of balancing the art and science of brewing. His *Brewer's Companion* is the result of hundreds of batches of beer, extensive research (most never done before), and more than six years of writing and design work. Like the beers he discusses, this book is a classic in the literature of beer and homebrewing.

CHARLES FINKEL
Seattle, Washington

Welcome to the revised edition of *The Brewer's Companion*. It was created in response to my own needs as a homebrewer—to have the tools to make my beer more consistent, better tasting, and more stylistically correct. All of which makes brewing more gratifying.

Why Brew?

Anyone not sleeping through this very modern age can see these are crazy times. Even if you don't take it all too seriously, it can tax your sanity. Brewing your own beer is a way to get back to something basic and honorable. As homebrewers, we can rightly feel connected to a most ancient tradition.

There are challenges, rewards, and even a simple spirituality to the act of making beer. But the mystical part is automatic—you don't have to work at it.

Science is the part you do have to work at. Not science, strictly speaking, but technology. It is an empirical activity. The ingredients and forces react with one another in predictable, repeatable ways. More or less.

These elements are at work as you brew (whether or not you know about them), so you may as well understand them. Alchemy as a hobby is fine fun, but the glorious heights of the brewer's art will not be reached without true understanding and control of the biochemical process.

Homebrewing is a real blessing for those of us who are wild about really good beer. It's an instant and inexpensive access to the world of great beers. Wonderfulness is within our grasp.

In fact, it's much easier to make world-class beer at home than to make world-class wine. Agricultural constraints shape the character of wine: soil, weather, cultivation. Wine is an intensely regional product, forever tied to the grapes of a particular region or even of a single vineyard. Modern viticulture has changed this somewhat, but not for what critics call "serious wines."

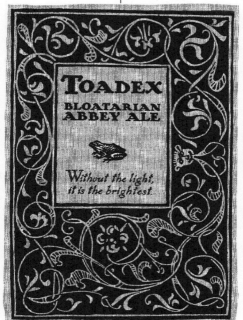

TOADEX
BLOATARIAN
ABBEY ALE

*Without the light,
it is the brightest.*

In beer these factors play a smaller role. It's even possible to create very different beers from identical ingredients. Or similar beers from different ingredients. It's the recipe and process that really matters.

As enlightened homebrewers, we can brew beers as good as any in the world. As rare or as strange as beer from the tiniest Belgian cottage brewery. No idea is too goofy to pursue.

And, just like the big brewers, we can brew with the seasons and for our market. But unlike the big guys, we can brew just to suit our whims. Unregulated, unstructured, uninhibited, unencumbered, but definitely not uninspired.

We can now get malt from Germany, hops from the Czech Republic, and yeast from Belgium. If we want to take the trouble, we can make our tap water match the water of Munich, Burton-on-Trent, or Edinburgh. We can even roast grains in our ovens to match malt types not made commercially anymore.

As homebrewers, we can be flexible with our equipment. It's no big deal just to put another pot on the stove and start decoction mashing.

About This Book

My hope is that *The Brewer's Companion* will give you information to improve the beer you brew. It covers all the main topics on beer and brewing.

The first three sections describe beer in its many forms. Next come several sections devoted to the ingredients in beer. After these are chapters on the brewing and fermentation process, a section on problems, conversion tables, and a glossary.

The worksheets are the core of this book and are the key to brewing exactly the kind of beer you want, time after time. In most cases there are two sets of each worksheet. Copy them as needed and begin building your own historical homebrewing record. Good luck and good brewing!

Getting Started

It's so simple.

Malt, hops, water, yeast. With just four ingredients, you can make almost any kind of beer.

It's so incredibly complicated.

Dozens of varieties of malts and hops, countless yeast strains, and innumerable biochemical reactions are involved in the creation of beer. The brewing process can be controlled to vary the proportions of more than 800 flavor chemicals in beer, making possible a truly limitless variety of distinctly different beers.

As homebrewers, we all face the problem of handling the tremendous complexity of the brewing process. How are we to unlock the secret of perfect beer? Art is vital, but it's not enough. Persistence is necessary, but insufficient. The key to the magical art of brewing is technology.

When you brew, you're really operating a tiny biochemical factory. Starting with raw materials, using enzymes, heat and other processes, you create something new from the materials you begin with. It's just too much to keep track of in your head.

Commercial breweries keep detailed records of all pertinent aspects of brewing, their aim being to repeat the same beer year in and year out. Homebrewers are more adventurous. Our goals are different. We might brew an American porter in one batch, try a German dunkel weizen, and follow that with an English bitter. What matters is not consistency so much as predictability. Also, we typically use more types of malt, hops, and yeast than a commercial brewery. We don't have the luxury of varying one thing at a time, batch after batch. Most of us like to keep our cellars filled with lots of differently delicious brews. We need something that works with our broad interests.

Before You Brew

Decide on the beer you want to brew. An ale or a lager, or something else? Fix the three big variables in your mind: color, original gravity, and hop-malt balance. Compare your mental picture to the various styles listed in **Section 2, Overview of Beer History & Styles**. Write down the numbers for International Bitterness Units (IBUs), Homebrew Color Units, and Original Gravity. These three parameters define the broad strokes of a beer's style.

In addition to these parameters, there is an overlay of national style that defines much of a beer's character. This is determined by choice of ingredients and techniques. There is a good deal of detail on recipe formulation in **Section 13–1, Beer Design**. After color, gravity, and bitterness, the three most important things are mash type, yeast, and hop varieties.

The mash technique, in turn, determines the type of malt to be mashed. Likewise, ale and lager yeast each have a working temperature range that produces the most characteristic flavor for their style.

All these things need to be decided in advance of brewing or recipe formulation.

Using the Worksheets

The next thing is to figure out how to hit your targets. Use the recipe worksheets (either a full sheet or a quarter-page sheet) in **Section 13.**

The page is broken into sections, which consider each process and type of

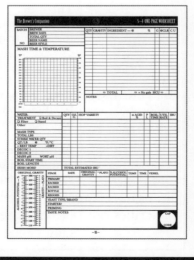

ingredient separately.

Start with **Section 6, Grains & Adjuncts** and write down the grain types you wish to use. Then, flip to the **Quick Reference Chart** (either **5–2** or **5–3**) that's the right size for the batch you're brewing. This is what you use to determine degrees of gravity from various grain types at different amounts. You'll need a calculator for this simple math. Be aware that the extract figures are theoretical maximums and that you will probably be brewing between 85 and 90 percent of these, so aim a little high. Add up the gravities contributed by the various ingredients to get a total.

Color

You can calculate color in a very simple way. Write the grain color number in the "@" column and multiply by the number of pounds; enter that product in the "Color Units" column. Add 'em up and divide by the number of gallons in the batch.

Hop bitterness can be figured in a similar simplified manner. For all hops boiled 20 minutes or more, multiply the hop alpha acid by the number of ounces in the brew. Multiply that number by a constant to give you a figure roughly equivalent to the Hop Bittering Units used by commercial breweries. To work backward from a known hop bitterness, use the **Hop Estimator, Section 8–3**.

Brewing It

You'll be filling out one worksheet for every batch you brew. **Section 5, The Worksheets** has detailed instructions. You can draw the temperature profile to follow during the mash on the mash chart and note the water treatment in the appropriate section. As the brew proceeds, you

BIG THREE COLOR VARIABLES

BEER COLOR	The darkness or lightness of beer is due to chemicals called melanoidins, formed during malt kilning and wort boiling. In practice, beer color comes from a mix of different pale and colored malts, which add up to a particular color. In this book, beer color is expressed in the American measurements, °SRM, and grain color in °Lovibond. °L grain color ranges from 1.2 for lager malt, to 1000 for black malt. Beer color ranges from 2°SRM for pale American lagers to 50+ for stouts.
ORIGINAL GRAVITY	This is the strength of the wort before it is fermented, a measure of all the carbohydrates present in the wort. These dissolved sugars and dextrins are denser than water, and so the wort can be measured by its specific gravity. The gravity of a beer determines much of its character and contributes to the alcohol content, flavor, intensity, head quality, and mouthfeel.
	There are many different scales used to measure specific gravity, but only a few are used in brewing. First is original gravity. This is really specific gravity, which is the density of a liquid expressed as a factor of the strength of water. A solution that has a specific gravity of 1.050 is 1.05 times the density of water. In brewing, it is customary to drop the decimal point, so 1.050 becomes 1050. When calculating, drop the "1", or you'll just get nonsense.
	The other two scales commonly used in brewing are Balling and Plato. Both express gravity as a percentage of pure sugar. Plato is the newer and more accurate of the two, but for homebrewing, they may be thought of as interchangeable.
HOP BITTERNESS	Bitterness provides a counterpoint to the sweet stickiness of malt. The yin to balance the malt's yang, if you want to get Taoist about it. Most beer types have a characteristic bittering level, a balance that strongly affects the overall flavor. What is most important is the malt-to-hop ratio. Stronger beers need to be more highly hopped to maintain their specific hop-malt balance.
	In breweries, hop bitterness is measured directly. The International Bittering Unit (IBU) is the content, in parts-per-million, of isomerized hop resins in beer. In homebrewing, this can be estimated. Homebrewers sometimes estimate the amount of alpha acids added to the wort, a very different figure (ounces x alpha acid % ÷ gallons = Homebrew Bittering Units, or Alpha Acid Units). To accurately estimate IBUs, it is necessary to calculate for the efficiency at which the hops are incorporated into the wort during boiling, a factor known as utilization. For more information, see **Section 8, Hops**.

can record specific data—times, temperatures, quantities and procedures—as well as track the progress of fermentation and conditioning. Later, you can perform analyses to figure the percentage of alcohol and efficiency of mashing.

Fudge Factors

Numbers, however, will only take you so far. There are many factors that are too much trouble to work out numerically, at least in a homebrew situation.

Hops

Variety, growing locality, and weather during the growing season all affect the flavor and bittering power (alpha acid percentage) of hops. Many suppliers have their hops analyzed and include an alpha acid percentage number along with the hop order. The alpha acid content declines with age, but generally, hops lose their bittering power slowly. Storage conditions and hop variety affect how well hops age. Once in beer, hop bitterness declines as the beer ages, with a half-life of about six to twelve months. During boiling, stronger worts tend to incorporate fewer alpha acids. This is why very strong beers seem to have ridiculously high bittering levels. Pellet hops end up being more bitter per unit of weight than whole hops. Brewing water composition also affects the way bittering components are taken up and expressed by your beer. The length and vigor of the boil also determine how much of the available bittering components are dissolved in the wort.

Wort Target Gravities

These figures are derived from laboratory measurements of the theoretical yield of various types of malt and other grains. You will find that a successful mash at home will yield between 80 and 95 percent of these target figures. Take this into account when you are formulating a recipe. Mash type, temperature, pH, duration, and dilution all affect your final gravity. I got really dramatic increases when I finally started getting my grain crushed properly. Sparging equipment and technique can also make a difference.

Color

Grain comes in many colors, as do beers. Commercially roasted grain is usually labeled with the color in either EBC (European) or °Lovibond (American). A crude predictor of beer color is to multiply color times pounds, then divide by gallons. I want to stress that this calculation is strictly unscientific, but, nevertheless, it may give you numbers you can use as a starting point to get you to the color range for the style you are brewing. See **Section 3–1, Beer Color & Gravity** for a comparison to °SRM.

Home-roasted grain adds to the unpredictability; see the **Grain Roasting chart** in **Section 6–5**).

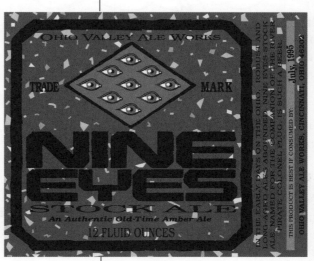

Decoction mashes are darker than infusion mashes. Long boils darken the wort. Water mineral content also affects the color of the finished beer, with high-carbonate water tending to make darker, redder beers. Color is also affected by oxidation during the hot stage of the brewing process. This "hot side aeration" has many negative effects on beer and care must be taken to avoid excessive stirring or splashing, which could introduce air into hot wort.

Bottle Pressure

Many things can affect this important parameter. The more priming sugar, the more pressure. Simple. At the same priming level, ales served at cellar temperature will be more highly pressurized than lagers served at 38°F/3°C. Also simple. Beers with large amounts of unfermentables also contain sugars that ferment very slowly, so priming them can be tricky. This is often a problem with fruit beers, such as cherry ale. Very tricky. It's best to let these beers sit for a long time before bottling. Split-priming—adding less sugar to part of the batch destined for long-term storage—is a way to hedge your bet on beers that will age a long time in the bottle (see **Section 12–1, Priming Guide**).

To Mash or Not to Mash

The vast majority of people brew mostly from extracts, and they are brewers just as much as those who labor over the mash tun. Extract beer, no less than mashed, can be really good or really bad, and it takes skill and experience to make the good stuff.

Wifey's Tender Ale

№. 117

A most supremely wonderful brew, correct and proper in every respect

Mashing is doing it the hard way, there is no doubt. It requires a solid base of brewing experience, some new equipment, considerably more brewing time, and perhaps even a little more room. But for those in search of brewing perfection, it has much to offer. The best of the extract beers are no match for the best of the mashed. The majority of the first-place winners in recent American Homebrew Association competitions have been all-grain beers, which should tell you something.

Total Control

Mashing gives you nearly the same amount of control as a commercial brewery. Unlike extract brewing, you'll know exactly what is in your beer: malt types and quantities, colors, hops, and on and on. Extract manufacturers are notoriously secretive about what's in their products. You can become familiar with different brands, but you'll probably never know exactly what's in them.

Lower Price

Even at full retail, mashed beers cost half as much per batch to make as extracts. If you buy larger quantities of grain, you can cut that in half.

Better Flavor

Even the best extract beers always have a slight wateriness in midtaste, along with a subtle tang that never shows up in mashed beers. Whether it's the wort composition, the plastic coating on the can, or the evaporation process, to my taste extract beers simply do not deliver the pure, uncluttered malt flavor that whole grains do. By mashing at home, you can equal the best beers in the world.

So Get Brewing!

Start with what you know. I suggest you master one section at a time before you move on. When you cover all the variables, you will have essentially the same control over your handcrafted product as the commercial brewer.

WAYS TO IMPROVE YOUR BEERS

Roughly arranged in order of increasing sophistication:

- Boil the full volume of your wort.
- Use malt only—no sugar.
- Use a two-stage fermentation arrangement.
- Dechlorinate tap water before using.
- Add specialty grains to your extracts.
- Rehydrate dry yeast before using.
- Use unhopped wort and add your own hops.
- Use liquid yeast.
- Make a yeast starter.
- Dry-hop, when appropriate.
- Treat your water to match beer style.
- Use a wort chiller.
- Ferment lagers at refrigerator temperatures.
- Harvest and reuse yeast from your beers.
- Actively aerate chilled wort before pitching.
- Use all-grain instead of extracts.
- Maintain active fermentation temperature control.
- Blend beers to match specific targets.
- Brew in a hermetically sealed, computer-controlled, solar-powered, electronically measured, steam-heated, self-cleaning, robotically mashing, continuous-flow titanium-clad brewhouse!

Simple, get-started-so-you-can-have-some-homebrew-while-you-read-this-book, instructions.

1. Get a basic equipment kit from your local homebrew shop (see **Section 15, Homebrew Equipment**).

2. Buy these ingredients:

> 2 3.3-pound cans malt extract, any kind, unhopped light, amber, or dark.
>
> 1.2-pound light, medium or dark crystal malt (whole or pre-crushed).
>
> 1 cheesecloth grain/hop boiling bag.
>
> 1–2 ounces hops: Saaz, Hallertau, Cascade, or Goldings (a little or a lot, according to taste).
>
> Enough bottle caps to do a little more than 2 cases.
>
> 2 packs of dry ale (not lager) yeast.

3. Put 6 gallons of tap water into sterilized plastic bucket(s); let stand overnight (or longer) to dechlorinate. Better yet, use a carbon filter.

4. Fill large (2- to 6-gallon) pot most of the way with some of the water you have standing in the bucket, then turn on the heat. When the water gets warm, pour in malt extract syrup. Use hot water to rinse remaining extract from can. Stir well.

5. Heat slowly and stir until all syrup is dissolved; syrup on bottom can scorch easily. Bring rapidly to a boil, but don't let it boil over.

6. Add half the hops. Just dump 'em in. Watch for boilover when hops are added. Continue boiling.

7. Sterilize carboy and fill partway with water, so that when the boiled wort is added, the total amount will be 4½ gallons (you need some headspace).

8. After 55 minutes, add the other half of the hops. boil 5 more minutes, then turn off the heat and cover pot. Allow to stand 5 minutes to settle.

9. Siphon (sterilize siphon hose first) or carefully pour hot wort through sterilized filter funnel (or cheesecloth) into carboy. If necessary, fill to within 1/2 gallon of top with water.

10. Cover carboy and let stand until wort cools to 90°F/32°C.

11. Sterilize hydrometer and measure the specific gravity. Note the temperature and make corrections, if needed (see **Hydrometer chart, 17–4**). Record gravity on your log sheet.

12. Rehydrate 1 or 2 packages of dry yeast in 100°F water for 10 minutes. Add and stir very vigorously with sterilized spoon to aerate.

13. Fit with sterilized fermentation lock (I like to fill mine with vodka), and put fermenter where the temperature will remain steady: 55°–70°F/13°–21°C. Note temperature on log sheet.

14. In 2 to 24 hours you should see fermentation as patches or gobs of frothy stuff on the surface.

15. Once it starts, the beer will go through 2 to 5 days of very active fermentation. Very vigorous activity may cause foam to ooze out of fermentation lock. Clean up the mess and replace with clean lock, if necessary. This is the primary stage. When surface clears, take specific gravity reading and record it.

16. Allow beer to sit in carboy for about 2 weeks. The bubbling will slow down and stop, and the beer will appear to darken as it clears. When this has happened, it is ready to bottle.

17. Check gravity with sterilized hydrometer. If over 1012, wait a few more weeks. For an extract beer of this strength, gravity should be at or under 1010 for bottling.

18. To bottle, put 3/4 cup of dry malt extract or corn sugar (dextrose) into a clean saucepan with 1 to 2 cups of water. Stir to dissolve well, boil for 10 minutes, cover, and cool.

19. Without splashing, siphon some beer into the saucepan (about half full). Put the rest into your sterilized primary and cover.

20. Gently add the beer-syrup to the beer in the primary. Stir well, but don't splash.

21. You need 34 (2 cases plus 10) nontwist-off beer bottles. Clean the bottles thoroughly: sterilize with chlorine, then rinse with three times with tap water. A turkey baster is useful for squirting sterilizer into the bottles.

22. Using the special bottle-filling tube on the end of the siphon, fill each bottle to within 1 inch of the top; top-up by pouring from a bottle if needed). Don't splash.

23. Cap, then rinse or sponge off bottles.

24. With a permanent marker, label the caps with a number 1 and, if you like, some sort of code for the type of beer it is, for example, "PA" for pale ale.

25. Store where you kept the secondary. After a couple of weeks, there should be enough pressure so you can drink it. The beer will continue to clear and improve for several weeks.

NOTE 1:

Start your second batch sooner than you think you need to. This first batch will be gone before you can say *Saccharomyces cerevesiae*. The maxim is: "The homebrew is ready when you've drunk the last bottle." The stronger the beer, the truer this is. If you've made a barley wine, stash a few bottles in the basement of a nondrinking relative and think about something else for a couple of years.

NOTE 2:

This goes against homebrew nature, but don't fuss over it *too* much. Give it a little time. If you've kept things clean, it will turn out OK.

NOTE 3:

You will have lots of new friends, once the people around you find out you can make beer. You may notice that these new friends seldom bring any beer when they come to visit.

NOTE 4:

Find some people who also brew beer to talk to. You'll bore your significant other—who won't even pretend to be all that interested, unless he or she is really crazy about you—with beer talk. There is likely to be a homebrew club in your area filled with people bursting at the crown caps with brewing knowledge. The local homebrew shop or the American Homebrew Association will know how to contact them.

NOTE 5:

Start tasting beers critically. Pay attention to appearance, aroma, flavor, body, and aftertaste. Do this with commercial beers, as well as your own. Try to figure out what ingredients and processes were used. A good book, such as one by Michael Jackson, can help educate you about brewing styles and traditions.

NOTE 6:

Enter a homebrewing competition. You'll get written commentary from someone who has tasted your beer blind, and can suggest techniques for improvement. You might even win a ribbon or two.

NOTE 7:

There are a million ways to start a siphon, including thermonuclear implosion, but this is how I do it: After sterilizing racking tube and hose, fit together and fill with cold tap water (hold both ends up at the same level). Use hose clamp to pinch tube shut. Quickly insert the racking tube into the full vessel, then place the hose into the receiving vessel. Release the clamp and the beer will start to flow.

NOTE 8:

You can set up your carboy with a blow-off tube arrangement, so if fermentation is very vigorous, foam can flow through tube into a receiving bucket without spilling. Simply take a 3-foot length of hose and attach one end to the little tube inside a plastic fermentation lock (leave the inside piece and lid off). Put the other end in a small bucket filled halfway with clean water. Once fermentation has begun, you can add a little bleach solution to the bucket, but don't do it while the wort is still warm, because when it cools, the change in pressure will draw bleach up into the beer, hindering fermentation.

OVERVIEW OF BEER
HISTORY & STYLES

2

We brewers have a long and glorious history. Barley grains have been discovered in a late Pleistocene context in Greece. This may not be too far from the emergence of true humankind, maybe 40,000 years ago.

It is possible that beer was being brewed 10,000 years ago. Primitive cultures in many parts of the world have elaborate fermentation traditions, involving almost every available grain, fruit, or

other source of extract. Agriculture based on wheat and barley gave rise to the first great civilizations—those in the fertile land between the Tigris and Euphrates rivers in Mesopotamia.

Unlike wheat, barley contains little gluten, which holds bread together. Since barley makes lousy bread, something else was called for. By about 3000 B.C. the techniques of malting and fermentation were practiced, if not well understood. At that time in Mesopotamia, barley accounted for about 60 percent of the cereal production, and up to 40 percent of total cereal production was used for brewing.

It is reasonable to assume that the cradle of civilization is also the cradle of beer. Clearly, civilization and beer are inseparable.

One of the Egyptian gods of beer was Seth, who appeared (I'm guessing to those who overindulged in his fruits) in the form of a hip-

popotamus. By the time of the Pharaohs, many kinds of beers were being brewed, using cakes of barley, which were broken up and steeped in water prior to fermentation. These early beers were augmented with such materials as dates, pomegranates, and mandrake root, which supposedly has a strong leek-like flavor. Whew!

Brewing in ancient Egypt was a big, if somewhat smelly, business. The brewery of one of the Pharaoh Ramses is said to have given 10,000 hectoliters of beer annually to the temple administration. That's about 300,000 bottles.

The Greeks never did catch on to beer.

The Roman Emperor Julian, upon sampling British beer sometime in the fourth century, wrote the following poem:

ON WINE MADE FROM BARLEY

Who made you and from what
By true Bacchus I know you not
He smells of nectar
You smell of goat.

Like many modern-day Americans, the Romans thought beer was suited only for working-class Visigoths, preferring instead the fruits of the vine. Their error was demonstrated some time later as the beer-drinking barbarians from the north swung down and trashed the place, as enthusiastic beer drinkers have been known to do.

The Dark (Beer) Ages

Preserved in a small museum in Alzey, in the Rhineland Palatinate, is the oldest bottle of beer in the world, dating from Roman times. It is a ceramic jug, and the beer is now a nasty dried deposit adhered to the bottom, solid evidence of the brewing genius of the ancient Germanic tribes. It is known that they were brewing by at least the first century B.C.

Like everything else in the Middle Ages, brewing must have been a crude process. Barley was

RECIPE FOR BABYLONIAN BEER

Take a quantity of grain—mostly barley, with some Emmer wheat. Pound in a mortar with a pestle. Form it into moist cakes. Bake at a high temperature until light or dark, as you like.

Cool, then soak in water at sparge temperatures. Drain and filter.

Place in a 44-gallon ceramic container, and allow to spontaneously ferment. Both yeast and *Lactobacillus* should be involved. Continue through primary fermentation. Cover with mats to help stabilize the temperature.

Transfer to smaller containers, 4 to 15 gallons, which are half-buried in the floor of the cellar. Allow secondary fermentation to proceed.

Drink whenever seems appropriate, without any carbonation, or bury in jugs to age.

malted, and then pounded by water-powered hammers prior to mashing. Several types of grains were used—wheat, oats, rye, with barley malt being preferred. Sparging as such was unknown. The mash was simply infused a number of times, the resulting runoff being weaker each time. In this way, three strengths of beer were brewed from the same batch. The strongest beer, *Prima Melior*, was very strong, usually over 1100 OG. An intermediate-strength brew, *Secunda*, was perhaps around 1060 or 1070 OG. The weakest, *Tertia*—or small beer—was a pitiful creation, probably as weak as a typical American beer of the 1980s.

The strongest beers were reserved for the monks and honored guests. The middle grades were served to the lay brothers and other employees of the monasteries, and the small beer was given to the numerous pilgrims who came seeking food and a place to stay.

Lacking a thermometer, strike-water temperature was gauged by the clarity of the reflection of the brewer's face. At the right temperature, the surface of the water becomes very still and clear. Water hardness was measurable and its effect on brewing was understood, with hard water being preferred. Yeast was collected and pitched, although its real nature was not even guessed at. Various herbs, many of which were bitter, were added. Bog myrtle, rosemary, and yarrow were among those used.

The Babylonians were using hops before A.D. 200. In Europe, the bittering and preservative powers of hops eventually came to be appreciated, at least on the Continent. The first European mention of hops is dated to the year 736, in the Hallertau district of Germany. In England, hops

were quite controversial, and were outlawed more than once.

In most places the beer was subject to taxation and various other governmental controls, which quite often led to conflicts and controversy. The first national tax affecting brewing in England was levied by Henry II in 1188. The following year, laws to control the location and operation of breweries, primarily for the protection of the public, were enacted in London.

Even out of this Dark Ages' gloom, some good beer was probably being made. Remember, these are the people who brought us the great gothic cathedrals of northern Europe.

There were brewers at the royal court of Charlemagne. And in the early Middle Ages, it is estimated that there were 400 to 500 monasteries brewing in what is now Germany.

Beer contributed greatly to the health of the medieval population. The Dark Ages are not known for being hygienic, and the drinking water could literally be deadly. Rich in carbohydrates, and preserved by hops and alcohol, beer was a safe and nutritious beverage.

The introduction of hops was opposed by every country in its turn. Even in Germany, hops were not widely used until the mid-14th century.

Without hops, ale needed to be strong in alcohol to be protected from microbial spoilage. With the preservative power of hops, alcoholic strength could be lowered without compromising the stability of the beer.

In 1516, the famous Bavarian beer purity law, the Reinheitsgebot, was passed. It restricted beer ingredients to malt, water, hops, and yeast (with the exception of wheat beers). The law remained in effect until 1987 when a European court decided it was restrictive to Common Market trade.

SAINT PAUL CATHEDRAL'S ALE

As reported in the *Domesday Book*
(to make 84,767.5 gallons, @ 1150 OG)

   175 Quarters of barley (78,400 lbs)

   175 Quarters of wheat (78,400 lbs)

   708 Quarters of oats (317,184 lbs)

This amounts to 5½ lbs of grain per gallon of ale!

DOUBLE BEER   (For 5 gallons)

From medieval Lorraine

1 septier (130–150 lbs.of malt   (19–22 lbs)

7.5 livres (lbs) hops   (1 lb)

1 hogshead water–67.5 gallons   (10 gal)

A writer in 1574 gives the rate of six pounds of grain per gallon of ale (about 1170 OG!), which was unhopped, and less than three pounds per gallon per beer (1075 OG), which was hopped. Beer and ale were obviously very different products.

Until the late 16th century, all breweries were brewpubs, although by the mid-1500s references were being made to regulations regarding beer exports from England. In London, breweries settled in the Southwark area, many of which remained into the 19th century. This was the start of brewing as a large-scale industry. Smaller cottage brewers were squeezed, but were never completely replaced, and are still brewing today.

In such far-flung countries as Norway, beer continued to be brewed in a medieval way until quite recently. Barley was malted in linen sacks, which were often placed in streams for steeping. The malt was dried over fires (with considerable risk) or dried in the sun. Fire-drying gave the desired brown coloring, but imparted a smoky taste. The only specialized piece of equipment was the mash tun, a special type of barrel, in which sticks were used to support a bed of straw, which did the actual filtering of the mash. Hot stones were used to heat the mash, as well as for boiling the wort. This stone-brewing technique has recently been revived at a brewery in Germany.

Because cool temperatures were necessary for fermentation, it was illegal to brew beer in Germany between April 23 and September 29. This lack of artificial temperature control led to the creation of the various types of seasonal brews we enjoy to this day.

Jacob Theodor von Bergzabern, also known as Tabernaemontanus, describing regional beers in 1588 wrote that Danzig beers were as thick as syrup, and a pleasing brown-red color— "...there is more strength and nourishment in a little mug of this than a whole measure of other beers." Beers from Hamburg were pale, made from wheat malt. Polish beers were also pale, and had a vinous flavor. He described Lubeck beer as "strong but unfriendly beer," causing headaches. "English beers are also extraordinarily good, especially English ale brewed from wheat."

The first recorded mention of bottom-fermented, or lager, beer occurs in a report of the Munich Town Council in 1420, although it wasn't until later that the lager style became dominant in Germany.

Enlightenment Comes To Brewing

In the late 1600s, the Fahrenheit thermometer, hydrometer, and steam engine were all invented. The first two offered a new measure of control over the product. Before the hydrometer, there was no way to determine the efficiency of the process. We still can only guess at the strength of beers brewed prior to this time. The hydrometer did not find common use in breweries until about 1760. The thermometer was the key to unlocking the complexities of the mashing process, but it also was not in common use until the mid-1700s.

TYPICAL ENGLISH BREW IN 1577
As reported by the author William Harrison (to make 5 gallons, @ 1100 OG)
12.8 lbs fine English pale malt
86 lbs. each of unmalted oats and wheat
2.5 ozs. hops

James Braverstock, an early user of the thermometer, had to hide it from his father, who violently opposed its use.

Many other facets of the brewing process were beginning to be understood by this time, including the differing varieties of barley malt (which was now the dominant brewing grain), techniques of malting and kilning, and water chemistry.

At this time there was a rise in interest in the clarity of beers, which was coincident with the introduction of the inexpensive glass drinking tumbler.

Bottled beer also appeared in this period. In England, in 1695, no less than three million glass bottles were manufactured, but stoneware bottles were also used. The bottles made it possible to carbonate beer at higher levels. Bottles also preserved export beers better than casks, which helped open up new markets outside of northern Europe.

The wild growth that was the Industrial Revolution applied to brewing as well, especially in England. The steam engine made it possible to build breweries on a scale we would recognize as modern. But for quite a some time to come, the smaller, country brewers held the reputation for quality. A Mr. R. Bradley wrote in 1727 that in the northern counties "...it is as rare to find ill malt liquors as it is to find good in London." Essentially, this remains true today. Industrialization has never been that great a thing for beer.

The first large-scale brewers were the porter breweries of London. According to brewing mythology, porter was created in London in 1722, by Ralph Harwood. Mixtures of beers were popular at the time. A

BEERS IN ENGLAND, 1785		
TYPE	OG	END
Strong Ale	1110	1052
Common Ale	1075	1025
Porter	1071	1018
Table Beer	1040	1004

mixture of pale ale, stale brown ale, and fresh brown ale was called "three threads." The new beer was in imitation of this mix and was called "Mr Harwood's Entire" or "Entire Butt." *Entire* refers to brewing only one style of beer from the various runnings of the mash, which were mixed and boiled together. The story further goes that the new beer was popular with working-class people and porters, and was named after them.

A number of well-known breweries began in this period: Truman's, in 1683; Smithwick, in 1710; Whitbread, in 1742; and Arthur Guinness leased St. James' Gate brewery in 1759.

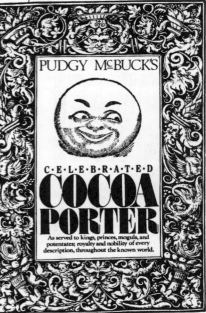

PUDGY McBUCK'S

C·E·L·E·B·R·A·T·E·D

COCOA PORTER

As served to kings, princes, moguls, and potentates; royalty and nobility of every description, throughout the known world.

By 1748, there were several large brewers. Sir William Calvert brewed 55,700 British barrels per year; his brother Felix, 53,600; Truman's brewed 39,400 British barrels; Parsons, 39,000; Thrale, 35,500; and Hope, 34,400.

The biggest breweries were those brewing porter: Barclay Perkins brewed 270,300 barrels of porter in 1812. Twelve breweries made 42 percent of all the strong beer and ale in London, which had more highly mechanized breweries than anywhere else in the world.

Porter was often adulterated by many different flavoring agents. In 1802, Alexander Morrice mentioned the following ingredients: Copper of sugar, "leghorn juice," *Fabia armara* (or bitter bean), quassia, honey, molasses, *Cocculus indicus,* Grains of Paradise, hops, *Calamus aromaticus,* stick licorice, Spanish licorice, elderberry juice, gentian, coriander, capsicum (hot red pepper), caraway, ginger, and salt. These were outlawed for commercial breweries about that time, but were common in homebrewing.

The first reliable records of actual gravities of beers were given by Richardson in 1785.

A patent for malt extract was filed in 1778, for the purpose of "...making good and wholesome beers at sea and in distant climes and countries."

Brewing Developments in Europe

Lager beer was consistently being brewed in Germany by the mid-1800s, when refrigeration equipment became a commercial reality. The great hero of German brewing was Gabriel Sedlmayr, Brewmaster of Munich's Spatenbrau, still one of the great breweries of the world. He didn't invent lager beer, but it was he who made it a commercial success. In the 1830s he visited Britain and returned to Germany full of ideas: the thermometer, the hydrometer, and steam power.

Also in the 1830s, scientists in several countries reached the conclusion that yeast was a plant organism. Louis Pasteur revolutionized everyone's thinking with a wealth of accurate, detailed data about yeast and fermentation. In the 1880s, Emil Christian Hansen of the Carlsberg Brewery in Denmark became the first to isolate and brew with a pure single-cell yeast culture, the way most lager brewing is done today.

The Dawn of American Beer

The first commercial brewery in the New World was built in Mexico, at the astonishingly early date

EARLY BREWERS IN U.S. CITIES

George Shiras, Pittsburgh, 1795

The Embree Brothers, Cincinnati, 1805

Jacques DeLassus de St. Vrain, St. Louis, 1810

William Lill & Co. in Chicago, 1833

Richard Owens & William Pawlett, Milwaukee, 1840

Adam Schuppert, San Francisco, 1849

of 1544, just 52 short years after Columbus made his voyage.

The first European brewer in North America was Sir Walter Raleigh, who malted maize for beer in 1587. The use of maize has remained a distinctly American brewing tradition, not to our credit. The Pilgrim fathers recorded their reason for landing at Plymouth Rock: they were out of beer, and needed to stop to make some more, right then and there. Indeed, the first permanent structure they built was the brewery.

Hops were being cultivated in America as early as 1625, and John Smith recorded two breweries in Virginia as early as 1629. The Netherlands West India Company was brewing beer in New Amsterdam (later New York) in 1632. The first commercial brewery opened in Charleston, Massachusetts, in 1637. And an ale named Red Lion was the first brand-name beer recorded in America, about 1660.

Beers brewed at that time were English-style ales and porters. George Washington was fond of porter, but the style never caught on here as it did in London. A document of the times records four strengths of beer: Small Beer, Ship's Beer, Table Beer, and Strong Beer.

Our Founding Fathers brewed beer. In 1814, Thomas Jefferson was ordering quart and half-gallon bottles by the gross for his home brewery.

In Canada, North America's oldest brewery was being built. In Montreal in 1786, John Molson brewed 4,000 gallons in his first year to satisfy the ale-thirsty British minority in a French, wine-drinking city.

As large cities evolved, brewing concentrated in them. As the frontier moved west, so followed the tide of beer.

Lager Comes to America

In 1840, a Bavarian brewer named Johann Wagner opened a brewery in Philadelphia. Until then, the American brewing style was mainly English, consisting of various ales and porters. The English tradition has still held on in the East, especially evidenced by the continued presence of cream ale, a product with characteristics of both ales and lagers. The oldest brewery in the United States, Yuengling (1829), still brews a porter.

BREWERIES BY CITY, 1905-1984							
CITY	1905	1933	1943	1953	1963	1973	1984
Albany, NY	20	3	3	1	1	—	—
Boston, MA	21	4	5	1	1	1	—
Brooklyn, NY	41	9	6	5	4	3	—
Buffalo, NY	19	6	8	5	1	—	—
Chicago, IL	59	15	16	14	7	1	—
Cincinnati, OH	23	6	7	5	4	4	2
Cleveland, OH	19	5	8	5	1	1	1
Detroit, MI	17	7	9	3	4	2	1
Louisville, KY	15	2	3	3	3	1	—
Milwaukee, WI	14	7	6	6	6	6	2
Minneapolis, MN	10	5	5	3	4	4	2
New Orleans, LA	10	4	6	4	3	3	1
New York, NY	43	8	8	4	1	—	—
Newark, NJ	19	na	5	3	3	2	2
Pittsburgh, PA	10	3	3	1	2	1	1
Rochester, NY	10	4	4	3	2	1	1
St. Louis, MO	27	5	7	5	3	2	1
San Francisco, CA	28	7	6	6	4	4	1
Syracuse, NY	11	4	1	1	1	—	—

When chaotic times brought thousands of German immigrants to America, two things they brought with them were a thirst for lager beer and the talent to brew it. By 1850, there were 431 breweries producing 23 million gallons of beer. Just 10 years later, in 1860, 1,269 breweries made 30 million gallons. This frenzy peaked in 1873, when 4,131 breweries brewed 9 million barrels.

By 1860, the majority of beer brewed in the United States was lager beer. Ice was cut from the rivers and lakes in winter and used throughout the summer to keep beer chilled during lagering. However, this was not possible in San Francisco, where the lack of freezing winters led to the development of a unique American style—steam beer. Traditional lager brewing methods were used except for fermentation, which was carried out at the natural temperatures of the region— about 60°F/15.5°C. The result was a beer with some ale characteristics, due to the warm fermentation. The word "steam" supposedly refers to the

TRADE MARK
CYCLONE
REGISTERED JUNE 29 1897

WRITE FOR
OUR HIGHGRADE
RED VELVET
RUBBER STOPPERS
FOR
WEISS BEER

clouds of vapor which escaped from the kegs when this highly carbonated product was tapped.

The introduction of refrigeration equipment in the 1880s ended all this silly ice cutting, and allowed breweries to brew any kind of beer they wished, no matter where they were located. This was the golden age of brewing in the United States.

Amalgamation and the Quality Slide

Sadly, the last hundred years has seen a steady march toward weakness and monotony. Both gravity and bittering levels have decreased dramatically as the economics of big business and the curious American desire for blandness conspired to reduce beer to mere barley-pop. Ingredient rationing during two world wars allowed drinkers to get used to lighter-weight beers. Perhaps the home refrigerator has cooperated by encouraging ice-cold serving temperatures.

The phenomenon of national brands began with the rise of the railroad. The 25 years between 1865 and 1890 saw a fivefold increase in the number of railroad miles in this country, forming the basis of a national distribution system for all kinds of industries, including brewing. Other factors, including the discovery of pasteurization, also allowed for greater stability during shipping.

John Painter invented the bottle cap in 1892, perhaps America's greatest contribution to the brewing world. We were also the inventors of canned beer. Kruger Beer, of Newark, introduced

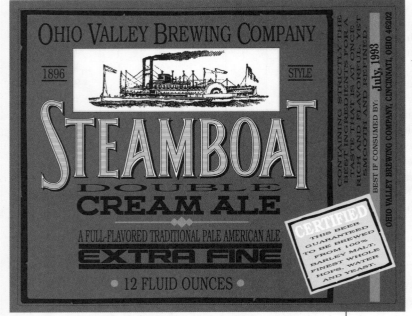

OHIO VALLEY BREWING COMPANY

1896   STYLE

STEAMBOAT DOUBLE CREAM ALE

A FULL-FLAVORED TRADITIONAL PALE AMERICAN ALE

EXTRA FINE

• 12 FLUID OUNCES •

CONTAINING STRICTLY THE BEST INGREDIENTS FOR A TASTE THAT IS AT ONCE RICH AND FLAVORFUL YET SMOOTH AND REFINED

BEST IF CONSUMED BY: July, 1993

OHIO VALLEY BREWING COMPANY, CINCINNATI, OHIO 46202

CERTIFIED THIS BEER GUARANTEED TO BE BREWED FROM 100% FINEST BARLEY MALT, HOPS, WATER AND YEAST.

the first canned beer on June 24, 1934. Coors introduced the world to aluminum cans in 1959.

The experiment of prohibition had many undesirable side effects. When it was enacted, there were 1,568 breweries. When it was over, only half remained. Oddly, some of the staunchest temperance advocates were the producers of malt extracts, which were used, as today, for beer brewing. Some estimates say that more alcohol was consumed during prohibition than before.

The Depression made it even more difficult for breweries to compete, so the slide continued. The chart on the previous page shows the drama of this situation. After prohibition, much of the loyalty to local beers had been eroded, and so the breweries that gained acceptance were those that were better-organized, better-funded, and usually, bigger. Other developments, such as the beer can, which eliminated the necessity of returnable containers, also benefitted the national brands.

In the modern corporate environment, the drive for bottom-line performance can overshadow everything else, sometimes even to the long-term detriment of the companies themselves. Legend has it that just such a pattern of activity

led to the demise of the Schlitz brand, once one of the mightiest in the nation, and now relegated to the shadows due to a disastrous attempt to implement a more rapid fermentation process.

This commodity-oriented thinking has not been kind to beer. Pasteurization increases shelf-life, but takes the life out of beer, reducing head-forming capabilities. Such has been the callousness of some American brewers that in the 1950s, compounds of the toxic metal cobalt were used as a heading agent until a horrified public caught on.

Customers must accept part of the blame for this situation, for if inferior products are tolerated, they will continue to be sold. Today, of course, the situation is improving. Not only is there a proliferation of microbreweries, but even some of the big brewers have made changes.

The Microbrewing Revolution

This really began with Fritz Maytag and the Anchor Brewery. It is not a new operation, but an old traditional West Coast brewery, the last of its kind. It was in deep decline when the young Mr. Maytag purchased it in 1968. After much hard work and replacing all the brewing equipment, Anchor is producing some of the very finest beers in this country, setting the standard of quality for the entire microbrewing revolution.

Since then, hundreds of these microbreweries have sprung up, with many more in various stages of planning and construction. This flurry of activity bodes well for all lovers of true beer. A similar blossoming happened with wine during the 1970s, and indicates the potential that awaits the brewer's art. American professional and homebrewers are now pushing the art, redefining every existing beer style and inventing many new ones. The movement is only in its infancy even now, and soon there could be thousands of little breweries offering quality, freshness, and individuality to their happy customers.

BEER STYLE	Original Gravity	°Plato of Wort	% Alcohol-Vol	Attenuation-%	Color-°SRM	Bitterness-IBUs	% Barley Malt	Yeast Type	Fermentation Temp	DESCRIPTION & COMMENTS
ORDINARY BITTER	1032 1038	8 9.5	3.2 3.9	60 67	8 12	20 40	70 100	Ale	65-75°F 18-24°C	A range of ales, the national drink of Britain. Various strengths. Not clearly defined categories; there is considerable overlapping commercial practice. Usually deep gold to amber color. Hops or malt may predominate (usually hops, especially in ordinaries).
BEST BITTER	1035– 1044	9 10.5	3.6 4.6	61 67	12 14	22 40	80 100	Ale	65-75°F 18-24°C	East Kent Goldings are choice for finishing. Fermented at warm temperatures, (70°F/21°C) using a variety of fermentation arrangements, some of them quite strange (see Burton Union).
EXTRA SPECIAL BITTER	1040 1056	10.5 12.4	4.1 5.2	59 64	12 14	25 45	85 100	Ale	65-75°F 18-24°C	Always served at cellar temperature, on draught, and should be naturally carbonated on the premises. Very lightly carbonated. Wheat Malt <7%, Corn <15%, Torrefied Barley <7%, Sugar <15% used.
PALE ALE (Bottled)	1043 1065	10.7 15.9.	4 7	65 70	6 14	25 50	85 100	Ale	62-67°F 17-19°C	A type of ale similar to those above, but normally stronger and bottled. A rather wide category encompassing a range of beers. Often noticeably hoppy, typically dry-hopped. Many U.S. microbreweries produce idiosyncratic versions.
INDIA PALE ALE	1055 1065	13.5 15.9	5 7	65 70	8 14	40 70	85 100	Ale	62-67°F 17-19°C	Much stronger version of pale ale, which originated as an export version. Higher gravity allowed it to survive shipboard passage to the tropical colonies. Often very bitter. Quite pale considering its strength. Traditionally dry-hopped. A touch of oak is appropriate in this style.
MILD ALE	1032 1037	8 9.3	2.8 3.6	55 62	15 35	12 18	75 100	Ale	56-62°F 13-16°C	A rich, brown ale usually served on draught. Pale versions exist, but are rare. Very light hopping allows malt to predominate. Very low in alcohol. Very lightly carbonated and served at cellar temperature. Up to 12% black malt.
BROWN ALE	1040 1045	10 11.2	4 5	60 67	14 22	14 22	85 100	AlE	62-67°F 17-19°C	Slightly stronger version of mild ale. Lightly hopped, lightly carbonated. The best available version in the U.S. is Samuel Smith's Nut Brown Ale, which is pale for the style. U.S. versions tend to be stronger and often much hoppier.
SCOTCH ALE 60' "Light"	1030 1034	7.5 8.5	3 3.4	58 62	10 15		90 100	Ale	56-62°F 13-16°C	Scottish-style ales, brewed in a range of strengths. Still designated by their original cost in shillings. Scotland being far from the hopfields of southern England, all Scotch ales are very lightly hopped, and so can have an overwhelming maltiness.
SCOTCH ALE 70' "Heavy"	1034 1038	8.5 9.3	3.2 3.7	56 62	12 17		90 100	Ale	56-62°F 13-16°C	Quite high in unfermentables as well. Similar to English bitters, but less estery, and generally darker, sweeter and maltier. Usually fermented cooler than English ales.

BEER STYLE	Original Gravity	°Plato of Wort	% Alcohol-Vol	Attenuation-%	Color-°SRM	Bitterness-IBUs	% Barley Malt	Yeast Type	Fermentation Temp	DESCRIPTION & COMMENTS
SCOTCH ALE 80' "Export"	1039 / 1043	9.7 / 10.7	4.1 / 4.5	58 / 64	14 / 18	15 / 20	90 / 100	Ale	56-62°F / 13-16°C	See previous page.
SCOTCH ALE 90' "Wee Heavy"	1070 / 1090	17.0 / 21.5	7 / 9.9	57 / 70	16 / 22	22 / 32	90 / 100	Ale	56-62°F / 13-16°C	
PORTER	1040 / 1060	10 / 14.7	3.7 / 5.5	60 / 70	24 / 36	25 / 35	92 / 100	Ale	65-75°F / 18-24°C	A deep brown ale, highly hopped, that originated in London in 1722. It was, in fact, the first product of large mechanized breweries. Roast flavor now comes from black patent malt (after 1820), but originally was from brown and amber malts. Not as dark as stouts. Recently revived in England, notably by Samuel Smith. There are two substyles: a pale brown version of modest gravity, and the stronger, darker type favored by U.S. micros. High-temperature ferment during early days, up to 1830.
SWEET STOUT MILK STOUT LONDON STOUT	1038 / 1042	9.5 / 10.5	2.7 / 3.8	50 / 58	30 / 50	18 / 25	90 / 100	Ale	56-70°F / 13-21°C	London-style stout, directly descended from porter. Very thick and sweet, sometimes from the addition of lactose sugar, which is unfermentable. Relatively low alcohol. Very dark color and roasted flavor comes from black patent malt.
OATMEAL STOUT	1040 / 1052	10 / 12.2	3.7 / 5	55 / 67	35 / 65	30 / 40	90 / 95	Ale	56-70°F / 13-21°C	A subset of stouts made with the addition of a small amount of oatmeal to the grist, which produces a rich smoothness, without the sweetness of the London style.
IRISH STOUT DRY STOUT	Draft 1037 / 1040 Bottle 1048 / 1060	Draft 9.3 / 10 Bottle 11.9 / 14.7	Draft 4.3 / 5.4 Bottle 4.2 / 5.5	60 / 70	35 / 70	25 / 50	94 / 100	Ale	56-70°F / 13-21°C	The national drink of Ireland, typified by Guinness. Very dark color with a creamy brown head. Very dry flavor, accentuated by a high hop rate. Roasted flavor comes from black roasted unmalted barley as opposed to patent malt. Served bottled or on draught. It is pressurized in the keg with nitrogen instead of CO_2, giving it a very creamy head. Served at cellar temperature. Draught versions lighter than bottled. Small amount of lactic fermentation added.
TROPICAL STOUT	1060 / 1080	14.7 / 19.3	5.75 / 7.5	65 / 72	40 / 60	30 / 60	90 / 100	Strong Ale	56-62°F / 13-16°C	Irish-style stout, brewed at higher gravities to survive shipment to the tropics. Invariably bottled. Often quite lactic, in imitation of earlier wood-aged beers.
OLD ALE STRONG ALE	1050 / 1075	12.4 / 18.2	4.5 / 7	55 / 64	22 / 85	12 / 30	85 / 100	Strong Ale	56-62°F / 13-16°C	A wide range of ales of varying strength, color and bitterness. These ales start where pale ale and bitter leave off, and end where barley wine begins. Typically deep coppery amber color. Usually bottled. Sometimes referred to as winter warmer.

BEER STYLE	Original Gravity	°Plato of Wort	% Alcohol-Vol	Attenuation-%	Color-°SRM	Bitterness-IBUs	% Barley Malt	Yeast Type	Fermentation Temp	DESCRIPTION & COMMENTS
BARLEY WINE	1075 / 1110	18.2 / 26	7 / 11.5	55 / 70	25 / 110	85 / 100		Strong Ale	56-62°F / 13-16°C	A very strong ale. Like old ale, this category is rather loosely defined. Typically rich, heavy and malty, but with a strong bitter finish. Long bottle aging is a must.
RUSSIAN STOUT IMPERIAL STOUT	1075 / 1120	18.2 / 28	7.2 / 12.5	60 / 70	50 / 150	90 / 100		Strong Ale	56-62°F / 13-16°C	Intensely bitter, strong stout originally brewed for the Russian imperial court by British brewers in the 19th century.
				NA	NA	NA	Ale	NA		
Bass, Dog's Head	1066	16.1	8.2	76					1901	
Bass Strong Ale	1102	24.2	8.7	48.3					1896	
Worthington Burton	1110	25.8	11.0	61.3					1890, sample 90 years old, brewed in 1800!	
Allsopp Lt. Dinner	1054	13.4	5.9	67					1896	
Allsopp Burton IPA	1061	15.1	6.9	70.5					1879	
MacEwan's Sparkling	1090	21.6	9.9	67.4					1901	
Guinness Extra	1073	17.6	7.1	59.6					1896	
Guinness Foreign	1075	18.2	8.0	65.4					1901	
Dublin Single Stout	1062	15.2	6.2	67.3					1879	
Dublin Double Stout	1086	20.6	9.1	64.9					1879	

BEER STYLE	Original Gravity	°Plato of Wort	% Alcohol-Vol	Attenuation-%	Color-°SRM	Bitterness-IBUs	% Barley Malt	Yeast Type	Fermentation Temp	DESCRIPTION & COMMENTS
PILSNER–Czech	1046 1051	11.5 12.5	4.3	54 60	3.5 4.5	25 45	100	Lager	45.5-47.5°F 7-8°C	A very dry pale lager. Czech versions richer, not as pale as German versions. Color and caramel taste contributed by long kettle boil. Dominant spicy Saaz hop aroma. Quite bitter. Saaz hops mandatory. Soft water important for smooth bitterness.
PILS–German	1044 1048	11 12	3.5 4.8	57 67	2.2 3.7	25 40	100	Lager	41-45.5°F 5-7°C	Serve at 46°F/8°C.
DORTMUNDER EXPORT	1051 1065	12.5 16	5 6.5	55 65	4 8	22 30	100	Lager	41-45.5°F 5-7°C	A pale lager, midway in the spectrum between pils and Munich light, but stronger than either. Rich pale straw color. Michael Jackson describes it as a cool blonde. More or less equal balance between hops and malt. Serve at 48°–50°F/9°–10°C.
MUNICH LIGHT Münchner Helles	1047 1055	11.5 13.5	4.4 5.5	52 64	2.6 4.5	18 25	100	Lager	41-45.5°F 5-7°C	Maltiest and richest and darkest of all the German pale lagers. Light hopping allows the malt flavors to dominate. High amount of unfermentables.
MUNICH DARK Münchner Dunkel	1048 1059	12 14.5	4.3 6	50 62	14 20	16 25	100	Lager	50-51°F 10-10.5°C	Style of dark lager once widely popular in Munich. Intense red-brown color. Aromatic malty flavor is a result of light hop rates and lots of Munich malt.
VIENNA	1048 1053	12 13	4.5 5.5	60 65	8 14	18 25	100	Lager	47.8-49°F 8.5-9.5°C	German amber lagers. Vienna is similar in gravity to the standard pils, Märzen is slightly stronger. When Germans were forbidden to brew in the summer, this was the last brew of the season—its strength allowed it to last until fall. Spaten Bräu is the originator of the Märzen style. Once the primary style of the city of Vienna. Authentic versions are brewed in Mexico, originally by Austrian brewmasters.
OKTOBERFEST MÄRZEN	1052 1061	12.9 15	5 6	60 65	10 16	22 30	100	Lager	47.8-49°F 8.5-9.5°C	
KULMBACHER	1061 1070	15 17	5 6	50 55	20 30	22 30	100	Lager	50-51°F 10-10.5°C	A very dark beer originating in the city of Kulmbach. About as strong as a Dortmund. Similar to München dunkel, but darker, with more of a roasty finish.
PALE BOCK MAIBOCK	1066 1070	16 17	6 7.5	62 68	4 6	22 35	100	Lager	41-45.5°F 5-7°C	A strong pale lager, now the most popular bock style in Germany. Hop/malt balance can be just on either side of the middle. Hop/malt balance like Munich or Dortmund, rather than pils.
DARK BOCK	1066 1074	16.1 18	5 7	50 60	18 28	20 35	100	Lager	50°-51°F 10-10.5°C	A strong, dark lager. Originally the popular bock style in Germany, now more or less supplanted by the pale version. Very hard to find in the United States for some reason.

BEER STYLE	Original Gravity	°Plato of Wort	% Alcohol-Vol	Attenuation-%	Color-°SRM	Bitterness-IBUs	% Barley Malt	Yeast Type	Fermentation Temp	DESCRIPTION & COMMENTS
DOPPELBOCK EISBOCK	1075 / +	18.2	6.5 / 11.5	50 / 60	12 / 30	25 / 45	100	Lager	50-51°F / 10-10.5°C	Extremely strong lager beer. Wide variety of gravities, colors, and bitterness levels. All share an intense malty flavor, and high alcohol content. Medium to dark brown.
DUSSELDORF ALT	1046 / 1051	11.5 / 12.5	4 / 4.7	65 / 75	10 / 18	30 / 55	100	Alt	60-65°F / 15.5-18°C	A distinctive ale, top-fermented, very highly hopped. Traditionally, Spalt hops are used. *Alt* literally means "old" in German, as in old style. It is cold-conditioned 3 to 8 weeks, lightly carbonated, and is served in small, tall glasses.
KOLSCH	1045 / 1049	11.2 / 12	3.5 / 4	62 / 67	3.5 / 5.5	22 / 30	90	Alt	64-72°F / 32-47°C	A crisp, pale, mild-mannered ale brewed (by law) only within the city limits of Köln (Cologne). Lightly carbonated and traditionally served at 50°F/10°C, in the same sort of tall little glasses as Düsseldorfer Alt.
SUDDEUTSCHE WEIZEN (WEISSBIER)	1051 / 1057	12.5 / 14	4.5 / 5.5	57 / 65	3 / 8	13 / 17	25 / 60	Wheat Ale	59-68°F / 15-20°C	A popular Bavarian specialty, often drunk in summer. Between 40 and 75 percent malted wheat is used in this brew, giving the beer a light thirst-quenching quality. A light clove aroma is also characteristic in this beer, which is traditionally pale and lightly hopped. Unique strains are used to impart the clove characteristic. Bottled with yeast (*hefe*) and without yeast (*hefefrei* or *kristal*).
DUNKEL WEIZEN	1051 / 1057	12.5 / 14	4.5 / 5.5	57 / 65	12 / 20	13 / 17	25 / 60	Wheat Ale	59-68°F / 15-20°C	Traditionally a drink of summer, when it is served in tall, vase-shaped glasses with a slice of lemon. Dark varieties exist, but are usually a light brown color, lighter than a München dunkel.
WEIZENBOCK	1065 / 1072	16 / 17.5	6.2 / 7.5	52 / 62	10 / 24	18 / 25	25 / 60	Wheat Ale	59-68°F / 15-20°C	Stronger, darker version of the wheat beer above. Has a dry crispness not usually associated with bock beers. Perilously drinkable.
BERLINER WEISSE	1030 / 1036	7.5 / 9	3 / 4	66 / 75	2 / 4	4 / 8	50 / 67	Ale + Lactobacillus	61-66°F / 64-77°F / 16-18.5°C / 17.5-25°C	A very light tangy brew that is, as the name suggests, the specialty of Berlin. Very pale, very low gravity, highly carbonated, and very tart. Originally made with unboiled wort. The yogurty tang is provided by a lactic acid fermentation. Served with a shot of either raspberry or woodruff syrup, in a large, bowl-shaped goblet.
Münchener	1057	13.9		66						1901, Löwen Brauhaus.
Kulmbacher	1072	17.6		45						1888
Einbecker Bock	1064	15.6		48						1893, Export.
Dort. Adambier	1103	26.4		49						1864, 33 years old when analyzed.
Mumme	1214	54.8		13						1899, Braunschweig (this is actually an herb beer/tonic, also popular in England).
Broyhan Alt	1032	7.95		21						1884, Single. Double @ 13.22 °P, 0.96 ABV.

BEER STYLE	Original Gravity	°Plato of Wort	% Alcohol-Vol	Attenuation-%	Color-°SRM	Bitterness-IBUs	% Barley Malt	Yeast Type	Fermentation Temp	DESCRIPTION & COMMENTS
ABBEY/TRAPPIST DUBBEL	1052 1063	12.9 15.4	5.5 7	68 70	10 25	16 25	90 100	Special Ale	65-85°F 18-29°C	Brown ale. Smooth, malty, lightly hopped. Brewed by genuine Trappists monks. The yeast strains give distinct fruity character. Chimay yeast is live and, when fresh, is easily cultured. Rich creamy head that lasts and lasts. On large bottles, date is stamped on the side of the cork. Candy or partially refined sugar sometimes added to kettle.
ABBEY/TRAPPIST SPECIAL	1070 1080	17 19.3	7 9	63 72	6-20	18 30	90 100	Special Ale	65-85°F 18-29°C	Amber strong ale. Strong, vinous, often highly hopped, and well-aged in the bottle. Unique spicy yeast character common to all Belgian abbey-type beers. Typically the middle beer in an abbey's range, but often the lightest in color.
ABBEY/TRAPPIST TRIPLE	1072 1100	17.5 26	7 10.5	61 70	10-25	20 40	90 100	Special Ale	65-85°F 18-29°C	Usually gold or amber, but sometimes deep amber, even brown. Many unique versions. Hallertau and Northern Brewer hops are common. Sssstrong.
AMBER ALE (Palm)	1053	13.2	5.2		12	27		Ale	65-85°F 18-29°C	Amber ale. Reddish amber color. Clean, fruity flavor, almost spicy. Decidedly caramelly. Very white head. Relatively light body.
STRONG PALE ALE (Duvel)	1083	20	8.2		4.5	52	100	Special Ale	65-85°F 18-29°C	Strong pale ale. Very light color comes from the use of pilsner malt. Much lighter in color and body than an abbey triple. Saaz and Styrian hops are used. Beer is conditioned both warm and cold. Very drinkable for such a strong beer. Serve chilled.
FLANDERS BROWN ALE (Liefman's)	1048 1052	12 13	4.6 5.6		15 18	23 27	100	Special Ale & Lactobacillus	Varies with season	Brown ale. A warm-fermented and -conditioned beer made in two strengths. Has a lactic tartness that may be quite intense. Dry taste. Young (6-week) beer is blended with a smaller quantity of beer that has been oak-aged 8 to10 months. The strong version is straight, and peaks at about 2 years. Vienna malt is often used.
BRABANT WHITE WITTE/WITBIER WHITE BEER	1044 1050	11 12.4	4.5 5.2	63 68	2 4	14 22	50	Ale & Lactobacillus	58-70°F 14-21°C	Pale wheat ale, usually spiced. The word *witte* means white. A medieval mashing technique is used to make this beer, which has about 50 percent unmalted wheat and 10 percent unmalted oats in it. This gives the beer an opalescent sheen, from which the name is derived. Flavored with coriander and orange peel (curaçao). Darker, stronger versions similar, but with additions of crystal and other colored malt for a sweet caramelly flavor. Other spices sometimes used in small amounts. The style was extinct until revived by Pierre Celis of Hoegaarden. There are other related styles, such as Peeterman, "Uytzet des Flandres," "l'Orge d'Anvers," "Diest," and "Zoeg." These were all very light-gravity beers 100 years ago.
STRONG WHITE BEER	1081	19.5	8 9		10 15	16 27	50-100	Special Ale	58-70°F 14-21°C	

BEER STYLE	Original Gravity	°Plato of Wort	% Alcohol-Vol	Attenuation-%	Color-°SRM	Bitterness-IBUs	% Barley Malt	Yeast Type	Fermentation Temp	DESCRIPTION & COMMENTS
SAISONS SEZOENS	1048 1059	12.5 14	5.0 6.0	50 65	6 9	30 45	90 100	Ale	50-54°F 10-12°C	French (Saisons) and German (Sezoens) spellings for related styles, which could be described as Belgian pilsner ales. Very crisp, bitter, and refreshing. Golden color. Stronger versions more amber. Fruity ale aromas also evident. Pretty straightforward, lacking the unusual microbial activity that gives many Belgian ales their bizarre character. Some versions spiced with orange and coriander.
SAISONS SPECIALE	1083	20	7.5	50 65	8 14	35 50	90 100	Ale	50-54°F 10-12°C	
LAMBIC — Straight; GUEUZE — Blended, old + new; FARO — Diluted, sweetened; KRIEK — Cherries; FRAMBOISE — Raspberries; AARDBIEN — Strawberries; DRUIVEN — Muscat grapes; PÊCHE — Peach	1048 1052	12 13	4.4 5.5	70 90	6 12	11-20	60-70, Malt, 30-40 Wheat	Wild, see below	Varies through year. Summers important.	The characteristic "wild" beers of the area around Brussels, Payottenland. Unique family of beers with a sharp, sour flavor. May have pH as low as 3 (very acidic). Fermented with wild yeast and other microbial flora unique to the region. Lambic is the basic product, made from barley malt and unmalted wheat. May take 3 years to make. Gueuze is a blend of old and young lambic. Faro is young lambic with candy sugar added. Others are fruit beers: Kriek has cherries; Framboise, raspberries; Aardbien, strawberries; and Druiven, grapes. Whew! Serve at 50°F/10°C. Reputed to be impossible to make outside the Payottenland region. Although reasonable facsimiles have been made by dedicated homebrewers, fermentation in wooden barrels inoculated with the appropriate microbes seems critical. Hops are used as a preservative only, and should be well-aged.
TRAPPIST (Orval)	1054	13.5	5.2 5.7	66	7 9	24	85-90 Malt + Sugar	Ale + Lager	59-72°F 15-22°C	A unique abbey ale, still made by monks. Brilliant orange-amber color. Unique, sharp, dry taste, very champagne-y. Three malts plus sugar are used, with a single-cell ale yeast during primary and secondary fermentation. Several lager yeasts are added at bottling, and then warm-conditioned. The beer is dry-hopped with Hallertau and Kent Goldings.
BIÈRE DU GARDE	1062 1075	14.5 18	5.5 6.5	60 65	6 15	24 32	100	Ale	55-60°F 12-15°C	Strong pale ales brewed in France. Brewed strong to age a year or two, they are generally malty and amber in color, although pale versions are becoming more common. Usually put up in corked champagne bottles.

LAMBIC FLORA (Partial):
- *Brettanomyces bruxellensis*
- *Brettanomyces lambicus*
- *Saccharomyces* sp.
- *Kloekeria* sp. (yeast)
- *Pediococcus*
- Enterobacteria

BEER STYLE	Original Gravity	°Plato of Wort	% Alcohol-Vol	Attenuation-%	Color-°SRM	Bitterness-IBUs	% Barley Malt	Yeast Type	Fermentation Temp	DESCRIPTION & COMMENTS
AMERICAN LAGER	1044 1048	11 11.9	4.0 4.8	63%	2.4 3.8	10.5 17	60–80	Lager	46-52 8-11°C 33-40 14°C	A light-tasting lager beer, originally patterned after the pilsner style, but now weaker, paler, and less bitter. Contains corn or rice adjuncts, the cheaper brands having more. Six-row malt is used because of its high enzyme levels. The present law limits adjunct content to 60 percent. The best examples are light, crisp, and taste good ice-cold on a hot day. The worst are thin, watery, with a soda pop texture, and a flavor of too much corn. Some brands are stabilized with ultrafiltration instead of pasteurization, greatly improving beer body and head retention. These are sometimes known as "bottled draft" (or canned). Cans have plastic coatings on the inside, which can affect beer flavor.
AMERICAN LIGHT LAGER	1031 1040	8 10	3.5 4.3	72%	1.9 3.5	7 18	60–80	Lager + Enzymes	46-52 8-11°C 33-40 14°C	An even lighter-tasting version of the same type of lager. Original gravities are less, and industrial enzymes are used to reduce dextrins almost completely to maltose, so attenuation is higher than normal beers. Continues to be a growing segment of total U.S. beer consumption. Difficult, if not impossible, for the homebrewer to make; a good thing—we really don't want to!
CREAM ALE	1046 1048	11.4 11.9	4.8 5.0	63%	2 4.4	12 25	60–80	Lager	58-70°F 14-21°C 33°F 1°C	Originated in the 1800s as a combination of fresh lager and old stock ale. Examples still survive, mostly in the East and Midwest. Very similar to American lager, they are usually bottom-fermented, hoppier, and slightly stronger than the regular beer. Some breweries still use ale and lager yeast combined.
CALIFORNIA COMMON BEER	1050	12.4	4.0	60%	16	40	60–80	Lager	60°F 15°C 50-53°F 10-12°C	Uniquely American style, indigenous to San Francisco, it is a lager beer fermented at ale temperatures. Originated in the days before refrigeration on the West Coast, which lacked frozen rivers and lakes from which to cut ice for lagering. Amber, highly carbonated, strongly hopped. Anchor Steam is the only surviving example. Anchor Steam is a registered trademark of the Anchor Brewing Company.
AMERICAN PALE ALE	1046 1062	11.4 15.2	5.3 6		8 20	17 40	90 100	Ale	58-70°F 14-21°C	New style of amber ales from American craft brewers. Fairly wide range of beers, not in exact imitation of British styles. Many have Cascade hops as a signature. Usually balanced toward the bitter side, often intensely. Dry-hopping common.
KENTUCKY COMMON BEER	1049	12.2	3.8		25	27	60 70	Ale	58-70°F 14-21°C	Style of dark beer once brewed in the lower Ohio Valley, especially near Louisville. Characterized by moderate lactic sourness, the result of controlled infection.

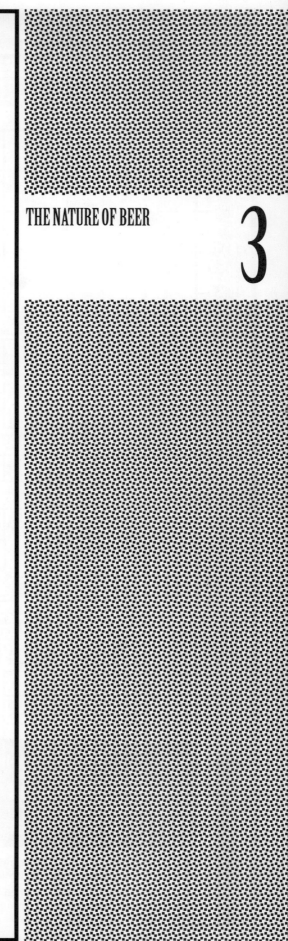

THE NATURE OF BEER

3

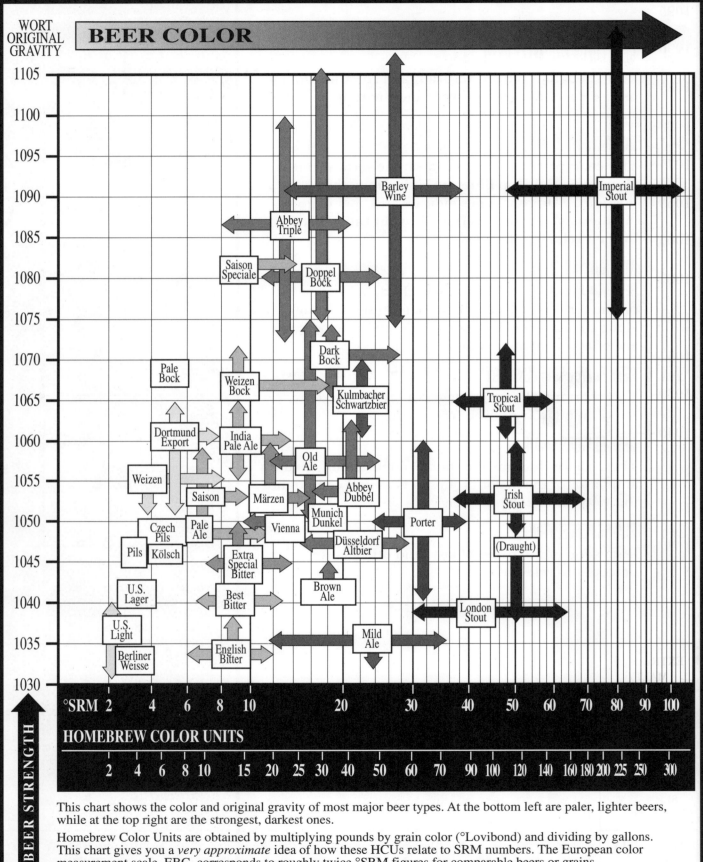

WORT ORIGINAL GRAVITY

BEER COLOR

BEER STRENGTH

This chart shows the color and original gravity of most major beer types. At the bottom left are paler, lighter beers, while at the top right are the strongest, darkest ones.

Homebrew Color Units are obtained by multiplying pounds by grain color (°Lovibond) and dividing by gallons. This chart gives you a *very approximate* idea of how these HCUs relate to SRM numbers. The European color measurement scale, EBC, corresponds to roughly twice °SRM figures for comparable beers or grains.

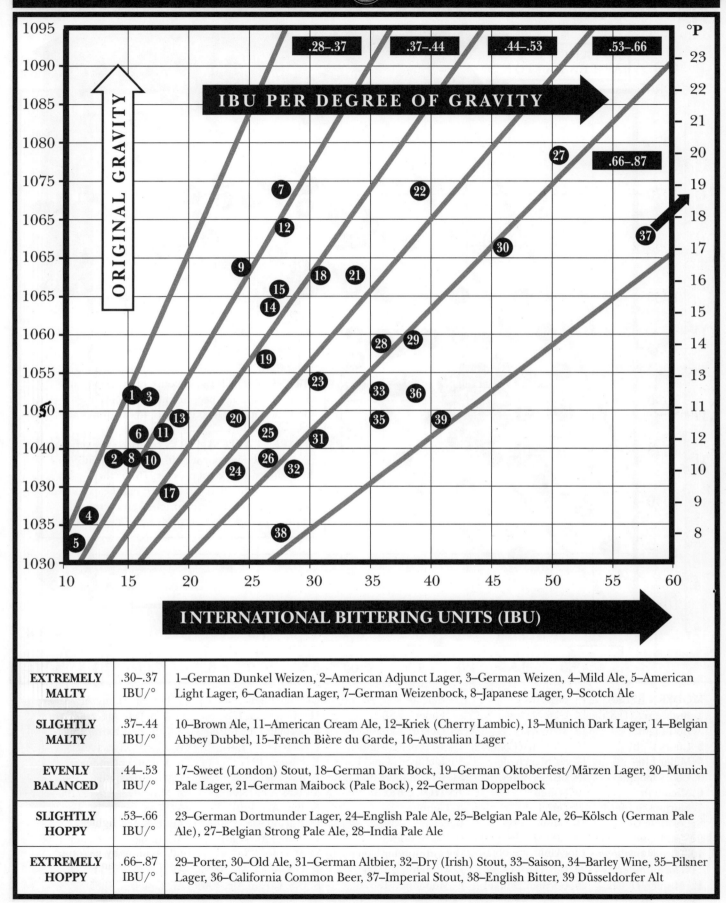

EXTREMELY MALTY	.30–.37 IBU/°	1–German Dunkel Weizen, 2–American Adjunct Lager, 3–German Weizen, 4–Mild Ale, 5–American Light Lager, 6–Canadian Lager, 7–German Weizenbock, 8–Japanese Lager, 9–Scotch Ale
SLIGHTLY MALTY	.37–.44 IBU/°	10–Brown Ale, 11–American Cream Ale, 12–Kriek (Cherry Lambic), 13–Munich Dark Lager, 14–Belgian Abbey Dubbel, 15–French Bière du Garde, 16–Australian Lager
EVENLY BALANCED	.44–.53 IBU/°	17–Sweet (London) Stout, 18–German Dark Bock, 19–German Oktoberfest/Märzen Lager, 20–Munich Pale Lager, 21–German Maibock (Pale Bock), 22–German Doppelbock
SLIGHTLY HOPPY	.53–.66 IBU/°	23–German Dortmunder Lager, 24–English Pale Ale, 25–Belgian Pale Ale, 26–Kölsch (German Pale Ale), 27–Belgian Strong Pale Ale, 28–India Pale Ale
EXTREMELY HOPPY	.66–.87 IBU/°	29–Porter, 30–Old Ale, 31–German Altbier, 32–Dry (Irish) Stout, 33–Saison, 34–Barley Wine, 35–Pilsner Lager, 36–California Common Beer, 37–Imperial Stout, 38–English Bitter, 39 Düsseldorfer Alt

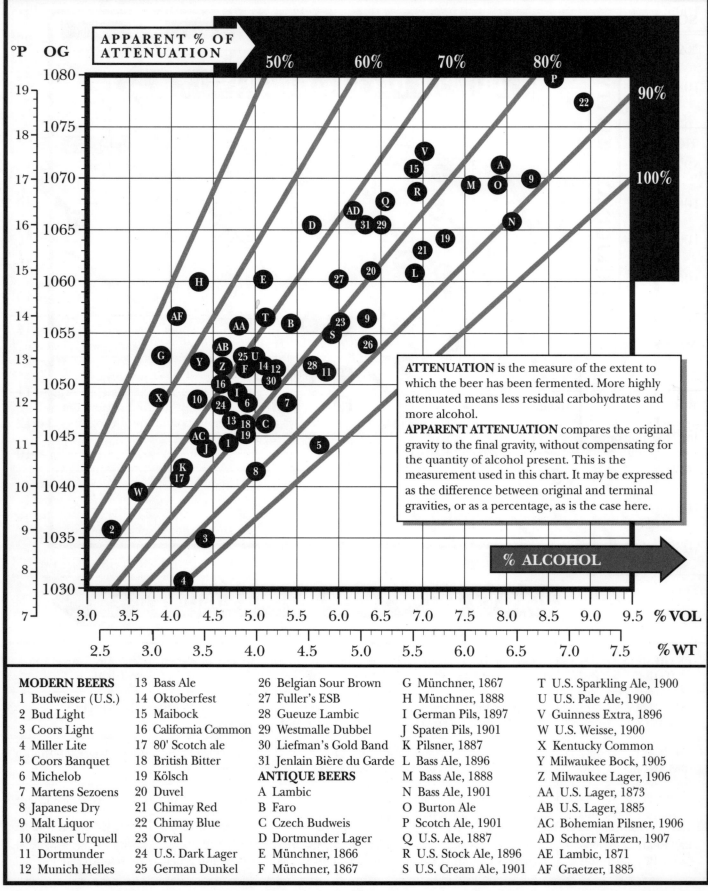

ATTENUATION is the measure of the extent to which the beer has been fermented. More highly attenuated means less residual carbohydrates and more alcohol.

APPARENT ATTENUATION compares the original gravity to the final gravity, without compensating for the quantity of alcohol present. This is the measurement used in this chart. It may be expressed as the difference between original and terminal gravities, or as a percentage, as is the case here.

MODERN BEERS
1 Budweiser (U.S.)
2 Bud Light
3 Coors Light
4 Miller Lite
5 Coors Banquet
6 Michelob
7 Martens Sezoens
8 Japanese Dry
9 Malt Liquor
10 Pilsner Urquell
11 Dortmunder
12 Munich Helles
13 Bass Ale
14 Oktoberfest
15 Maibock
16 California Common
17 80' Scotch ale
18 British Bitter
19 Kölsch
20 Duvel
21 Chimay Red
22 Chimay Blue
23 Orval
24 U.S. Dark Lager
25 German Dunkel
26 Belgian Sour Brown
27 Fuller's ESB
28 Gueuze Lambic
29 Westmalle Dubbel
30 Liefman's Gold Band
31 Jenlain Bière du Garde

ANTIQUE BEERS
A Lambic
B Faro
C Czech Budweis
D Dortmunder Lager
E Münchner, 1866
F Münchner, 1867
G Münchner, 1867
H Münchner, 1888
I German Pils, 1897
J Spaten Pils, 1901
K Pilsner, 1887
L Bass Ale, 1896
M Bass Ale, 1888
N Bass Ale, 1901
O Burton Ale
P Scotch Ale, 1901
Q U.S. Ale, 1887
R U.S. Stock Ale, 1896
S U.S. Cream Ale, 1901
T U.S. Sparkling Ale, 1900
U U.S. Pale Ale, 1900
V Guinness Extra, 1896
W U.S. Weisse, 1900
X Kentucky Common
Y Milwaukee Bock, 1905
Z Milwaukee Lager, 1906
AA U.S. Lager, 1873
AB U.S. Lager, 1885
AC Bohemian Pilsner, 1906
AD Schorr Märzen, 1907
AE Lambic, 1871
AF Graetzer, 1885

SOURCE	CHEMICALS	DISCUSSION	
BARLEY MALT	Starch, sugar, and carbohydrates	Mostly important as fuel for yeast growth. Dextrins that remain in beer contribute to mouthfeel and caloric content.	
	Proteins and amino acids	Important in yeast nutrition. Contribute greatly to body and character. Combine with polyphenols to form chill-haze.	
HOPS	Humulone (alpha acids), lupulone (beta acids)	Hard and soft resins of hops. Give beer its bitterness. During the boil, these resins isomerize (rearrange chemically) and become soluble.	
	Humulene, linalool, geraniol, myrcene, and others	A range of volatile oils called terpenes. These chemicals vary widely by hop type, determining the nature of hop character in the beer. Flavor fades rapidly with time. Also present in oils are ketones, aldehydes, and others.	
	Polyphenols	Tannins. Harsh, astringent taste. Mostly combine with protein fractions and drop out of beer at various stages. Involved in chill-haze.	
WATER & MINERAL IONS	Calcium, magnesium, sulfate, carbonate, chloride, sodium, etc.	Indirect flavor influence (carbonate makes hops taste harsh). Affect mash chemistry, pH. Carbonate/sulfate ratio influences hop flavor. Minerals are necessary for yeast nutrition. Chloride gives full, rich flavor to sweet brown ales. Sulfate gives crisp, dry taste.	
BROWNING During grain kilning/roasting and wort boiling	Melanoidins	Powerful brown pigments present in caramelized sugars. Formed by heating carbohydrates and nitrogenous compounds together. Polymeric, nonvolatile. Important in head retention.	
	Pyrazines Pyranones Furanones Pyridines Pyrroles	Huge range of powerful aromatic chemicals formed during browning reactions, when carbohydrates are heated in the presence of nitrogen. Amazing range of flavors including all those associated with roasting, toasting, caramelizing, etc. Specific chemicals formed from combinations of specific sugars and amino acids. Controllable by the homebrewer by varying the time, moisture, and temperature of grain roasting, and by using many roasted malt types in one beer.	
FERMENTATION	Aldehydes	Acetaldehyde = green apple aroma. Others have woody, cardboardy smells of oxidation.	All formed as by-products of yeast metabolism, as well as bacterial activity. Hundreds of different compounds are known in beer, many are very powerful. Generally, more are produced at higher temperatures (diacetyl excepted), hence the spicier, more complex aroma and flavor of ales. Differing organisms and conditions give a unique profile to every brew.
	Alcohol (ethanol)	Intoxicant. Tasteless under 8 percent.	
	Carbon dioxide	Provides fizz, some acidity.	
	Diacetyl	Butterscotch aroma. A defect when strong.	
	Esters	Fruity notes, especially desirable in ales.	
	Fusel oils (alcohols)	Complex alcohols. Solventy smells.	
	Lactones	Fruity, peachy, musky aromas.	
	Organic acids	Provide tartness, other flavors—goatiness, sweatiness. Often a sign of contamination.	
	Sulfur compounds	DMS and others. Usually vegetal aromas.	

SOURCE	QTY	CHEMICALS	FLAVOR/EFFECTS/COMMENTS
ACETALDE-HYDE	1 to 15 ppm	The principle volatile acid in beer. An intermediate step in the production of acetic acid and other more highly flavored compounds. 10 ppm taste threshold.	Acetaldehyde has a "green apple" aroma, present in yogurt and unlagered beer. Other aldehydes give woody, papery, and cardboardy flavors associated with oxidation.
ACIDS	Varies	Acetic and lactic acids are present, and may be from bacteria rather than yeast. Caprylic and other fatty acids (<10 ppm) are often indicative of spoilage.	Responsible for the acidity in beer. (pH 3.8–4.2). Caprylic and other fatty acids contribute a "goaty" aroma, a common sign of *Lactobacillus/Pediococcus* infection.
ALCOHOL Ethanol	2% to 12%	A waste product of yeast metabolism. Produced in rough proportion to the starting gravity.	The intoxicating component of beer. Relatively tasteless, except in strong beers. Usually perceived as a warming sensation. Taste threshold in water is 8 percent.
CARBON DIOXIDE	0.3% to 0.6%	A colorless gas, soluble in water, a by-product of yeast respiration. Forms carbonic acid when dissolved in water (or beer).	Gives beer its fizz. Much more gas dissolves when liquid is cold. In brewing water, its presence allows carbonate ions to be dissolved in the form of bicarbonates—HCO.
DEXTRINS	1.5% to 6%	A group of carbohydrates, intermediate between starch and sugar. Unfermentable by brewer's yeast.	Not sweet. Gives beer some mouthfeel, but is tasteless. Tests have shown it is not the primary component in beer body. Fills you up, though. Can be used as an additive.
DIACETYL	0.02 to 0.5 ppm	A powerful aromatic, produced by yeast and bacteria, especially *Streptococcus*. Worts with insufficient nitrogen (too much sugar) may cause problems.	Subtle or strong buttery/butterscotch aroma, depending on amounts. A defect over 1 ppm in ale, and .5 ppm in lager beers. Kraeusening helps keep levels low.
DIMETHYL SULFIDE	11 to 70 ppb	In small quantities, from malt. In larger amounts, from bacteria. Other sulfurous compounds contribute to flavor in beer—hydrogen sulfide, mercaptans, and others.	Cooked-corn aroma. Taste threshold 30 ppb. Precursor present in malt, slow wort cooling exacerbates. Yeast by-product, varies by strain. Produced by *Obesumbacterium* bacteria.
ESTERS	27 to 82 ppm	Family of powerful aromatics, produced by yeast. More are produced at higher temperatures. Major ones include ethyl acetate (30 ppm), isoamyl acetate (2 ppm), and ethyl formate.	A wide range of chemicals with fruity aromas. Give ales much of their "aley" taste. Yeast strains vary widely in their synthesis of various esters. Hundreds known in beer.
ETHYL ACETATE	15 to 40 ppm	Produced during fermentation, especially at higher temperatures.	The chemical in nail polish remover. Has a "solventy" aroma that can be felt in your eyes, as well as smelled.
4-VINYL GUIACOL	sub ppm	Phenolic compound produced by weissbier yeast strains. Taste threshold 0.3 ppm.	Clovelike flavor that is a keynote of authentic German-styled weissbiers. Regarded as a defect in any other context.
FUSEL OILS Higher alcohols	60 to 200 ppm	Volatile, oily liquids produced by yeast. Various alcohols, including N-amyl, isoamyl, active amyl, and isopropyl. High ferment temperature may double fusel oil content. Ales have more than lagers.	Present in all fermented drinks. Contribute flowery, fruity, aromatic flavors to beers. Excessive amounts can cause headaches and thirst. A convulsive poison in large amounts.

CHEMICAL	QTY	SOURCE/COMPOSITION	FLAVOR/EFFECTS/COMMENTS
HOP OILS (Aromatics)	50 to 2,000 ppb	A mix of volatile compounds, mostly terpenes, including linalool, humulene, that occur as oil in hop cones. Humulene is predominant. Esters, organic acids, ketones, aldehydes, and higher alcohols are also present in hop oil.	Much of hop character comes from this group of chemicals. Floral, green, spicy, and other aromas are all associated with terpenes. The other chemicals present have many individual aromas.
ISOAMYL ACATATE "Banana" ester	1.2 to 6 ppm	A higher alcohol, technically. Produced by certain yeast strains, especially at higher temperatures. Common in weissbiers.	Has the solventy aroma of ripe bananas. In small amounts, may be pleasant, especially in weissbiers, but a defect if it stands out.
MALTOSE	0 to 0.5% (in beer)	The main fermentable sugar of wort. Formed by the breakdown of starch by enzymes in the mash. Split by maltase, an enzyme present in yeast and barley.	Mostly fermented by yeast, but some beers— sweet stouts and some German lagers—have residual sweetness due to maltose.
MELANOIDINS	Low ppb	Complex nonvolatile polymers formed by heating sugar with nitrogen. Improve head formation and responsible for color in beer.	The prime color contributor to beer. Develops mostly during malt roasting, but also occurs during the boil to a lesser extent.
MERCAPTANS	Under 0.05 ppb	One of this group is responsible for the "skunky" off-flavor of beer exposed to sunlight or other harmful light. Formed from hop components.	Flavor defect, an aroma with skunky, rubbery character. Often happens to beer in green bottles in retail cooler cases. May happen quickly. Brown bottles are good protection.
PHENOLS	Sub ppm	Group of generally unpleasant chemicals produced by wild and brewing yeast. Weissbier yeast produces a "clove-y" one.	Harsh, medicinal aromas in beers infected by wild yeast. Clove-flavored 4-vinyl guiacol gives weissbier its characteristic aroma.
POLYPHENOLS Tannins	Low ppm qty	Complex group of chemicals leached from barley husks during sparging, or from hops. Highly reactive.	Astringent qualities. Mostly important for its interactions. Combines with proteins during the boil and either precipitates to form the hot break or remains to cause chill-haze.
PYRAZINES Also pyridines, pyrroles, fura- nones, and pyra- nones	Low ppb.	Powerfully aromatic chemicals derived from the browning reaction. Formed mostly over 212°F/100°C. Over 100 pyrazines are known, some tastable at less than .002 ppb.	Very large group of powerful flavor chemicals with many flavors. Flavors of caramel and roasted grains—nutty, bready, toasty, malty, and on and on.
RESINS From hops: alpha and beta acids, and their isomers	8 to 75 ppm	A variety of similar but different resins. Iso-acids are the soluble ones, formed from insoluble resins by heat during the boiling process.	Bitterness, mostly. Recent studies have shown that there is some relationship between hop resin components and hop character in beer.
SODIUM CHLORIDE	5 to 150 ppm	Common table salt, present in brewing water. Rarely used as an additive.	Adds fullness, richness in small amounts. High levels (>20) appropriate only for dark, sweet beers.
TERPENES Geraniol, lina- lool, humulene	50 to 2000 ppb	Volatile, aromatic oils, primarily derived from hops. Includes all the hop aromatics.	Fresh, green, hoppy, floral aromas. Humulene is the most abundant. Linalool is a major component of lavender oil. Geraniol is a major component of rose oil.

Ultimately, you'll drink your beer. This simple act sets off a complex chain reaction of neural events that eventually leads to some sort of conscious perception of taste, texture and aroma.

Taste

Taste, narrowly defined, is a much simpler process than smell. The tongue is covered with small bumps that are actually specialized chemical detectors, or receptors. There are only four types of receptors, located on different parts of the tongue. These receptors respond to specific flavor effects: salty, sour (acid), sweet, and bitter. When combined in different ways, these primary flavors—all present in varying amounts in beer—create a wide range of flavor effects. Interestingly, the tastebuds receptive to bitterness are about 50 times as large as the other three types, and they respond much more slowly to the bitter sensation. Perhaps this is why bitterness lingers on the tongue far longer than other tastes.

In addition to the four primary flavors, the tongue can also detect other nonaroma sensations, such as astringency, cooling (minty/menthol), peppery, and mouth-coating. Some of these sensations play an important role in the way we perceive beer flavor. Astringency comes mainly from hop tannins and is especially noticeable in bitter pale beers made from alkaline water.

Aroma

The nose is lined with a staggering array—tens of thousands—of incredibly sensitive chemical receptors, each sensitive to a single chemical. Threshold of aroma perception varies by chemical, but some thresholds are amazingly low, even in the parts-per-quintillion. Most important beer flavor chemicals have sensitivities in the parts-per-million or parts-per-billion. With many chemicals, perception varies enormously by quantity, with the flavor actually changing according to the concentration. One malt chemical tastes like malt at parts-per-trillion quantities, tacos at parts-per-million, and concord grapes at parts-per-thousand. It is, in fact, the chemical used in grape soda.

In addition, aromas interact in unpredictable ways. DMS, for example, smells very different in dark beers than in pale ones.

Smell is not always perceived as such. Much of what we think of as taste is actually aroma. In addition to conscious sniffing, much smell comes as aromas are breathed out after swallowing.

Temperature has an enormous effect on the way flavors are perceived. Higher temperatures cause aromatic chemicals to volatilize at higher rates, making more of the stuff available to your sensory apparatus. Full-flavored ales taste very bland and lifeless if served at cold temperatures. Likewise, beers designed to be served cold don't do well at warmer temperatures. Much of their flavor profile is created by high levels of carbonation, which is lost when the product is warmed.

Interestingly, the sense of smell is wired into the brain differently than the other senses. The olfactory nerves run deep inside to a very ancient part of the brain—the lizard brain, if you will. The ability of aromas to trigger emotions is attributed to this.

Mouthfeel

Tasting beer invokes a number of sensations that are neither taste nor smell, but affect the total taste experience nevertheless. "Body" is a prime example. What we experience and describe as "body" is a reaction of the mouth to colloidal protein complexes that make beer a dilute gel, with a much higher viscosity than water. The presence of unfermented dextrins in the beer contribute to this effect also, but to a lesser extent than the proteins. Generally, the experience of "body" increases with beer gravity, unless the beer is fortified with a proteinless substance, such as honey.

Alcohol has a very high taste threshold, about 8 percent in water. It has a slightly sweet character, but more noticeable is a warming sensation as it goes down the throat. Strong ales are not called "winter warmers" for nothing. The level of carbonation also affects the perception of taste. High levels of dissolved CO_2 tend to mask beer flavors, especially hops. But a totally flat beer will taste rather drab and lifeless.

Other Senses

Strange as it seems, sight can also affect the way we perceive taste. In a way, our eyes set up expectations for our tastebuds, making unbiased judgments difficult. In competitive tastings, out-of-style color can reduce the score of a beer far beyond the two points allotted to it on the scoring sheet. Experience, memories, and even such things as packaging and advertising have an effect on our perception that is more powerful than we might like.

Rules for Serious Tasting

1. Taste in a room free of distracting odors, especially tobacco smoke. If you are a smoker, don't smoke for a couple of hours before a tasting. And, don't wear clothes you've smoked in. Perfumes are also a problem. For those allergic to pets, their presence can be disastrous. Colds or nasal congestion can also bring your taster to a grinding halt.

2. Have good lighting. Avoid strong or uneven lighting. Fluorescent lighting affects the color of beer in a negative way; incandescent seems to make the beer look better. Some recommend the use of candles to help judge the clarity of beers. Many people bring penlights to judging sessions for the same purpose.

3. Use proper glassware. Wide-mouth cups or glasses allow you to get a better noseful of the beer aroma. Wine glasses work very well. If you use plastic, be sure there is no residual smell.

4. Pour the beer straight down the middle. Don't tilt the glass and pour gently. You want to create a good head of foam and volatilize the aromatic chemicals, making them available to your senses.

5. Smell first. Some aromas are highly volatile and dissipate fast. Get a whiff before you evaluate appearance or taste.

6. Serve the beer at the proper temperature. Lagers at 38°–45°F, ales at 50°–60°F. Generally, lighter beers can be served cooler than stronger ones. This is sometimes difficult, especially with ales, but flavor is enormously affected by temperature. Have a thermometer available to check the temperature of the beers you're sampling.

7. Work at it. Swirl the beer around in your mouth and aspirate (as they say in wine-tasting circles), by breathing in and up into your nose while your mouth has beer in it. This will give you much more exposure to the aromatics. It's noisy, but fun.

8. Taste with purpose. Whether it's a homebrew competition or a commercial tasting, it helps to have some kind of scoring system, based on aroma, appearance, flavor, and aftertaste. Scoring helps to focus your attention on the specifics.

9. Taste blind. Your perception of beer depends on many things, including your memories and judgments about the beer's brand personality or the person who brewed it. The only fair way to evaluate a beer is not to know what it is.

10. Have palate-cleansers available. French bread or saltine crackers work best, along with pure water, preferable dechlorinated. Avoid anything that is greasy or too salty. Also, the crust on the bread should not be too dark.

11. Limit the number of beers you taste. An experienced judge can do justice to about 25 samples per day. For the rest of us, 10 to 12 beers is considered maximum for a serious tasting. Beyond that, your tastebuds wear out. If you going for a second round, allow your senses a break before resuming. Schedule your judging sessions accordingly.

12. Expand your taste vocabulary. Discriminating tasting is a process that can be learned. It is extremely helpful to know the important flavor chemicals responsible for beer flavors and defects—DMS, diacetyl, phenol, aldehydes, skunkiness, etc. Once you know these, you can quickly, pick them out and understand the variations in process that created them.

13. Dump it. If you're tasting in a competition, don't feel compelled to drink it all. Have an

empty pitcher to dump out the excess. Nobody will be offended or think less of you.

Serious Homebrew Judging

The American Homebrew Association and the Home Wine and Beer Trade Association cosponsor a national Beer Judge Certification Program. A written and judging test is the entry vehicle, and various levels are attainable, depending on your test score and experience points. You can accumulate points for organizing and judging in homebrew competitions. This program is well worth getting into and is the best way to really get to know about beer flavor evaluation. For more information, contact: BJCP Administrator, c/o American Homebrew Association, Box 1670, Boulder, CO 80302.

Talk to your local homebrew shop or club, as they probably know of tests in your area.

Beer Judging Checklist

In homebrew competitions, every aspect of beer character is judged against the standards for a particular style. This means that judges must have a good understanding of the range of parameters for each of the 30 or so beer styles typically included in homebrew contests. And, of course, for styles such as "specialty," the specifics are very loosely defined. In tastings of commercial beers, adherence to style is not so critically judged, and the beers are judged on their own merits.

Appearance
Clarity
Color
Depth of color*
Carbonation level
Head retention

Aroma
Malt
Hops
Fermentation characteristics
Off-flavors
Specialty ingredients—spices, fruits, smoke, etc.
Overall effect

Taste
Hops—character and bitterness level
Malt
Balance
Sweetness
Fermentation character
Specialty ingredients
Off-flavors

Mouthfeel
Body—thick or thin
Warming/alcoholic

Aftertaste
Intensity
Quality
Astringent
Off-flavors

Overall Impression
Drinkability
Uniqueness
Finesse
Intensity
Free from defects

*Depth of color is a term that applies to the apparent richness of the beer color. Generally, beers that are colored with a small amount of very dark malt will have less "depth" than ones colored with a larger amount of lighter malt. Refractivity, or the liquid's ability to bend light, is also a factor. High-gravity beers will invariably look very rich, as both alcohol and dextrins are highly refractive compared to water.

OVERVIEW OF BREWING

4

COUNTRY	BEER TYPES	GRAINS	MASH	HOPS	COMMENTS
GERMAN Also Czech Republic, Scandinavia	Lagers, pale, dark, bock, and amber. Doppelbock, alt, wheat ales, Kölsch.	Two-row malt, mostly. High %N, less complete modification than English malts.	**Decoction**—Part of the mash is removed, boiled, then returned to raise temperature. $90° \rightleftharpoons 122° \rightleftharpoons 142° \rightleftharpoons 170°F / 32° \rightleftharpoons 50° \rightleftharpoons 61° \rightleftharpoons 77°C$.	Hallertau, Spalt, Tettnanger, Hersbrucker, Saaz (Czech), Northern Brewer. Also, Perle, recently.	Lager yeast and cold fermentation is used with lager beers. Primary is 5–14 days at 45°F/7.5°C. A long secondary lagering period at 34°F/2°C is used. Long aging needed with lagers. Wide range of bitterness. Paler beers usually more bitter, darker ones more malty. Only malt, hops, water and yeast used. Ales (altbiers) are still made in some places.
ENGLAND Also Ireland, Scotland	Ales of all colors and strengths. Bitter, pale ale, strong or old ales. Porter, stout, mild and brown ales. Scotch ales.	Two-row malt, very highly modified. Lower %N than lager malt. Pale ale malt, darker than lager most common.	**Infusion**—Hot water is mixed with grain to raise temperature, then held between 145°–165°F / 63°–74°C.	Fuggles, Bullion, Goldings, E. Kent Goldings, Brewer's Gold, Progress, Target Challenger, Northdown.	Ale yeast with high fermentation temperature gives characteristic fruity ale quality. Beers are typically cask-conditioned, lightly carbonated, served on draught. Malt character usually evident, even in bitter beers. Stout is the drink of Ireland—dark and dry. The ales of Scotland are amber to brown and very malty.
BELGIUM	Huge variety of idiosyncratic ales, some medieval types, lambic abbey ales, pale ales, sour beers, fruit ales.	Two-row malts, mostly, often from France, Germany, Czech Republic. Unmalted wheat, oats used.	**Step mash**—Grain is mixed with water, then heated in a tun, usually with steam.	Northern Brewer, Hallertau, Saaz, Styrian, Goldings. Some hops grown in France.	Beers in amazing variety are brewed. Mostly ale yeasts, but wild yeasts and bacterial cultures are used to give certain ales their uniqueness. Some very bizarre and ancient techniques are used, especially in the production of witbiers, lambics and sour brown ales. Monastic ales important.
United States Also Canada, Japan, Australia, Mexico & others	Mostly pale, light lagers, lightly hopped. Cream ale plus a few weak bocks. Warm-fermented lagers a California tradition. Microbreweries a recent boom, reinventing many styles.	Six-row malt, traditionally. Very high enzyme levels allow up to 50 percent corn and/or rice. (precooked) U.S. 2-row malts also high in protein, enzymes.	**Step mash**—Corn and rice well-cooked before being added to mash. Temperature raised with steam. Enzymes commonly added, especially to adjunct mash.	Cluster, now being replaced with high-alpha types: Nugget, Galena, Chinook, and Eroica. To finish, Cascade and European types, such as Hallertau.	Industrial brewing technique usually centers on getting maximum alcohol from the minimum ingredients. Lightness, shelf stability, and all-day drinkability are the most important qualities sought after. Generally, in superficial imitation of German pils style. Most new microbreweries are in German or English tradition, although new American styles are emerging. Typically a 6- to 9-day primary at 50°–55°F/10°–13°C. Then held at 41°F/5°C. Craft breweries all over the map.

STAGE	PRACTICE	THEORY
MALTING	Selected grades of barley are moistened and allowed to sprout. When rootlet is from one-half to the full length of the corn, growth is stopped by drying.	Enzymes in barley are unleashed to attack the starch granules and make them soluble as food for the young plant. Texture changes from hard to crumbly. Protein is also attacked by enzymes, breaking it up into smaller units.
KILNING	Malt is heated by hot air to a predetermined moisture content, to stop malting activity and bring out malt flavor. Some types are further roasted to develop color and caramel flavors.	Pale malt types are dried at low heat to minimize color change. In roasted types, sugars and nitrogen compounds interact to form a wide spectrum of caramelly, malty, roasted flavors.
MILLING	Specialized roller-mills crush the starchy middle, leaving the husks more or less intact.	Malt starch should be ground finely to maximize extract, husks left coarse, to serve as filter bed.
MASHING	Crushed malt is mixed with water and pre-cooked adjuncts (if used) and taken through a series of temperature steps. Typically, a protein rest at 122°F/50°C, and a starch-conversion rest at 145°–165°F/63°–74°C.	Diastatic enzymes break starch into dextrins and then sugars, mainly maltose. Malt and grains are combined for flavor, color and other qualities. Time, temperature, pH, dilution, and water chemistry affect the outcome.
SPARGING	Mash is put into a vessel with a perforated false bottom. Hot water at 180°F/82°C is slowly sprinkled on top, and allowed to trickle through, rinsing fermentable sugars from the spent grains.	Husks form a filter bed for the draining wort. Remaining starch gels at 180°F/82°C, can clog mash, creating haze. Wort increases in tannins, silica, and other bad stuff toward end of sparge.
BOILING	Liquid collected from the sparge—wort—is boiled vigorously in a kettle for 1 to 2 hours. Hops are added in stages for bittering. Wort is filtered through hops at end, to remove coagulated protein (trub).	Temperatures over 170°F/76°C destroy enzymes, fixing sugar/dextrin ratio. Hop resins isomerize and become soluble. Wort caramelizes, darkens. Heat sterilizes. Protein fractions precipitate with hop resins as the hot break.
CHILLING	Boiled wort is chilled rapidly with a heat exchanger to the temperature of primary fermentation. Wort is splashed into fermenter to allow oxygen to dissolve.	More protein coagulates as temperature drops and forms the cold break. Rapid cooling aids this and limits the vulnerability of the wort to bacteria and wild yeast, and also limits DMS production.
PRIMARY FERMENT	Yeast is added to chilled wort, and fermentation begins. A thick head of foam develops and lasts about 1 week for ale, 3 weeks for lager.	Yeast multiplies by budding until oxygen is used up, then fermentation begins. Maltose, abundant and easily metabolized, is consumed first.
SECONDARY FERMENT	Yeast slows down, but continues to ferment complex sugars. The beer clears as yeast drops to bottom in 3 weeks to 6 months or more.	Maltose gone, yeast eats other sugars in the wort, but slowly. Yeast drops out and autolyses (self-digests). Fining is done at end of this stage.
CONDITIONING	In casks or bottles, an added dose of sugar starts fermentation again. Pressure develops with CO_2, giving beer its fizz. Flavor mellows and dries out. Hop bitterness decreases.	Fermentation restarts and CO_2 gas dissolves in the beer. Flavor spectrum changes with time. Off-flavors may develop from oxidation, autolysis, light exposure, and other processes.
DRINKING	Beer is deftly poured and a magnificent head develops as myriad tiny bubbles dance their way upward. The glass is tilted, thirsty lips receive the treat, and the brewer is at last rewarded.	Theory? What theory? Who gives a fig about theory? Just drink the stuff and enjoy the multitudinous pleasures of homebrewing.

There are a few biochemical concepts you need to be familiar with because they form the basis for all brewing processes.

Enzymes

Enzymes are complex molecules that act as catalysts for a wide variety of chemical reactions in brewing and elsewhere. Think of them as elegant facilitators, helping reactions occur with a minimum input of energy. Enzymes make it possible for highly specific chemical changes to take place at temperatures and energy levels far lower than if the same reaction were initiated through brute force (heat + acids, for example).

Enzymes are involved in all the key reactions in brewing: dissociation of proteins and texture change during malting, further protein degradation and conversion of starch to sugar during mashing, and within the yeast cells, metabolism of various sugars.

Catalysts (which enzymes are) speed up chemical reactions but remain unchanged themselves. When the reaction is over, the quantity and chemical form of the catalyst remain the same as before the reaction.

Chemical reactions may be thought of as a change from one state to another. Between these two stable states is a condition of instability, a transition that can be looked at as a wall, or barrier, of energy. In order for a reaction to happen, energy must be applied to push the reaction over the "wall" that separates the two stable states.

For some reactions that energy may be quite high. When the reaction is at midpoint, the chemical state is highly unstable. One theory holds that enzymes help "stabilize" the transition state of the reaction, thereby lowering the energy needed to proceed from one stable state to another.

The proteins that form enzymes are extraordinarily complex. The primary chains of amino acids twist and turn back on themselves forming knotted, looping structures, like so much wadded-up string. Side chains protrude here and there, adding to the apparent chaos.

Although a seeming tangle of atoms, the shapes formed by these proteins have very specialized functions. In the case of enzymes, a "pocket" is formed on one part of the molecule. This pocket is perfectly shaped to accept not the stable endpoints of a given reaction, but the wild, turbulent midpoint.

The molecules' shape at the transition point fits the pocket on the enzyme like a hand fits a glove. This physical configuration allows the reaction to happen at a fraction of the energy normally needed to make it go.

For some reactions (such as the hydrolysis of proteins), this one action is insufficient. The catalysis proceeds step-by-step, with side chains swinging in and out like blades on a Swiss army knife, each tailored to an intermediate step, and the reaction catalyzed one small step at a time. These multistep enzymes can reduce the energy needed by millions, or even billions of times.

Polymers

Polymers are classes of chemical compounds formed by the connecting together of simple molecular subunits. They are quite common in natural and manmade substances, including all the familiar plastics and rubbery substances. In brewing, two main types are involved: carbohydrates, which are polymers of sugars, and proteins, which are a very complex type of polymer, created from the connection of amino acids into vast tangles, often with molecular weights in the hundreds of thousands. Amino acids are, in turn, moderately sized molecules, a common feature of which is the presence of nitrogen.

Colloids

A colloid is a suspension of polymers, such as proteins, which, when dispersed throughout, give a viscosity or "body" out of proportion to their actual concentration. It is highly dependent on the action of static electricity, which is responsible for many of its qualities.

Proteins create the colloidal state that is beer. This is why protein plays such a big role in mouthfeel and body. When the colloidal suspensions destabilize, the result is either chill-haze, or in the case of overaged beer, flakes of protein material that settle like snow to the bottom of the bottle.

One process, adsorption (not to be confused with absorption), is centrally involved in the colloidal state. This is an electrostatic attraction between particles and figures most prominently in the fining of beer.

Atomic Weight

Atomic weight is a measure of the mass of particular types of atoms. Atoms with a high molecular weight (lead, for example) have fewer atoms per unit of mass than lighter ones (such as hydrogen). So, in any given amount of mass, there are fewer atoms of those elements with higher atomic weight.

ATOMIC WEIGHTS	
Hydrogen	1.008
Nitrogen	14.008
Oxygen	16
Carbon	12.01
Sulfur	32.066
Phosphorus	30.975
Potassium	39.1
Calcium	40.08
Sodium	29.997
Iron	55.85

Molecular weight is simply the sum of the atomic weights of the atoms present in any given compound: $H_2O = 2x (H) + O$. This becomes important when calculating chemical reactions between molecules, in water chemistry, for example.

Metabolism

This is the life-sustaining processing of food materials into cellular energy that sustains us all. There are a wide variety of specific metabolic reactions. Microorganisms represent a broad range of different metabolic types, each with specific reactions. So much so, that many (if not most) of the tests designed to differentiate microbes are based on nutritional likes and dislikes. Some need air. Some will tolerate alcohol. Others have specific vitamin requirements, or need the presence of amino acids.

MICROBIAL METABOLIC TYPES
Facultative aerobe—will tolerate the absence of oxygen
Obligate aerobe—must have oxygen
Facultative anaerobe—will tolerate absence of oxygen
Obligate anaerobe—must have oxygen

Yeasts have complex nutritional requirements that include oxygen (only during the reproductive phase—not toward the end of fermentation), vitamins, amino acids, and a variety of minerals, including sodium, potassium, carbon, nitrogen, copper, zinc, and many others.

For the opportunistic microbes that can infect beer, metabolic likes and dislikes determine when they are most apt to attack a beer. Some bacteria, such as *Obesumbacterium*, need the same amino acids as yeast, so after the yeast have eaten them all, there aren't any left for the poor *Obesumbacterium*. Its only chance is to attack early, as the wort cools, before the yeast gets a chance to take hold. Acetic acid bacteria oxidize alcohol in their respiratory cycle, so they must wait until after the yeast has produced alcohol before they can infect beer.

While the major metabolic processes are complex, the bulk of the products involved in them are mostly simple ones: sugar + oxygen = alcohol + CO_2.

But, there are hundreds of by-products created by yeast (as well as infecting microbes) that figure prominently in the flavor profile of beer. Some of these chemicals are so powerful that they are detectable to the senses at around one part per billion (!) or less.

pH

This is a measure of acidity or alkalinity. The abbreviation *pH* stands for *percent hydrion*, and is the measure of the quantity of hydrogen ions in a solution. It is a 14-point scale, and is logarithmic, with the neutral point at the middle. Logarithmic means that each number up or down the scale is 10 times the acidity or alkalinity of the number preceding it. Lower numbers are acidic, higher numbers are alkaline. pH may be measured by a controlled dilution called *titration* with electronic meters, or less accurately with paper test strips. Temperature affects and distorts pH readings on instruments or paper test strips. Better meters have a built-in temperature compensation.

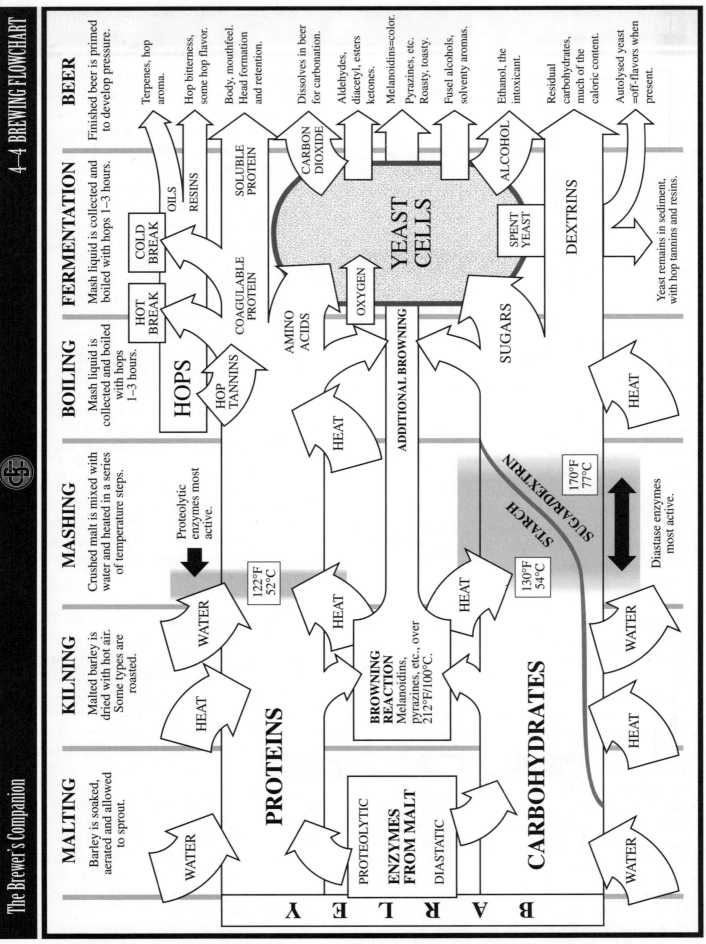

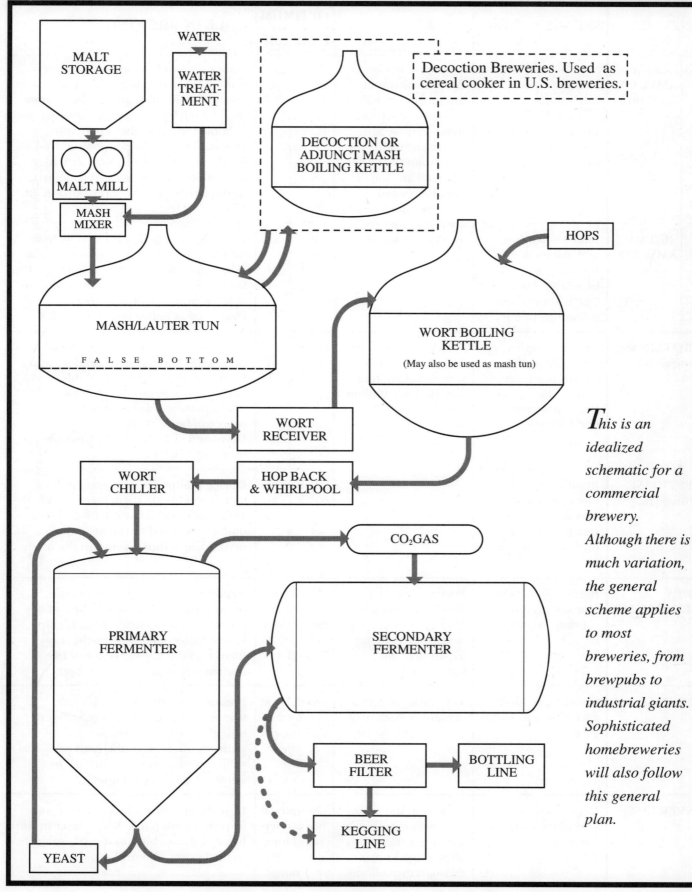

MALT
STORAGE

WATER

WATER
TREAT-
MENT

Decoction Breweries. Used as
cereal cooker in U.S. breweries.

MALT MILL

DECOCTION OR
ADJUNCT MASH
BOILING KETTLE

MASH
MIXER

HOPS

MASH/LAUTER TUN

F A L S E   B O T T O M

WORT BOILING
KETTLE

(May also be used as mash tun)

WORT
RECEIVER

WORT
CHILLER

HOP BACK
& WHIRLPOOL

*This is an
idealized
schematic for a
commercial
brewery.
Although there is
much variation,
the general
scheme applies
to most
breweries, from
brewpubs to
industrial giants.
Sophisticated
homebreweries
will also follow
this general
plan.*

CO_2 GAS

PRIMARY
FERMENTER

SECONDARY
FERMENTER

BEER
FILTER

BOTTLING
LINE

KEGGING
LINE

YEAST

ENZYME	BREAKS DOWN	SOURCE	OPTIMUM		ROLE IN BREWING
			TEMP	pH	
ALPHA AMYLASE Amylolytic (DIASTASE)	Starch—Amylose and amylopectin into random lengths, including maltose, glucose, and alpha-limit dextrins.	Present in barley. Becomes active in the sprouting malt to convert the seed's starch reserve into usable sugars for the plant embryo. Other nonmalt amylolytic enzymes (usually derived from fungus) are sometimes used as brewing additives.	158°F 70°C	5.3 to 5.7	Chops up starch molecules randomly into hunks that beta amylase can attack. Physically degrades starch granules, liquefying the starch and making it vulnerable to further enzymatic action. Mash temperature optimized for this enzyme gives a wort with high percentage of unfermentable dextrins, giving a rich, filling beer. Destroyed at 175°F/79°C.
BETA AMYLASE Amylolytic (DIASTASE)	Starch—Amylose and amylopectin into maltose and beta-limit dextrins. The main maltose-releasing enzyme.		140° to 149°F 60° to 65°C	5.3	Degrades starch, dextrin into maltose. Attacks the ends of the molecules only. When mash temperature is optimized for this enzyme, wort is highly fermentable, making a dry-tasting beer. Destroyed at temps over 160°F/72°C.
PROTEINASE Proteolytic	Breaks complex, insoluble proteins into intermediate-length chains—peptones, proteoses, and polypeptides.	Present in barley and malt. There are 5 varieties of proteinase, 10 types of peptidase known in barley and malt.	122°F 50°C	4.6 to 5.0	In malting and the mash, protease breaks whole proteins at random into fragments that are more soluble, and needed for nutrition by the yeast. These protein hunks are the main source of body in beer. Destroyed at 150°F/66°C. Unstable over 140°F/61°C.
PEPTIDASE Proteolytic	Breaks the intermediate protein products above into smaller, soluble units—amino acids.		122°F 50°C	7.8 to 8.0	During malting, attacks protein fragments and breaks them into individual amino acids, which are soluble. Peptidase is destroyed by the heat of malt-drying and is thus inactive in the mash.
BETA GLUCANASE	Breaks down beta glucans, gummy substances present in malt.	Present only in lightly kilned malts. Higher kilning temps destroy this enzyme in Munich and similar malts.	At low end of mash, especially in 90°F/32°C dough-in.		Action is not always evident to the brewer, but its absence can be a major problem in beers made from highly kilned malts, such as Munich. Mash turns into thick, jellylike mess. Use low-temp dough-in for such beers.
MALTASE	Converts maltose and maltotriose into glucose.	Very small amounts present in barley. Very active in yeast.	Operates at normal malting pH & temps: 59°F 15°C		Present in small amounts in malt, where it reduces any maltose present into glucose. Active as a key part of yeast metabolism, in the yeast cells. Not subject to the brewer's control. Just knowing it's there is enough.
INVERTASE	Converts sucrose into glucose and fructose.	Present at the yeast cell surface, to break the larger sugars to allow them to pass through the cell wall.	Operates at normal ferment temperature & pH range.		In yeast, invertase breaks sucrose into its component parts. A big player in the brewing game, but not directly subject to the brewer's control.

5–1 WORKSHEET INSTRUCTIONS

This page shows how to use the worksheets, section by section.

5–2 QUICK REFERENCE CHART: 5 Gallons

5–3 QUICK REFERENCE CHART: 15 Gallons

Handy guides to refer to when formulating recipes. Includes charts to calculate strength of extract for various grain types, grain color numbers, typical alpha acid content for varieties of hops, and some assorted conversion information.

5–4 ONE-PAGE WORKSHEETS

Worksheet with a small mash time and temperature chart included. Useful for recipes using grains as adjuncts to an extract base.

5–5 TWO-PAGE WORKSHEETS

The standard worksheet for mashing or advanced extract brewing. Includes information on water chemistry/treatment and a large chart for recording temperature during the mash. Fermentation information is on the back.

5–6 FOUR-PAGE WORKSHEET

This is an expanded worksheet with lots of room for ingredients and a large mash chart. Includes three fermentation sections, suited to large split-batch recipes. The fourth page is a flavor section, similar to those used for professional taste panel evaluations.

5–7 BREW SUMMARY

Use this section to record vital information on the beers you brew. The format makes it easy to compare the different beers. Post in your cellar or near the refrigerator.

5–8 CARBOY TAGS

Cut these apart and attach to your carboys to keep track of batch, type, location, temperature, and other vital stats.

BREWING WORKSHEETS

5

This worksheet is designed to allow you to record all important aspects of the brewing process. By using it, you will have control over the strength, color, bitterness, and water chemistry of your beer, all the things that make one style of beer different from another. Using this chart, you can repeat your successes, and avoid repeating your errors.

MASH SECTION

This is a time and temperature chart used to record specifics of the mashing process. Note the temperature at regular intervals during the mash and record them; connect these points with lines for a complete record. Decoctions are usually recorded with a dotted line. Record your start time at the bottom, below "Hours."

WATER INFORMATION

Record water quantity and treatment here. Boiling removes carbonate ions. "Stand" lets you note how long you let water sit to allow free chlorine to evaporate.

MASH INFORMATION

Use this section to record specifics of strike water and temperature and other mash and boil parameters. Use "Decoc" sections to record quantities removed and boiled during decoctions. Anything that doesn't have a line can be recorded in the "Notes" section.

GENERAL INFORMATION

This section is for really general stuff like batch number, your name, the beer name, and a description of the style of beer.

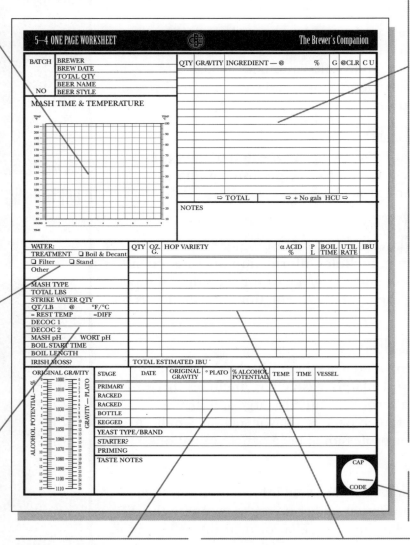

Enter all fermentable ingredients in this section. Use the **Quick Reference Chart** of the appropriate batch size to determine potential extract and color. Remember, you will only get 75–85 percent of the potential extract, so estimate a little higher than where you want to be. After brewing, enter the actual gravity on the line provided. Efficiency can be found by dividing actual gravity by the target. Use the "Grind" setting to keep track of settings on your grain grinder. "@ CLR" are the grain color figures taken from the **Quick Reference Chart, 5–2.** "Color Units" are simply grain color times pounds. To find Homebrew Color Units, add up all the Color Units, and divide by total gallons. Note that this does not really correspond to °SRM beer color scale. See **Section 3–1, Beer Color & Gravity** for a comparison of HCU to °SRM.

CAP CODE

Show what you put on the cap to identify the batch.

FERMENTATION SECTION

Use this to record gravity and other information at various times in the fermentation and conditioning process.
- "Time" means time from start of fermentation.
- Chart at left can be used to translate gravity measurements.

HOP SECTION
- "% Alpha" can be taken from the numbers supplied by your hop merchant or, less accurately, from the numbers shown elsewhere in this book.
- IBUs (International Bitterness Units) To approximate, add HBUs and correct for utilization. See **Sections 8–4 and 8–5, Hop Utilization.**
- P/L is used to indicate pellets or leaf hops.
- Utilization Rate is the efficiency with which hop resins are incorporated into the boil. For more information see **Section 8, Hops,** especially **8–3** and **8–4.**

Use this chart as a handy reference for use in filling out the Brewing Worksheet when developing recipes. Make sure you use the one for the batch size you are brewing. The extract figures (degrees x pounds) are laboratory maximums (Hot Water Extract). You'll get only 75 to 90 percent of these. Decoctions will produce a higher yield than infusions.

ORIGINAL — POUNDS PER 5-GALLON BATCH

INGREDIENT	1/4	1/2	1	2	3	4	5	6	7	8	9	10	11	12	13
Dextrose, Dry Malt Extract	10024	10047	10094	10188	10282	10376	10470	10564	10658	10752	10846	10940	10134	11128	11222
Malt Extract Syrup	10020	10040	10080	10160	10240	10320	10400	10480	10560	10640	10720	10800	10880	10960	11040
Corn, Rice	10020	10039	10079	10158	10237	10316	10395	10474	10553	10632	10711	10790	10869	10948	11027
Wheat Malt	10020	10039	10078	10156	10234	10312	10390	10468	10546	10624	10702	10780	10858	10936	11014
English 2-Row Lager, Pale	10019	10037	10075	10150	10225	10300	10375	10450	10525	10600	10675	10750	10825	10900	10975
English Mild Ale Malt	10018	10036	10072	10144	10216	10288	10360	10432	10504	10576	10648	10720	10792	10864	10936
German 2-Row Pilsner Malt	10018	10035	10070	10140	10210	10280	10350	10420	10490	10560	10630	10700	10770	10840	10910
German 2-Row Munich Malt	10017	10034	10069	10138	10207	10276	10345	10414	10483	10552	10621	10690	10759	10828	10897
Light Crystal, Dextrine Malt	10016	10032	10065	10130	10195	10260	10325	10390	10455	10520	10585	10650	10715	10780	10845
Brown, Amber Malt	10016	10032	10064	10128	10192	10256	10320	10384	10448	10512	10576	10640	10704	10768	10832
US, Canadian 6-Row	10016	10031	10063	10126	10189	10252	10315	10378	10441	10504	10567	10630	10693	10756	10819
Chocolate Malt, Dk Xtl.	10015	10030	10061	10122	10183	10244	10305	10366	10427	10488	10549	10610	10671	10732	10793
Black Malt, Roast Barley	10015	10030	10060	10120	10180	10240	10300	10360	10420	10480	10540	10600	10660	10720	10780

HOP ALPHA ACID %—Use to calculate bitterness level of finished beer.

VARIETY	% Alpha	VARIETY	%Alpha	VARIETY	% Alpha
Brewer's Gold	7–10	Fuggles	4–6	Nor. Brewer	7–9
Bullion	7–10	Galena	12–14	Nugget	12–14
Cascade	4.5–7	Golding	3.5–5	Perle	7–9.5
Centennial	9.5–11.5	Hallertau	3.5–7	Saaz	3.5–6
Chinook	12–14	Hersbrucker	3–6	Styrian Goldings	4.5–7.5
Cluster	5.5–9	Kent Golding	4–6	Spalt	3.5–6.5
Crystal	2–4.5	Liberty	7–10	Tettnanger	4–5.5
Eroica	11–13	Mt. Hood	12–14	Willamette	4–6

GRAIN COLOR

INGREDIENT	°Lovibond
Corn, Rice	0
Pilsner, Lager	1.2/1.4
Pale Ale	2.5
Mild Ale	3
Munich	7
Wheat Malt	2.7
Amber	35
Light Crystal	20
Brown	100
Dark Crystal	90
Chocolate	400
Roast Barley	700
Black Malt	900

SUGAR WT/VOLUME

CUPS =	Oz	Gm
1 Tbsp	0.4	13
1/8 Cup	0.8	23.7
1/4 Cup	1.6	47.3
1/3 Cup	2.2	63.2
3/8 Cup	2.5	71.0
1/2 Cup	3.3	94.7
5/8 Cup	4.1	118
2/3 Cup	4.4	126
3/4 Cup	5.0	142
7/8 Cup	5.8	166
1 Cup	6.6	189
1-1/4 Cup	8.3	237
1-1/2 Cup	10.0	284

BITTERNESS (IBUs)

Estimation: Alpha acid x number of ounces multiplied by 3.4 (5-gallon batch size, @ 23% utilization).

HOMEBREW COLOR

Multiply grain color by number of pounds, then divide by number of gallons. See **Section 3–1, Beer Color & Gravity** to compare to °SRM.

PRIMING RATES

ALE — Lt. 0.6 oz/gal
      Med. 0.8 oz/gal
LAGER — Lt. 0.9
      Med. 1.1 oz/gal

Conversion scales:

°F: 212, 210, 200, 190, 180, 170, 160, 150, 140, 130, 120, 110, 100, 90, 80, 70, 60, 50, 40, 32

°C: 100, 95, 90, 85, 80, 75, 70, 65, 60, 55, 50, 45, 40, 35, 30, 25, 20, 15, 10, 5, 0

O.G.: 1100, 1095, 1090, 1085, 1080, 1075, 1070, 1065, 1060, 1055, 1050, 1045, 1040, 1035, 1030, 1025, 1020, 1015, 1010, 1005, 1000

°PLATO: 24, 23, 22, 21, 20, 19, 18, 17, 16, 15, 14, 13, 12, 11, 10, 9, 8, 7, 6, 5, 4, 3, 2, 1, 0

OZ.: 200, 190, 180, 170, 160, 150, 140, 130, 120, 110, 100, 90, 80, 70, 60, 50, 40, 30, 20, 10, 0

GRAMS: 7.0, 6.5, 6.0, 5.5, 5.0, 4.5, 4.0, 3.5, 3.0, 2.5, 2.0, 1.5, 1.0, 0.5, 0

Use this chart as a handy reference for use in filling out the Brewing Worksheet when developing recipes. Make sure you use the one for the batch size you are brewing. The extract figures (degrees x pounds) are laboratory maximums (Hot Water Extract). You'll get only 75 to 90 percent of these. Decoctions will produce a higher yield than infusions.

ORIGINAL — POUNDS, PER 15 GALLON BATCH

INGREDIENT	1/2	1	2	3	4	5	6	8	10	12	14	16	18	20	22
Dextrose, Dry Malt Extract	10016	10031	10063	10094	10125	10157	10188	10251	10313	10376	10439	10501	10564	10627	10689
Malt Extract Syrup	10013	10027	10053	10080	10107	10133	10160	10213	10267	10320	10373	10427	10480	10533	10587
Corn, Rice	10013	10026	10053	10079	10105	10131	10158	10211	10263	10316	10369	10421	10474	10527	10579
Wheat Malt	10013	10026	10052	10078	10104	10130	10156	10208	10260	10312	10364	10416	10468	10520	10572
English 2-Row Lager, Pale	10013	10025	10050	10075	10100	10125	10150	10200	10250	10300	10350	10400	10450	10500	10550
English Mild Ale Malt	10012	10024	10048	10072	10096	10120	10144	10192	10240	10288	10336	10384	10432	10480	10528
German 2-Row Pilsner Malt	10012	10023	10047	10070	10093	10117	10140	10187	10233	10280	10327	10373	10420	10467	10513
German 2-Row Munich Malt	10012	10023	10046	10069	10092	10115	10138	10184	10230	10276	10322	10368	10414	10460	10506
Light Crystal, Dextrine Malt	10011	10022	10043	10065	10087	10108	10130	10173	10220	10260	10308	10352	10396	10430	10484
Brown, Amber Malt	10011	10021	10043	10064	10085	10107	10128	10171	10213	10256	10299	10341	10383	10427	10469
US, Canadian 6-Row	10011	10021	10042	10063	10084	10105	10126	10168	10210	10252	10294	10336	10378	10420	10462
Chocolate Malt, Dk Xtl.	10010	10020	10041	10061	10081	10102	10122	10163	10203	10244	10285	10325	10366	10407	10447
Black Malt, Roast Barley	10010	10020	10040	10060	10080	10100	10120	10160	10200	10240	10280	10320	10360	10400	10440

HOP ALPHA ACID % — Use to calculate bitterness level of finished beer.

VARIETY	% Alpha	VARIETY	%Alpha	VARIETY	% Alpha
Brewer's Gold	7–10	Fuggles	4–6	Nor. Brewer	7–9
Bullion	7–10	Galena	12–14	Nugget	12–14
Cascade	4.5–7	Golding	3.5–5	Perle	7–9.5
Centennial	9.5–11.5	Hallertau	3.5–7	Saaz	3.5–6
Chinook	12–14	Hersbrucker	3–6	Styrian Goldings	4.5–7.5
Cluster	5.5–9	Kent Golding	4–6	Spalt	3.5–6.5
Crystal	2–4.5	Liberty	7–10	Tettnanger	4–5.5
Eroica	11–13	Mt. Hood	12–14	Willamette	4–6

GRAIN COLOR

INGREDIENT	°Lovibond
Corn, Rice	0
Pilsner, Lager	1.2/1.4
Pale Ale	2.5
Mild Ale	3
Munich	7
Wheat Malt	2.7
Amber	35
Light Crystal	20
Brown	100
Dark Crystal	90
Chocolate	400
Roast Barley	700
Black Malt	900

SUGAR WT./VOLUME

CUPS =	Oz	Gm
1 Tbsp	0.4	13
1/8 Cup	0.8	23.7
1/4 Cup	1.6	47.3
1/3 Cup	2.2	63.2
3/8 Cup	2.5	71.0
1/2 Cup	3.3	94.7
5/8 Cup	4.1	118
2/3 Cup	4.4	126
3/4 Cup	5.0	142
7/8 Cup	5.8	166
1 Cup	6.6	189
1-1/4 Cup	8.3	237
1-1/2 Cup	10.0	284

BITTERNESS (IBUs)

Estimation: Alpha acid x number of ounces, total, then multiply by 1.13 (15 gallon batch size, @ 23% utilization).

HOMEBREW COLOR

Multiply grain color by number of pounds, then divide total by number of gallons. See **3–1, Beer Color x Gravity** to compare to °SRM.

PRIMING RATES

ALE —   Lt. 0.6 oz/gal
            Med. 0.8 oz/gal
LAGER — Lt. 0.9 oz/gal
            Med. 1.1 oz/gal

Conversion scales

°F	°C	O.G.	°PLATO	OZ.	GRAMS
212 / 210	100	1100	24	200	7.0
200	95	1095	23	190	6.5
190	90	1090	22	180	
180	85	1085	21	170	6.0
170	80	1080	20	160	5.5
160	75	1075	19 / 18	150	
150	70	1070	17	140	5.0
140	65	1065	16	130	4.5
130	60	1060	15 / 14	120	
120	55	1055	13	110	4.0
110	50	1050	12	100	3.5
100	45	1045	11	90	3.0
90	40	1040	10	80	
80	35	1035	9	70	2.5
70	30	1030	8	60	2.0
60	25	1025	7	50	1.5
50	20	1020	6 / 5	40	1.0
40	15	1015	4 / 3	30	0.5
32	10 / 5	1010 / 1005	2 / 1	20 / 10	
	0	1000	0	0	0

BATCH	BREWER
	BREW DATE
	TOTAL QTY
	BEER NAME
NO	BEER STYLE

MASH TIME & TEMPERATURE

TEMP °F   TEMP °C

210 — 100
200 — 90
190
180 — 80
170
160 — 70
150
140 — 60
130
120 — 50
110
100 — 40
90 — 30
80
70 — 20
60
50 — 10

HOURS 0 1 2 3 4 5 6 7 8

TIME

QTY	GRAVITY	INGREDIENT — @	%	G	@CLR	C U
		⇨ TOTAL	⇨ ÷ No gals HCU ⇨			

NOTES

WATER:	QTY	OZ. G.	HOP VARIETY	α ACID %	P L	BOIL TIME	UTIL RATE	IBU
TREATMENT ❑ Boil & Decant								
❑ Filter ❑ Stand								
Other								
MASH TYPE								
TOTAL LBS								
STRIKE WATER QTY								
QT/LB @ °F/°C								
= REST TEMP =DIFF								
DECOC 1								
DECOC 2								
MASH pH WORT pH								
BOIL START TIME								
BOIL LENGTH								
IRISH MOSS?	TOTAL ESTIMATED IBU							

ORIGINAL GRAVITY

ALCOHOL POTENTIAL — %   GRAVITY — PLATO

0 — 1000 — 0
1 — 1010 — 1,2,3
2 — 4
3 — 1020 — 5,6
4 — 1030 — 7,8
5 — 9
6 — 1040 — 10,11
7 — 1050 — 12,13
8 — 1060 — 14,15
9 — 16
10 — 1070 — 17,18
11 — 1080 — 19,20
12 — 1090 — 21,22
13 — 23
14 — 1100 — 24,25
15 — 1110 — 26

STAGE	DATE	ORIGINAL GRAVITY	° PLATO	% ALCOHOL POTENTIAL	TEMP.	TIME	VESSEL
PRIMARY							
RACKED							
RACKED							
BOTTLE							
KEGGED							
YEAST TYPE/BRAND							
STARTER?							
PRIMING							
TASTE NOTES							

CAP

CODE

MASH TIME & TEMPERATURE

BATCH	BREWER			QTY	GRAVITY	INGREDIENT — @	%	G	@CLR	C U
	BREW DATE									
	TOTAL QTY									
	BEER NAME									
NO	BEER STYLE									

⇨ TOTAL | ⇨ ÷ No gals HCU ⇨

NOTES

WATER:		QTY	OZ. G.	HOP VARIETY	α ACID %	P L	BOIL TIME	UTIL RATE	IBU
TREATMENT ❏ Boil & Decant									
❏ Filter ❏ Stand									
Other									
MASH TYPE									
TOTAL LBS									
STRIKE WATER QTY									
QT/LB @ °F/°C									
= REST TEMP =DIFF									
DECOC 1									
DECOC 2									
MASH pH WORT pH									
BOIL START TIME									
BOIL LENGTH									
IRISH MOSS?		TOTAL ESTIMATED IBU							

ORIGINAL GRAVITY

STAGE	DATE	ORIGINAL GRAVITY	° PLATO	% ALCOHOL POTENTIAL	TEMP.	TIME	VESSEL
PRIMARY							
RACKED							
RACKED							
BOTTLE							
KEGGED							

YEAST TYPE/BRAND

STARTER?

PRIMING

TASTE NOTES

CAP
CODE

BATCH	BREWER
	BREW DATE
	TOTAL QTY
	BEER NAME
NO.	BEER STYLE

WATER SOURCE

QTY   ❑ BOILED   ❑ FILTERED   ❑ STAND

MINERAL IONS (ppm)	Ca	Mg	Na	SO$_4$	Cl	HCO$_3$
PRE TREATMENT						
POST TREATMENT 1						
POST TREATMENT 2						
TO MATCH						

CHEMICAL	g	g/15gal	Ion	ppm	Ion	ppm
CaSO$_4$ Gypsum			Ca		SO$_4$	
MgSO$_4$ Epsom Salts			Mg		SO$_4$	
NaCl Table Salt			Na		Cl	
KCl Potassium Chloride			K		Cl	
CaCl Calcium Chloride			Ca		Cl	

QTY	GRAVITY	INGREDIENT – @	%	G	@CLR	C U

⇨ TOTAL   ⇨ ÷ No gals HCU ⇨

NOTES:

GRAVITY	O.G.	°P
COLOR		HCU
BITTERNESS		IBU
BOIL LENGTH		HRS
YEAST		

NOTES:

QTY	OZ GM	HOP VARIETY	α ACID %	P L	BOIL TIME	UTIL RATE	IBU

TOTAL ESTIMATED IBU ➜

ORIGINAL GRAVITY

STAGE	DATE	ORIGINAL	°PLATO	% ALCOHOL POTENTIAL	TEMP.	TIME	VESSEL
PRIMARY							
RACKED							
RACKED							
BOTTLED							
KEGGED							

TASTE NOTES

ALCOHOL POTENTIAL–% / GRAVITY–°PLATO scale: 0–15 | 1000–1110 | 0–26

MASH TYPE						
TOTAL POUNDS		STRIKE WATER—QT/LB		STRIKE WATER QTY:	QT	GAL
STRIKE TEMP		= REST TEMP OF	TEMP DIFFERENCE		MASH pH	WORT pH

MASH CHART

TEMP °F

TEMP °C

HOURS 0   1   2   3   4   5   6   7   8

TIME

DECOCTION NO	% OF MASH	BOIL TIME	TEMP DIFF	SPARGE TEMP		QTY	❏ ACIDIFIED?
FIRST				**A**	BOIL START	BOIL LENGTH	❏ I MOSS?
SECOND				**B**	BOIL START	BOIL LENGTH	❏ I MOSS?
THIRD				❏ WORT CHILLER		CHILL TIME	

MASH NOTES:

BATCH	BREWER	
	BREW DATE	
	TOTAL QTY	
	BEER NAME	
NO.	BEER STYLE	

WATER SOURCE						
QTY ❑ BOILED ❑ FILTERED ❑ STAND						

MINERAL IONS (ppm)	Ca	Mg	Na	SO$_4$	Cl	HCO$_3$
PRE TREATMENT						
POST TREATMENT 1						
POST TREATMENT 2						
TO MATCH						

CHEMICAL	g	g/15gal	Ion	ppm	Ion	ppm
CaSO$_4$ Gypsum			Ca		SO$_4$	
MgSO$_4$ Epsom Salts			Mg		SO$_4$	
NaCl Table Salt			Na		Cl	
KCl Potassium Chloride			K		Cl	
CaCl Calcium Chloride			Ca		Cl	

QTY	GRAVITY	INGREDIENT – @	%	G	@CLR	C U
		⇨ TOTAL	⇨ ÷ No gals HCU ⇨			

NOTES:

GRAVITY	O.G.	°P
COLOR		HCU
BITTERNESS		IBU
BOIL LENGTH		HRS
YEAST		

NOTES:

QTY	OZ GM	HOP VARIETY	α ACID %	P L	BOIL TIME	UTIL RATE	IBU

TOTAL ESTIMATED IBU →

STAGE	DATE	ORIGINAL	°PLATO	% ALCOHOL POTENTIAL	TEMP.	TIME	VESSEL
PRIMARY							
RACKED							
RACKED							
BOTTLED							
KEGGED							

ORIGINAL GRAVITY

ALCOHOL POTENTIAL–%

GRAVITY–°PLATO

0	1000	0
1	1010	1 / 2 / 3
2	1010	4
3	1020	5
4	1030	6 / 7 / 8
5	1040	9 / 10
6		11
7	1050	12 / 13
8	1060	14 / 15
9	1070	16 / 17
10	1080	18 / 19 / 20
11	1090	21 / 22
12	1090	23
13	1100	24 / 25
14	1110	26
15		

TASTE NOTES

MASH TYPE				
TOTAL POUNDS	STRIKE WATER—QT/LB	STRIKE WATER QTY:	QT	GAL
STRIKE TEMP	= REST TEMP OF	TEMP DIFFERENCE	MASH pH	WORT pH

MASH CHART

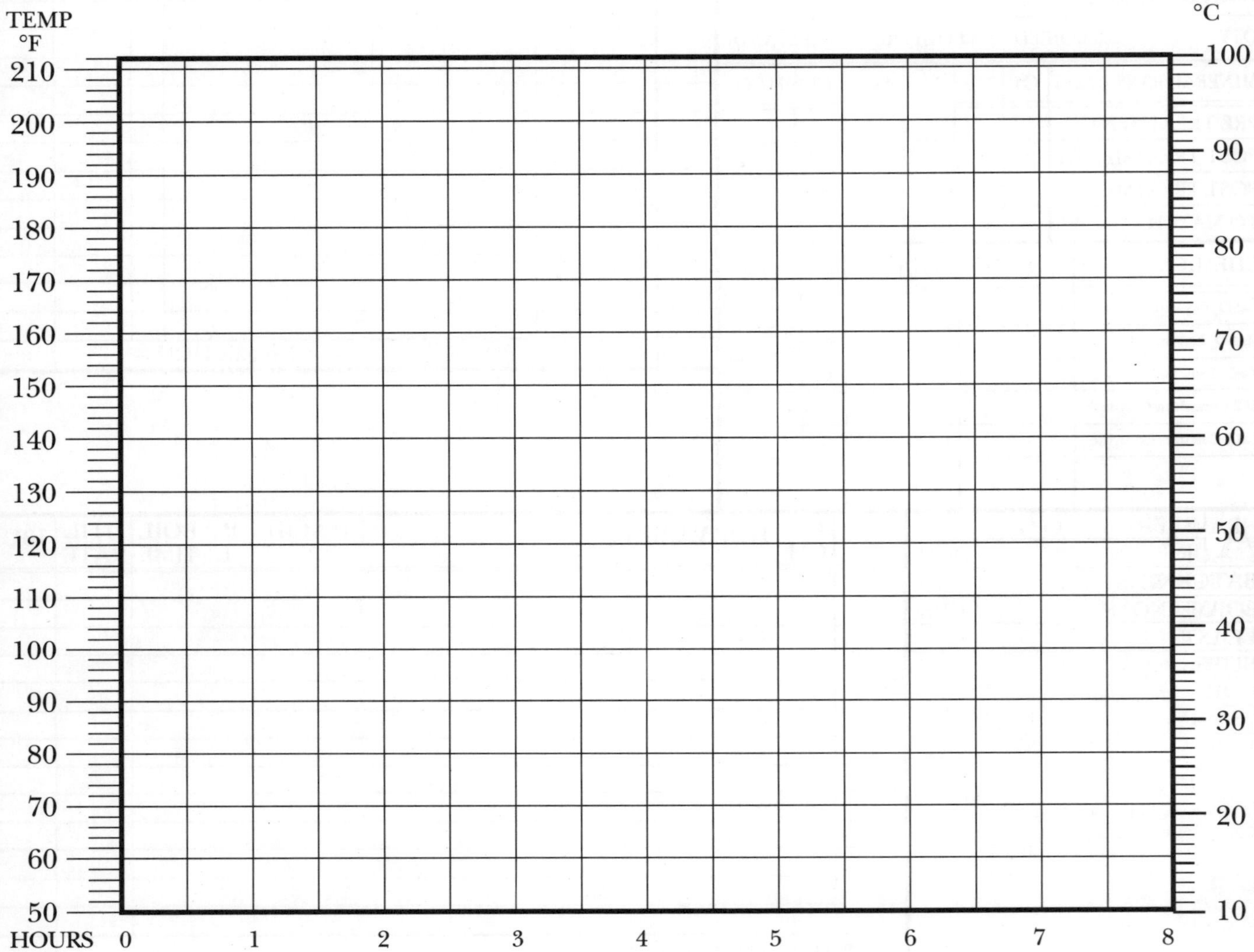

TEMP °F

TEMP °C

HOURS 0   1   2   3   4   5   6   7   8

TIME

DECOCTION NO	% OF MASH	BOIL TIME	TEMP DIFF	SPARGE TEMP	QTY	❏ ACIDIFIED?
FIRST				**A** BOIL START	BOIL LENGTH	❏ I MOSS?
SECOND				**B** BOIL START	BOIL LENGTH	❏ I MOSS?
THIRD				❏ WORT CHILLER	CHILL TIME	

MASH NOTES:

BATCH	BREWER					
	BREW DATE					
	TOTAL QTY					
	BATCH GRAVITY		OG			°P
NO.	BEER STYLE					HCU

WATER SOURCE

QTY	❏ BOILED	❏ FILTERED	❏ STAND

MINERAL IONS (ppm)	Ca	Mg	Na	SO$_4$	Cl	HCO$_3$
PRE TREATMENT						
POST TREATMENT 1						
POST TREATMENT 2						
TO MATCH						

CHEMICAL	g	g/15gal	Ion	ppm	Ion	ppm
CaSO$_4$ Gypsum			Ca		SO$_4$	
MgSO$_4$ Epsom Salts			Mg		SO$_4$	
NaCl Table Salt			Na		Cl	
KCl Potassium Chloride			K		Cl	
CaCl Calcium Chloride			Ca		Cl	

QTY	GRAVITY	INGREDIENT – @	%	G	@CLR	C U
		⇨ TOTAL	⇨ ÷ No gals HCU ⇨			

NOTES:

A

BEER	
TYPE	
BATCH SIZE	GAL
GRAVITY O.G.	°P
COLOR	HCU
BITTERNESS	IBU
BOIL LENGTH	HRS
YEAST A	
NOTES:	

QTY	OZ GM	HOP VARIETY	α ACID %	P L	BOIL TIME	UTIL RATE	IBU
			TOTAL ESTIMATED IBU ➜				

B

BEER	
TYPE	

C

BEER	
TYPE	
BATCH SIZE /	GAL
GRAVITY O.G.	°P
COLOR	HCU
BITTERNESS	IBU
BOIL LENGTH	HRS
YEAST B	
YEAST C	
NOTES:	

QTY	OZ GM	HOP VARIETY	α ACID %	P L	BOIL TIME	UTIL RATE	IBU
			TOTAL ESTIMATED IBU ➜				

MASH TYPE				
TOTAL POUNDS	STRIKE WATER—QT/LB		STRIKE WATER QTY:	QT GAL
STRIKE TEMP	= REST TEMP OF	TEMP DIFFERENCE	MASH pH	WORT pH

MASH CHART

HOURS   0   1   2   3   4   5   6   7   8

TIME

DECOCTION NO	% OF MASH	BOIL TIME	TEMP DIFF	SPARGE TEMP		QTY		❑ ACIDIFIED?
FIRST				**A**	BOIL START	BOIL LENGTH		❑ I MOSS?
SECOND				**B**	BOIL START	BOIL LENGTH		❑ I MOSS?
THIRD				❑ WORT CHILLER		CHILL TIME		

MASH NOTES:

BEER NAME   STYLE

STAGE	DATE	ORIGINAL	°PLATO	% ALCOHOL POTENTIAL	TEMP.	TIME	VESSEL / LOCATION
PRIMARY							
RACKED							
RACKED							
BOTTLED							
KEGGED							

BATCH A

YEAST TYPE/BRAND

STARTER?   QTY   DATE

PRIMING

CAP / CODE

BEER NAME   STYLE

STAGE	DATE	ORIGINAL	°PLATO	% ALCOHOL POTENTIAL	TEMP.	TIME	VESSEL / LOCATION
PRIMARY							
RACKED							
RACKED							
BOTTLED							
KEGGED							

BATCH A

YEAST TYPE/BRAND

STARTER?   QTY   DATE

PRIMING

CAP / CODE

BEER NAME   STYLE

STAGE	DATE	ORIGINAL	°PLATO	% ALCOHOL POTENTIAL	TEMP.	TIME	VESSEL / LOCATION
PRIMARY							
RACKED							
RACKED							
BOTTLED							
KEGGED							

BATCH A

YEAST TYPE/BRAND

STARTER?   QTY   DATE

PRIMING

CAP / CODE

ORIGINAL GRAVITY

ALCOHOL POTENTIAL–%

0	1000	0
1	1010	1
		2
		3
2	1020	4
		5
3		6
4	1030	7
		8
5	1040	9
		10
6		11
7	1050	12
		13
8	1060	14
		15
9		16
10	1070	17
		18
11	1080	19
		20
12	1090	21
		22
13		23
14	1100	24
		25
15	1110	26

GRAVITY–°PLATO

NOTES

BATCH	BEER NAME	NOTE	CAP
	TYPE		
	BREW DATE		CODE
COLOR			
GRAVITY			
BITTERNESS			
HOP CHARACTER			
BODY/SWEETNESS			
YEAST/FERMENT			
PROBLEMS			

BATCH	BEER NAME	NOTE	CAP
	TYPE		
	BREW DATE		CODE
COLOR			
GRAVITY			
BITTERNESS			
HOP CHARACTER			
BODY/SWEETNESS			
YEAST/FERMENT			
PROBLEMS			

BATCH	BEER NAME	NOTE	CAP
	TYPE		
	BREW DATE		CODE
COLOR			
GRAVITY			
BITTERNESS			
HOP CHARACTER			
BODY/SWEETNESS			
YEAST/FERMENT			
PROBLEMS			

BATCH	BREWER					
	BREW DATE					
	TOTAL QTY					
	BATCH GRAVITY		OG		°P	
NO.	BEER STYLE				HCU	

WATER SOURCE						
QTY	❏ BOILED	❏ FILTERED	❏ STAND			

MINERAL IONS (ppm)	Ca	Mg	Na	SO_4	Cl	HCO_3
PRE TREATMENT						
POST TREATMENT 1						
POST TREATMENT 2						
TO MATCH						

CHEMICAL	g	g/15gal	Ion	ppm	Ion	ppm
$CaSO_4$ Gypsum			Ca		SO_4	
$MgSO_4$ Epsom Salts			Mg		SO_4	
NaCl Table Salt			Na		Cl	
KCl Potassium Chloride			K		Cl	
CaCl Calcium Chloride			Ca		Cl	

QTY	GRAVITY	INGREDIENT – @	%	G	@CLR	C U
		⇨ TOTAL	⇨ ÷ No gals HCU ⇨			

NOTES:

A	BEER		QTY	OZ GM	HOP VARIETY	α ACID %	P L	BOIL TIME	UTIL RATE	IBU
	TYPE									
BATCH SIZE		GAL								
GRAVITY	O.G.	°P								
COLOR		HCU								
BITTERNESS		IBU								
BOIL LENGTH		HRS								
YEAST A										
NOTES:										
					TOTAL ESTIMATED IBU ➜					

B	BEER		QTY	OZ GM	HOP VARIETY	α ACID %	P L	BOIL TIME	UTIL RATE	IBU
	TYPE									
C	BEER									
	TYPE									
BATCH SIZE	/	GAL								
GRAVITY	O.G.	°P								
COLOR		HCU								
BITTERNESS		IBU								
BOIL LENGTH		HRS								
YEAST B										
YEAST C										
NOTES:										
					TOTAL ESTIMATED IBU ➜					

MASH TYPE				
TOTAL POUNDS	STRIKE WATER—QT/LB	STRIKE WATER QTY:	QT	GAL
STRIKE TEMP	= REST TEMP OF	TEMP DIFFERENCE	MASH pH	WORT pH

MASH CHART

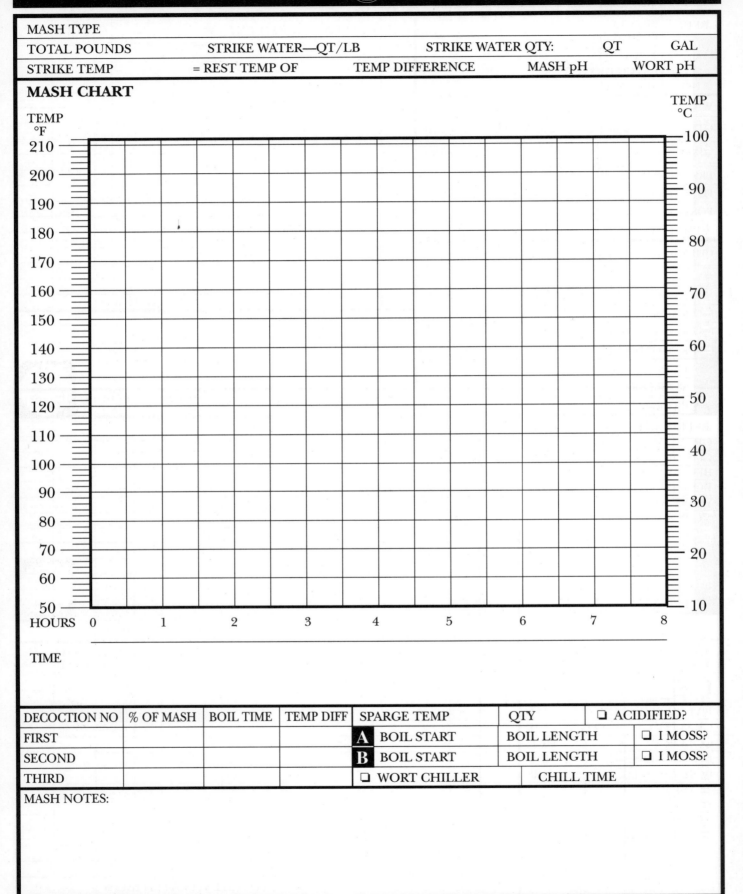

TIME

DECOCTION NO	% OF MASH	BOIL TIME	TEMP DIFF	SPARGE TEMP		QTY	❏ ACIDIFIED?
FIRST				**A**	BOIL START	BOIL LENGTH	❏ I MOSS?
SECOND				**B**	BOIL START	BOIL LENGTH	❏ I MOSS?
THIRD				❏ WORT CHILLER		CHILL TIME	

MASH NOTES:

BEER NAME   **STYLE**

STAGE	DATE	ORIGINAL	°PLATO	% ALCOHOL POTENTIAL	TEMP.	TIME	VESSEL / LOCATION
PRIMARY							
RACKED							
RACKED							
BOTTLED							
KEGGED							

BATCH A

YEAST TYPE/BRAND

STARTER?   QTY   DATE

PRIMING

CAP CODE

BEER NAME   **STYLE**

STAGE	DATE	ORIGINAL	°PLATO	% ALCOHOL POTENTIAL	TEMP.	TIME	VESSEL / LOCATION
PRIMARY							
RACKED							
RACKED							
BOTTLED							
KEGGED							

BATCH A

YEAST TYPE/BRAND

STARTER?   QTY   DATE

PRIMING

CAP CODE

BEER NAME   **STYLE**

STAGE	DATE	ORIGINAL	°PLATO	% ALCOHOL POTENTIAL	TEMP.	TIME	VESSEL / LOCATION
PRIMARY							
RACKED							
RACKED							
BOTTLED							
KEGGED							

BATCH A

YEAST TYPE/BRAND

STARTER?   QTY   DATE

PRIMING

CAP CODE

ORIGINAL GRAVITY

ALCOHOL POTENTIAL–%

0	1000 — 0
1	1010 — 1,2,3
2	1020 — 4,5,6
3	1020 — 5,6
4	1030 — 7,8
5	1040 — 9,10
6	11
7	1050 — 12,13
8	1060 — 14,15
9	16
10	1070 — 17,18
11	1080 — 19,20
12	1090 — 21,22
13	23
14	1100 — 24,25
15	1110 — 26

GRAVITY–°PLATO

NOTES

Batch 1

BATCH	BEER NAME	NOTE	CAP
	TYPE		CODE
	BREW DATE		

COLOR

GRAVITY

BITTERNESS

HOP CHARACTER

BODY/SWEETNESS

YEAST/FERMENT

PROBLEMS

Batch 2

BATCH	BEER NAME	NOTE	CAP
	TYPE		CODE
	BREW DATE		

COLOR

GRAVITY

BITTERNESS

HOP CHARACTER

BODY/SWEETNESS

YEAST/FERMENT

PROBLEMS

Batch 3

BATCH	BEER NAME	NOTE	CAP
	TYPE		CODE
	BREW DATE		

COLOR

GRAVITY

BITTERNESS

HOP CHARACTER

BODY/SWEETNESS

YEAST/FERMENT

PROBLEMS

BATCH NUMBER	DATE	BEER NAME	BEER STYLE	GRAV. O.G.	% ALC.	COLOR (HCU)	BITTER (IBU)

BATCH NUMBER	DATE	BEER NAME	BEER STYLE	GRAV. O.G.	% ALC.	COLOR (HCU)	BITTER (IBU)

BATCH NO.	❑ PRIMARY
	❑ SECONDARY
	❑ OTHER

BEER NAME	
TYPE	
BREW DATE	
DATE TRANSFERRED	
GRAVITY	
DATE TO TRANSFER	
GRAVITY	
TEMP	DATE
TEMP	DATE
TEMP	DATE
TEMP	DATE
TEMP	DATE
NOTES	

BATCH NO.	❑ PRIMARY
	❑ SECONDARY
	❑ OTHER

BEER NAME	
TYPE	
BREW DATE	
DATE TRANSFERRED	
GRAVITY	
DATE TO TRANSFER	
GRAVITY	
TEMP	DATE
TEMP	DATE
TEMP	DATE
TEMP	DATE
TEMP	DATE
NOTES	

BATCH NO.	❑ PRIMARY
	❑ SECONDARY
	❑ OTHER

BEER NAME	
TYPE	
BREW DATE	
DATE TRANSFERRED	
GRAVITY	
DATE TO TRANSFER	
GRAVITY	
TEMP	DATE
TEMP	DATE
TEMP	DATE
TEMP	DATE
TEMP	DATE
NOTES	

BATCH NO.	❑ PRIMARY
	❑ SECONDARY
	❑ OTHER

BEER NAME	
TYPE	
BREW DATE	
DATE TRANSFERRED	
GRAVITY	
DATE TO TRANSFER	
GRAVITY	
TEMP	DATE
TEMP	DATE
TEMP	DATE
TEMP	DATE
TEMP	DATE
NOTES	

BATCH NO.	❑ PRIMARY
	❑ SECONDARY
	❑ OTHER

BEER NAME	
TYPE	
BREW DATE	
DATE TRANSFERRED	
GRAVITY	
DATE TO TRANSFER	
GRAVITY	
TEMP	DATE
TEMP	DATE
TEMP	DATE
TEMP	DATE
TEMP	DATE
NOTES	

BATCH NO.	❑ PRIMARY
	❑ SECONDARY
	❑ OTHER

BEER NAME	
TYPE	
BREW DATE	
DATE TRANSFERRED	
GRAVITY	
DATE TO TRANSFER	
GRAVITY	
TEMP	DATE
TEMP	DATE
TEMP	DATE
TEMP	DATE
TEMP	DATE
NOTES	

BATCH NO.	❏ PRIMARY
	❏ SECONDARY
	❏ OTHER

BEER NAME

TYPE

BREW DATE	
DATE TRANSFERRED	
GRAVITY	
DATE TO TRANSFER	
GRAVITY	
TEMP	DATE
TEMP	DATE
TEMP	DATE
TEMP	DATE
TEMP	DATE
NOTES	

BATCH NO.	❏ PRIMARY
	❏ SECONDARY
	❏ OTHER

BEER NAME

TYPE

BREW DATE	
DATE TRANSFERRED	
GRAVITY	
DATE TO TRANSFER	
GRAVITY	
TEMP	DATE
TEMP	DATE
TEMP	DATE
TEMP	DATE
TEMP	DATE
NOTES	

BATCH NO.	❏ PRIMARY
	❏ SECONDARY
	❏ OTHER

BEER NAME

TYPE

BREW DATE	
DATE TRANSFERRED	
GRAVITY	
DATE TO TRANSFER	
GRAVITY	
TEMP	DATE
TEMP	DATE
TEMP	DATE
TEMP	DATE
TEMP	DATE
NOTES	

BATCH NO.	❏ PRIMARY
	❏ SECONDARY
	❏ OTHER

BEER NAME

TYPE

BREW DATE	
DATE TRANSFERRED	
GRAVITY	
DATE TO TRANSFER	
GRAVITY	
TEMP	DATE
TEMP	DATE
TEMP	DATE
TEMP	DATE
TEMP	DATE
NOTES	

BATCH NO.	❏ PRIMARY
	❏ SECONDARY
	❏ OTHER

BEER NAME

TYPE

BREW DATE	
DATE TRANSFERRED	
GRAVITY	
DATE TO TRANSFER	
GRAVITY	
TEMP	DATE
TEMP	DATE
TEMP	DATE
TEMP	DATE
TEMP	DATE
NOTES	

BATCH NO.	❏ PRIMARY
	❏ SECONDARY
	❏ OTHER

BEER NAME

TYPE

BREW DATE	
DATE TRANSFERRED	
GRAVITY	
DATE TO TRANSFER	
GRAVITY	
TEMP	DATE
TEMP	DATE
TEMP	DATE
TEMP	DATE
TEMP	DATE
NOTES	

GRAINS & ADJUNCTS

6

Barley Botony

Barley is a cereal, *Hordeum sativum*, a grass. Of all grains known, it is the most perfectly suited for brewing. When malted (sprouted), it contains an abundance of various enzymes crucial to the brewing process. It also has the right components for yeast nutrition, wonderful flavor, and a coarse, tightly-adhering husk which plays an important role in brewing.

Barley is a monocotyledon, or a simpler type of plant than, say, an oak tree. The plant is a series of shafts with long, blade-like leaves. Each shaft bears a flower spike, which holds the individual kernels. Modern varieties are 60 to 90 centimeters tall. The stalks rise from a root crown that supports the plant and provides water and nutrients from the soil. It is self-pollinating (about 99 percent so). Some cross-pollination can happen, but usually doesn't.

Of all barley grown, only one-quarter or less is used for malting; the rest goes for animal feed.

Where and When

Barley grows in a wide belt around the planet, roughly from North Africa to Scandinavia in latitude, as well as in certain areas in the Southern Hemisphere. In general, the six-row barleys are grown in the more extreme climates, such as the arid conditions in the north of Africa and the blustery fields of the Dakotas and Canada.

Some varieties are sown in the spring; others at the end of the farming year, which then winter over and come up the following spring.

Why Barley?

A number of reasons make barley well suited for malting and brewing. Its husk is not easily removed at threshing, serving to protect the sprouting shoot, and acting as a mechanical filtering aid during sparging. Its high complement of enzymes unleashes its stored supply of starch. Its low fat content eliminates problems of rancidity. Plentiful proteinaceous material is important for yeast nutrition, head retention and other aspects of brewing. Other grains are malted, including wheat, oats and millet, but today these are specialty grains and are not part of mainstream brewing.

Varieties of Barley

There are two major types of barley raised today: *Hordeum distichum*, or two-row barley, and *Hordeum hexastichum*, or six-row barley.

To distinguish these two types from one another, look at the flower heads from above. On both varieties there are seeds or seedlike structures, in groups of three, one group on either side of the stalk. In six-row barley, all of the flowers in these clusters are fertile, creating six seeds at every node on the flower head. In two-row barley, only the central flowers on each side of the stem produce seeds; the adjacent flowers are sterile, producing tiny, withered husklets which are not used in brewing.

Two-row barley has fuller, plumper kernels than six-row. Because of this, malted two-row barley yields a higher extract—a larger percent of the malt kernel is convertible to soluble starch and sugar. Six-row barley, with less-plump kernels and more husk per kernel, yields less material into the mash.

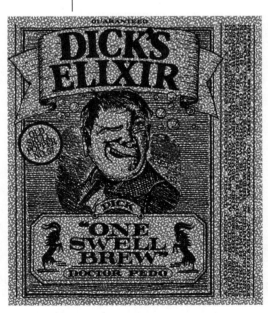

Two-row barley is the standard for brewing in all of Europe, including Great Britain. It is generally regarded as having a higher quality flavor than six-row.

The cream of the crop of British two-row barley is Maris Otter, a difficult-to-raise grain with full, plump kernels. High-quality two-row barleys are also grown in Germany, France, and the Czech Republic. Generally, the British and European malts produce beers with more intense malt flavors than their American counterparts, but this may have more to do with malting methods than barley varieties.

Some six-row malt is used in Europe, but it is treated as more of a specialty malt—usually added to increase diastatic activity, add nitrogen, or to provide extra husks for filtering during sparging.

Six-row malt has much higher levels of diastatic enzymes and protein than European two-row, making six-row the perfect malt to use when co-mashing adjuncts, such as corn or rice, which are lacking in both materials. A beer brewed with 100 percent six-row is likely to have some serious chill-haze due to excess protein.

In earlier times, all the barley grown in the United States was six-row. Now, some two-row is cultivated in California and the northern Midwest. Klages malt is a California variety often available to the homebrewer. U.S. two-row barleys are intermediate in protein content between American six-row and European two-row. There are many cultivated varieties of each, developed for particular characteristics, not all of which have to do with brewing. Traits such as disease resistance and adaptation to certain climates have little relevance to brewing, except in economic terms.

An expert can tell the varieties apart by examining details of the grains and husks, but for homebrewing purposes the basics of type and national origin are knowledge enough.

Structure and Function of the Barleycorn

There are a several structures that together form the barley grain. On the outside, the husks cling tightly to the kernels, especially when compared to other grains. This keeps the shoot, or acrospire, from breaking off as it emerges during malting. The next layer inward, the aleurone, is a thin protein shell three cells thick, surrounding almost the entire grain. It provides a semipermeable barrier, allowing respiration but protecting the embryo and starch reserve from invading microbes. The aleurone is pierced at the embryo end to allow gas and moisture to move in and out of the embryo. It is also secretes starch-degrading enzymes when stimulated during germination by the plant hormones, or gibberellin.

Within the kernel there are two main divisions, the embryo, and the starch reserve, or endosperm.

The embryo is the germ of the plant; it contains the motive force of life, orchestrating the complex changes that occur during germination and growth. Present are structures that grow to become the rootlet and the acrospire, or shoot. The embryo releases a complex of hormones, known collectively as gibberellin, which triggers complex changes in nearby tissues.

Adjacent to the embryo, and serving as a bulkhead to separate it from the starchy endosperm, is a membrane called the scutellum. During malting, the scutellum secretes proteolytic and amylolytic enzymes, which attack the starch grains in the endosperm, solubilizing them and making their reserves of carbohydrates available to the growing plant.

The endosperm itself is a large packet of starch contained in nonliving cells, which are filled with two discrete sizes of starch grains. These grains, large and small, are enclosed by a thin capsule of protein which protects the starch. During malting, these grains have their protein coatings perforated by proteolytic enzymes. This makes the starch inside vulnerable to further enzymatic attack. The result is a change in texture from glassy and flinty to soft and friable.

Onward to Malt

The maltster is looking for certain characteristics from barley. Uniform kernel size ensures uniform malting. High viability is essential—98 percent of the kernels must sprout when malted. Protein content must be appropriate. Polyphenol and beta glucan levels must be low, or they can cause problems in brewing or beer flavor.

The Malting Process

Very simply, the malting of barley is the process of controlled sprouting and drying.

The proper varieties having been selected, the grains are soaked in water, at 59°F/15°C for 12 to 24 hours. The water is then drained in what is called an "air rest" for a few hours. The next 24 to 36 hours continues the alternation of air and water until about 42 percent moisture content is reached. During this period, the embryo comes to life and respiration begins. In the presence of air, oxygen is consumed, along with some of its starchy reserves; CO_2 and water are released at this stage. In the absence of oxygen, an inefficient anaerobic respiration occurs, converting food reserves to CO_2 and alcohol—which in certain concentrations is toxic to the young plant.

After the steeping period, the barley was traditionally piled on the floor of the malthouse to a depth of about 10 inches. The grains were turned periodically by hand or with special machinery. All the while, the temperature was maintained at 59°F/15°C, which meant cooling the malthouse in the summer.

Pneumatic malting methods eliminate this labor-intensive flooring by using a special enclosure with a false bottom. The barley is piled up three to four feet deep and air is blown up through holes from below.

After four to six days, the shoot reaches half to three-quarters the length of the kernels. When the desired length is reached, the process is stopped by drying.

The exact length of the acrospire reached during malting is an indicator of the degree of modification, the extent to which starches and proteins within the grain have been broken down by enzymatic activity. The degree of modification is critical to the brewing process. Highly modified malts are crumbly and have a high percentage of soluble nitrogen.

It is essential to use highly modified malts with the British infusion process. Less highly modified malts are better suited to the decoction method, where the harder kernels are gelatinized during the periods when portions of the mash are boiled.

After malting has proceeded to the desired degree, the grain is dried with warm air. For most malts, the temperature is never allowed to rise above 100°F/38°C. A long, cool drying keeps enzyme activity high. A shorter, hotter drying sequence tends to destroy enzymes.

Specialty malts are further heated to create the flavor and color of toasting and roasting.

This roasting involves a number of reactions collectively known as nonenzymatic browning, also called Maillard browning. This is the basic caramel reaction, involving the combination of amino acids (protein fragments) with sugars and other carbohydrates. These reactions only occur above the boiling point, and create a huge range

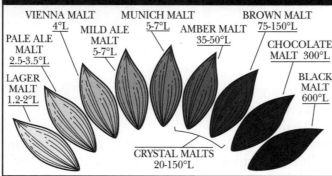

THE RAINBOW OF MALT

VIENNA MALT 4°L
MUNICH MALT 5-7°L
BROWN MALT 75-150°L
PALE ALE MALT 2.5-3.5°L
MILD ALE MALT 5-7°L
AMBER MALT 35-50°L
CHOCOLATE MALT 300°L
LAGER MALT 1.2-2°L
BLACK MALT 600°L
CRYSTAL MALTS 20-150°L

of flavors, each associated with a particular combination of nitrogen/carbohydrate. The colors are due to compounds called melanoidins, which are complex, polymeric, brown pigments.

The aromatic chemicals form at different temperatures, so two malts of the same color roasted at different temperatures won't possess the same spectrum of flavors. A small amount of very dark malt will not produce the same flavor as a large amount of a slightly dark malt, even if the total color is the same. This is an important fact to remember when formulating recipes.

Crystal malts are produced by heating the undried or "green" malt to mashing temperatures of 155°F/68°C and standing for a time to allow the grain to actually mash in the husk; the temperature is then raised to allow the appropriate color development. When the sugary mass cools, it turns to a glassy state, giving the grain its name. Dextrine malt is similar, but is dried at low temperatures to prevent color development.

Constituents of Malt

Barley contains two types of starch: amylose and amylopectin, which form the energy reserve the young plant uses for growth. During malting, some of this starch is degraded by enzymes into simple sugars and used by the embryo during germination. This loss of extract amounts to a few percent and is referred to as malting loss.

Amylose is a straight chain of dextrose molecules hooked together end to end to form structures that are 1,000 to 4,000 dextrose units long. These straight chains actually bend into long coils.

Amylopectin is a branched chain of dextrose molecules formed from shorter chains hooked together end-to-middle. It's a slightly larger molecule, from 2,500 units up. Because the branching structure creates many chain ends where beta amylase attacks, amylopectin is degraded preferentially over amylose.

Proteins are so complex that it is impossible to know or list them all. Barley proteins are categorized by solubility in laboratory tests into four broad types, each containing a large group of specific proteins. Besides the obvious structural qualities of proteins, the most important function in brewing is as enzymes—specialized protein molecules designed to facilitate chemical reactions. So powerful are they that they can gelatinize starch at as low a temperature as 59°F/15°C, even though the normal gelatinization temperature of barley starch is 126°–138°F/52°–59°C.

GRAIN TYPE & COUNTRY	BREWING USAGE	Extract	Color EBC	Color °L	Max % of Batch	Diast Power	% Protein	% PSN	Must Mash?	COMMENTS & DESCRIPTION
PILSNER MALT (Two-row) Continental Europe	Pilsners and other pale lagers. Also ultra-high gravity pale bocks and European ales. This is the palest two-row malt available. Suitable for all lagers.	1.0070 lb/5 gal	2	1.2 to 2.0	100	70	1.82	61	Yes	Almost greenish in color. Mash with decoction or step mash. 122°F protein rest critical to avoid chill-haze. Fine grind important to assure efficient yield. High diastatic power allows mashing with up to 40 percent grain adjuncts.
LAGER MALT (Two-row) U.S. (Klages, etc.)	Pale lagers, and darker lagers in combination with darker malts. Also American ales, all-malt lagers and steam beer.	1.0073 lb/5 gal	2.5	1.4 to 2.0	100	63	1.65	.66	Yes	Must be mashed with decoction or step mash. 122°F protein rest critical to avoid chill-haze. High diastatic power allows mashing with up to 35 percent grain adjuncts.
LAGER MALT (Six-row) U.S., Canada	American lagers with high percentage of adjuncts. Use as an additive to increase diastatic strength when needed.	1.0061 lb/5 gal	2	1.4 to 2,2	60	100 – 200	2.30	.60	Yes	Extremely high diastatic power makes this malt ideally suited to the co-mashing of rice or corn adjuncts, up to 60 percent. Generally viewed as inferior in flavor to two-row. Decoction or step-mash critical to avoid chill-haze.
VIENNA MALT Continental Europe, U.S., Canada	The malt of choice for Vienna, Oktoberfest, and Märzen lagers. Adds amber color and malty taste to any lager beer. Good as main malt in darker beers.	10072 lb/5 gal	9.4	4	100	30			Yes	Adds malty caramelly richness and sweet maltiness, along with pale amber color. Enzyme content very low, but sufficient for self-conversion.
MUNICH MALT (Two-row) Continental Europe, U.S., Canada	Traditional in Munich dunkel. Adds color and nutty flavor to lighter beers. Adds body and sweetness to any beer. Very dark versions sometimes called "Aromatic."	1.0070 lb/5 gal	16	5 to 7	100	22	1.8	.62	Yes	Imparts malt aroma and gentle toasty taste, and amber color. Roasted moist for rich aroma. Gives beer a reddish color, in quantity. Not enough enzymes to co-mash adjuncts, but will convert itself. Dough-in at 90°F/32°C.

GRAIN TYPE & COUNTRY	BREWING USAGE	Extract	Color EBC	Color °L	Max % of Batch	Diast Power °Lintne	% N	% PSN	Must Mash?	COMMENTS & DESCRIPTION
PALE ALE MALT England, Belgium	All English ales. Pale, light, bitter, brown, porter, Scotch, and old ales. This is the work-horse grain of British brewing.	10075 (1.80°P) lb/5 gal	4.5 to 6	2.5 to 3.5	100	36	1.35	0.50	Yes	Infusion mash, typically. Low % N makes protein rest unnecessary. Not well-suited to the co-mashing of adjuncts.
MILD ALE MALT England	Darker English ales such as mild. Adds body and sweetness to pale ales and other beers. Could be used as a substitute for Munich malt.	10072 (1.71°P) lb/5 gal	6 to 8	5 to 7	85	33	1.5	0.51	Yes	Darker color, sweeter, nuttier taste than pale ale malt. Low diastatic power makes this malt poorly suited to the co-mashing of grain adjuncts. Protein rest unnecessary.
AMBER MALT BISCUIT MALT England, Belgium	All amber and darker beers, but very good in brown ales. Not to be confused with crystal malt. Adds color and maltiness. Assists in clarification of the wort during the boil.	10064 (1.53°P) lb/5 gal	65	35 to 50	20	8 to 10	NA	NA	Yes	Toasty/nutty flavor, without the strong aroma of Munich malts. Roast wetted (not soaked) pale ale malt at 200°F for 15–20 minutes, then raise to 250°–300°F for a few more minutes. Recently made available in the U.S.
BROWN MALT England	All dark ales and beers. Much lighter than chocolate malt. Adds characteristic smoky flavor to beers. Traditionally used to brew porter, before the invention of black patent malt.	10064 (1.53°P) lb/5 gal	230	75 to 150	15	—	NA	NA	Yes	Traditionally made by rapidly heating pale ale malt to 350°F over an oak fire, and held for 2 hours or until a rich brown color is reached. A very old product that is not much used anywhere these days. Try roasting at home.
CHOCOLATE MALT England, Continental Europe, U.S., Canada	All dark beers. Adds sharply pungent roasted taste and deep color.	10061 (1.45°P) lb/5 gal	750 to 1100	300 to 450	15	—	NA	NA	No	Made by roasting pale ale malt until a deep chocolate color is reached. Sometimes harsh; black patent malt is darker, but usually smoother tasting.

GRAIN TYPE & COUNTRY	BREWING USAGE	Extract	Color EBC	Color °L	Max % of Batch	Diast Power °Lintne	% N	% PSN	Must Mash?	COMMENTS & DESCRIPTION
BLACK PATENT MALT England, Continental Europe, U.S., Canada	Adds deep color and intense roasted flavor to all dark beers, except for Irish dry stout (Guinness). Used for color adjustment in paler beers.	10060	1200 1500	600 900	15	—	1.5	NA	No	The most pungent and bitter of all malts. Made by roasting pale malt at a high temperature until nearly black, but not burned. Some versions are debitterized for smoothness.
ROASTED BARLEY England, U.S.	Use in any type of dark beer, just like black malt. Used especially in Irish dry stouts.	10060	1200	700	15	—	NA	NA	No	Similar to black malt, but barley is unmalted. Has drier, less pungent character. Very dark color.
LIGHT CRYSTAL England, U.S., Germany, Belgium, etc.	Adds unfermentable dextrins for body and richness. Has distinctive nutty flavor. Often added to extract beers. Good for pale ales, amber lagers.	10065	20 50	10 25	20	—	NA	NA	No	Partially "premashed" at roasting. Soaked whole malt is heated to mash temps, held, then raised to roasting temps. When cooled, sugars harden and give it a crystalline texture. May be made from two- or six-row barley. Contains high proportion of unfermentable dextrins. There are a wide variety of crystal malts, each with a unique flavor profile. Very useful in adding personality to beer.
DARK CRYSTAL Everywhere	Adds unfermentable dextrins for body and richness. Has distinctive nutty flavor. Often added to extract beers.	10061	50 190	25 150	15	—	NA	NA	No	
CARA-PILS DEXTRINE MALT Everywhere	Used in pilsners and other light-colored beers to give additional body. Contributes no color.	10065	5	2	20	—	NA	NA	No	Similar to crystal malt, but processed in a way that does not darken the malt. Adds richness to beer without adding color.
DIAMBER MALT	Adds color, flavor and body to all kinds of darker beers. Used where high level of diastatic activity is needed.	10067	175	100			NA	NA	Yes	Similar to crystal malt, but processed to retain some diastatic activity. Not normally available to homebrewers.

GRAIN TYPE & COUNTRY	BREWING USAGE	Extract	Color EBC	Color °L	Max % of Batch	Diast Power °Lintne	% N	% PSN	Must Mash?	COMMENTS & DESCRIPTION
WHEAT MALT	35–65 percent of extract in Bavarian weizens (wheat ales). 30 percent in Berliner weisse beers. Important in Belgian lambics. 5 to 10 percent as adjunct in other beers. Improves head retention.	10078	5	2.7	65	49	1.6	.53	Yes	Contributes a spicy flavor, refreshing quality to weiss beers. (40–60 percent wheat). In small amounts, aids head retention in any beer. Protein rest used, to avoid chill-haze. Huskless, so sparging may be sluggish in high percentage of wheat beers.
OATS	Adds a creamy head and a grainy taste to English stouts. Used in Belgian witbiers (white ales), as 5 percent of the grist.	10050	4.5	2.2	10	21	2.0	.49	Yes	Oat diastase reduces starch exclusively to maltose (as opposed to dextrins). Aids in head retention when used in small quantities. Unmalted oats also used. Delicious when lightly toasted.
RICE	American and Japanese lager beers. Oddly regarded as a "premium" ingredient by such brewers as Budweiser. May be added in small quantities to English pale ales. Cleaner taste than corn.	10079	0	0	25	0	1.12	0	Yes	Adds alcohol, but little body or flavor. Makes a crisp, light-tasting beer. Must be mashed with a malt with high diastatic power, like six-row. Must be cooked before using. Grind first, then cook as for eating.
CORN	American and Canadian lager beers. Sometimes as high as 60 percent in cheap beers. Sometimes added in small quantities to English pale ales.	10079	0	0	10	0	1.15	0	Yes	Adds alcohol, but contributes little else. Not as clean a flavor as rice. Very inexpensive. Must be cooked before using. Grind first, then cook as you would rice. I don't see much to recommend it, except for its cheapness.
WHEAT (Unmalted)	Key ingredient (45 percent of grist) in Belgian witbiers. Important to use low-protein varieties. May be added directly to the mash, with no preboiling.	10078	5	2.7	50	NA	NA	NA	Yes	Unmalted wheat has more intense wheat flavor than malted versions. Much cheaper than malted wheat. Always available at health food stores.

Proper crushing of the malt is crucial to brewing. The most important effect is upon yield. I have personally witnessed a 30 percent improvement in yield achieved simply by changing the grind of the malt. Sparging may be dramatically improved as well.

For brewing, the object is to reduce the starchy malt endosperm to a fine state, while leaving the husks intact. Brewing experts suggest a mix of 1/3 flour, 1/3 fine grits, and 1/3 husks. The problem is to balance between the fineness of starch needed for efficient conversion, and the coarseness of husks necessary for an easy sparge.

The more finely the endosperm is ground, the more vulnerable it is to attack by the enzymes present in the hot mash; but an excess of flour can cause the mash to become sticky and set. It takes specialized equipment to crush the endosperm without cutting up the husks.

Commercial breweries use sophisticated roller mills, sometimes with as many as six sets of rollers and arrays of screens to assure a perfect grind. To a brewery, getting the maximum efficiency is a very important financial consideration, as even a small percentage gained or lost can mean big money for a commercial operation.

The widely available Corona grain mill is adequate but slow, especially for larger batches, because it is cranked by hand. If you have access to a machine shop, you may want to undertake the construction of a roller mill, but it is definitely not a project for the amateur. If you're designing your own roller mill, remember that breweries use large-diameter rolls, up to nine inches in diameter. This forms a narrow angle between the rollers and helps draw the malt down into the mechanism for grinding. Large, but narrow rollers probably is the way to go with a small mill.

There are some new, reasonably priced homebrew grain mills that grind the grain nearly as well as a brewery can. If you're doing larger batches, the ability to motorize is a must. If you're looking at one of these, make sure it is adjustable, because each malt must be milled at a specific setting to ensure optimum results.

Many homebrew suppliers sell malt in a precrushed state, which is fine, but crushed malt tends to go stale much faster than whole malt. In storage, preground malt tends to absorb water, which can interfere with efficient mashing. If you don't store the preground malt for any length of time, it works just fine. If you do need to store ground malt for a long period, put it in an airtight container. In some areas of the country, bugs can be a problem. Be on the lookout. Airtight containers are a must under such circumstances, but be aware that the grain bugs sometimes come with the grain.

Tips on Grain Crushing

Your grinder adjustment should be marked with some sort of calibration, like numbers from one to ten. Record the grinder settings for each grain in the space (G) provided on the worksheet.

Crystal, chocolate, and other dark-roasted grains may be more coarsely ground than pale ones, and if you're only using them as adjuncts for flavor it isn't really all that important how they're ground.

However, for real mashing and sparging, it does matter quite a bit. Lager and pilsner malts, being less highly modified, need to be more finely ground than pale ale malt. Munich malt is in between.

Corn, rice, and unmalted wheat, barley, and other grains must be very finely ground prior to cooking. The precautions about the husks don't apply, as the husks have been removed in these products anyway.

You can add great depth of flavor to your beers by roasting your own malt. Many types of malt common in the past are now unavailable to the homebrewer, but excellent versions may be easily made in your oven at home.

By controlling two simple variables, time and temperature, you can make anything from Munich to chocolate, as well as smoked and crystal malts.

Theory

The object of roasting grains is to develop certain flavor and color chemicals that form when sugars are heated in the presence of nitrogen compounds. The resulting pyrazines and related chemicals form a huge category (see the **Beer Flavor Sources chart, Section 3—4,**) with flavors ranging from "biscuity" to "caramelly" to "toasty" and beyond. Different chemicals are formed by specific combinations of amino acids and sugars, and different flavor profiles develop from different temperatures and moisture levels during roasting. Color is from a mysterious group of polymers known as melanoidins.

Be aware that the high temperatures of roasting will destroy the enzymes present in malt (see the **Grain Roasting chart, Section 6—5**). This is of concern when using large percentages of highly roasted malts, such as Munich, which may take twice as long to reach complete starch conversion during mashing as lager malt.

Home Roasting Technique

Start with unground pale ale malt or lager malt. Spread it out in a shallow baking pan, cake pan or cookie sheet, not more than an inch deep. Preheat your oven and put in the malt. Use a timer, or note the time. Stir as you see fit, trying to roast the malt evenly. Follow the chart (**6—5**) for times and temperatures to produce various types of roasted grains. Roasting moist enhances aroma development; mist the grain with a spray bottle and allow it to sit an hour or so to absorb the moisture. Color will be less than dry grains, at the same time and temperature.

Toaster ovens work just as well as big ovens, but, of course, they don't hold as much. Set control on "Bake," not "Broil." In a toaster oven, malt may scorch more easily than in a big oven, so watch it carefully.

Be sure to check the progress of your malt as you approach the finish time. Take a few grains out of the oven and bite through the middle to check the color. When you get what you want, stop.

Homemade Crystal Malt

Crystal malt is processed differently than other malt types. The malted, wet grains are raised to starch conversion temperatures and held for a while, then raised to roasting temperatures to develop color and ultimately dry out. The malt actually mashes right in the husk, creating a large percentage of long-chain dextrins that are unfermentable by yeast. Moist-roasting allows a whole different set of flavor chemicals to form, quite different from ordinary colored malt.

Roasting Procedure for Crystal Malt

1. Soak pale or lager malt in spring water or dechlorinated tap water for 24 hours.

2. Place in a deep baking pan, such as a bread pan, and heat slowly in an oven to 150°F/65°C. Hold for 1 hour or more.

3. Raise oven temperature to 170°/77°C, and hold for 30 minutes.

4. Raise oven temperature to 350°F, and hold until desired color has been reached. This could take a couple of hours.

5. Allow to mellow 1 to 2 weeks or before brewing.

Tips for Roasting and Usage

• When using large amounts of roasted grains in a recipe, you may want to use some six-row, as for co-mashing unmalted cereals.

• Always keep a record of time and temperature of your various types of roasted grains.

• Calibrate your oven with an accurate thermometer. It is also useful to know how long it really takes for your oven to preheat.

• Allow the roasted grain to sit for a week or two to mellow after roasting. *This is very important.* Otherwise you will get some very harsh flavors, and the beer may be reluctant to clear.

OVEN TEMPERATURE

| 5 | COPPER | 6 | DEEP COPPER | 7 | BROWN | 8 | LT. CHOCOLATE |

450°F 230°C

400°F 200°C

350°F 175°C

300°F 150°C

10 MIN.   20 MIN.   30 MIN.   40 MIN.   50 MIN.   60 MIN.   70 MIN.

| 1 | PALE GOLD | 2 | GOLD | 3 | AMBER | 4 | DEEP AMBER |

No	COLOR	°LOVIBOND	FLAVOR/DESCRIPTION
1	PALE GOLD	10	Aromatic, nutty. Not toasted-tasting. Enzymes still active. Yellow-gold color.
2	GOLD	20	Malty, caramelly, rich. Not toasted-tasting. Limited enzyme activity. Brilliant gold color.
3	AMBER	35	Lightly toasted taste. Nutty, malty, caramelly. Enzymes pretty much inactive. Orange.
4	DEEP AMBER	65	Pronounced toasted taste. Nutty, toffeelike. Reddish-copper color.
5	COPPER	100	Very strong toasted flavor. Nutty. Dark ruby-copper color.
6	DEEP COPPER	125	Roasted flavor, not toasted. Lingering, smooth, porter-y, coffeelike. Ruby-brown.
7	BROWN	175	Sharply roasted flavor. Smooth, rich, lingering. Ruby-brown.
8	LT. CHOCOLATE	300	Very rich, smooth, roasted taste. Dark ruby-brown.

ROASTING PROCEDURE

1. Preheat oven to desired temperature. Be sure oven is set on "Bake," not "Broil." Regular or toaster ovens are OK. Watch toaster ovens more carefully for scorching.

2. Use whole malt—pale or lager. Put desired amount on cookie sheet or cake pan. Spread out to 1" deep.

3. Place in oven for the appropriate time. Check progress by biting through malt kernels as you approach the end.

4. Remove when done. Store in a cool, dry place. Allow the malt to mellow for a couple of weeks before using. This allows harsh aromatic chemicals to escape.

5. Use as you would any other colored grain. Using more than one roasted grain in a recipe will give the beer a richer, more complex flavor. This applies equally to both light and dark beers.

MALT EXTRACT TYPE	GRAVITY 1 pound per 5 gallons	ALPHA x OUNCES per pound	BEER BITTERNESS 1 CAN per 5 gallons	BEER BITTERNESS 2 CANS per 5 gallons	MALT COLOR °Lovibond	BEER COLOR 1 CAN per 5 gallons	BEER COLOR 2 CANS per 5 gallons	COMMENTS & DESCRIPTIONS
LIQUID — UNHOPPED								
LIGHT LAGER (American Style)	10080	0.5-1.5	5.6-17	11-34	4-6	3-4	5.5-7	Often contains corn syrup to lighten body.
EUROPEAN PALE LAGER/PILSNER PLAIN LIGHT	10080	1.5-4.0	17-45	34-90	6-7	3.5-5	6-8.5	Supposed to be 100 percent malt, but aren't always. The amber and darker types are sometimes colored with tasteless caramel coloring, rather than with roasted malt. Bitterness designed for one 3.3-pound can per batch, so doubling the malt will double the bitterness. Hop bitterness often comes from hop extract; hop character and aroma usually lacking, and so need to be added. Age seems to affect malt extract syrups in a negative way, creating sherry-like oxidized tastes in stale malt extracts.
PALE ALE OR PLAIN AMBER	10080	2.5-3.5	28-40	28-40	10-14	6-12	10-20	
BITTER ALE	10080	4.0-4.5	35-50	70-100	10-16	7-12	12-20	
BROWN ALE OR MILD ALE	10080	1.0-3.5	12-40	24-80	25-35	12-35	20-40	
DARK LAGER PLAIN DARK	10080	1.5-2.5	18-25	36-50	30-40	17-25	30-40	
STOUT	10080	3.5-5.0	25-30	50-60	125-400	30-70	50-120	
LIQUID — HOPPED								
DIASTATIC (DMS)	10080	—	—	—	4-6	3.5-5	6-8.5	Contains active diastatic enzymes. Useful to add to mashes with corn or rice.
LIGHT	10080	—	—	—	5-7	3.5-5	6-10	Similar to above, without hop bitterness, so hops need to be added. If boiling only a portion of the wort, hop at a higher rate (1.5–2 times as high) to compensate for the higher-gravity wort, which does not incorporate hop resins as well as lower-gravity wort.
AMBER	10080	—	—	—	12-16	6-15	10-25	
DARK	10080	—	—	—	30-50	15-25	25-45	
DRY — HOPPED								
PALE	10094	—		—	6-8	4-5.5	8-10	Same as above, but without the water. Note that it is stronger on a per-weight basis. Seems to keep better, does not develop sherry-like/ballpoint pen oxidized qualities.
AMBER	10094	—		—	15-35	12-20	20-35	
DARK	10094	—		—	40-100	25-50		

EXACT BRAND & STYLE	COMMENTS

MALT/GRAIN	DATE OF PURCHASE	SOURCE	NOTES

MALT/GRAIN	DATE OF PURCHASE	SOURCE	NOTES

MALT/GRAIN	DATE OF PURCHASE	SOURCE	NOTES

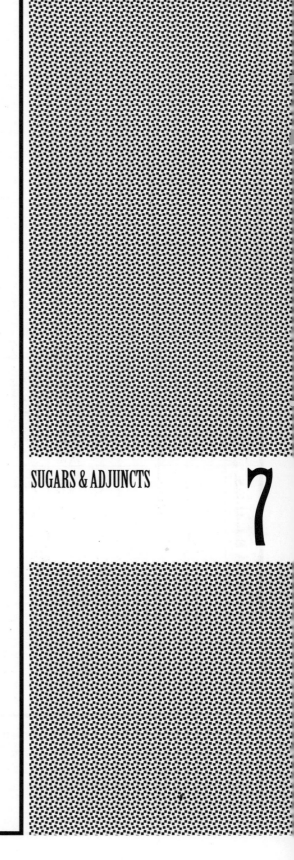

SUGARS & ADJUNCTS

7

	CARBOHYDRATE	No. of Sugar Units	% Total Carbohydrates			Ferment-ability	ROLE IN BREWING
			Malt	Wort	Beer		
S U G A R S	**DEXTROSE GLUCOSE** Corn Sugar $C_6H_{12}O_6$	1	<2	8–10	.5–1	Very good	A common monosaccharide, the building block for dextrins, starches, and other sugars. Yeast uses an enzyme to split maltose into this simpler sugar before metabolizing it.
	FRUCTOSE Fruit Sugar $C_6H_{12}O_6$	1	<1	1–2		OK	The most common naturally occurring sugar in nature, but not too important in brewing. Differs from glucose in structure only. Difficult to ferment.
	MALTOSE Malt Sugar $C_{12}H_{12}O_{11}$	2	<2	41–53	6–10	Very good	The main constituent of wort. Derived from the enzymatic splitting of starches and dextrins. Consists of two glucose molecules, joined.
	SUCROSE Cane Sugar $C_{12}H_{12}O_{11}$	2	3-5	5.5	>0.5	Fair	Not found naturally in wort. Consists of one molecule of glucose and one molecule of fructose, joined. Sometimes added for cheap fermentables. Difficult to ferment. Not recommended.
	MALTOTRIOSE	3	<1	14	7–11	Slow	More complex sugars that ferment slowly during secondary stage. Both are fermentable by lager yeast. Ale yeast can only handle maltotriose.
	MALTOTETRAOSE	4	<1	6	6–12	Lager only	
DEXTRINS	**ALPHA & BETA-LIMIT DEXTRINS**	5–20	—	17–29	65–75	Wild yeast only	Flavorless polysaccharides intermediate between sugars and starches, which provide (with alcohol) much of the caloric content in beer. Beta-limit dextrins are the little chunks of stuff left over at the site of the end-to-middle joints after amylopectin has been degraded.
	MALTODEXTRINS	20	—				
STARCHES	**AMYLOSE** Insoluble Starch	1000 to 4000	58-60	—	—	Wild yeast only	20-sugar subunits in long chains. Insoluble in water. Blue-black iodine reaction. Usually 20–30 percent of malt starch.
	AMYLOPECTIN Soluble Starch	Over 100,000		—	—	Wild yeast only	Larger branched structures. Forms stable colloidal solutions (gels) in water. About 20 units between branches. Reddish-purple iodine reaction. 70–80 percent of malt starch.
GUMS	**BETA GLUCANS**					No	Carbohydrates with a structure that gives them a very high viscosity (gooey, gummy) in water solutions. Present to some degree in all barley. With some varieties, they can be a problem in the mash, causing low yield/slow runoff.

Carbohydrates are the class of chemicals that includes simple sugars and the polymers formed from two or more single-sugar units, or monosaccharides. There are several types of monosaccharides, but dextrose is the only one that has an important role in brewing. Raffinose, a sugar found in very small quantities in malt, is used as a positive diagnosis for lager yeast, which can ferment it, whereas ale yeast cannot.

SUGAR TYPE	FERMENT-ABILITY BY BREWER'S YEAST	GRAVITY			APPLICATION
		Pounds	Per Gallon	Per 5 Gallons	
DEXTROSE GLUCOSE **Corn Sugar**	Very good	.1 .25 .5 .75 1 2 3 4 5 6	10047 1009 1018 1023 1047 1094 1141 1188 1235 1282	10009 10024 10047 10071 10094 10188 10282 10376 10470 10564	Common corn sugar, known to all homebrewers. Industrially used to produce light, inexpensive beers. Adds no flavor in small quantities, but larger amounts can cause a thin, cidery flavor. More evident in paler beers, especially with high fermentation temperatures. Sometimes used commercially. Less than 10 percent shouldn't do too much harm. Fine for priming, but I have a dim perception that dry malt extract gives a creamier head when used for priming.
SUCROSE **Cane Sugar** **Candy Sugar** **Beet Sugar** **Demerara*** **Turbinado*** ***Partly refined**	OK, but slow	.1 .25 .50 .75 1 2 3 4 5 6	10047 1009 1018 1023 1047 1094 1141 1188 1235 1282	10009 10024 10047 10071 10094 10188 10282 10376 10470 10564	Sometimes used by brewers in England, Belgium, and elsewhere, in the form of candy sugar. Less easily fermented by brewer's yeast than dextrose or maltose. May be used in a pinch for priming, but bottles may take longer to become fully pressurized. Used in some strong Belgian ales, such as abbey triples, to thin down the syrupyness possible in strong beers. In lighter beers, less than 10 percent probably won't be too offensive.
LACTOSE **Milk Sugar**	Non				Derived from milk, this sugar is completely unfermentable by brewer's yeast. Composed of two molecules of galactose, joined. The traditional sweetening in milk stout, it is typically added at the rate of 1–3 ounces per gallon.
MALTO-DEXTRIN	Non				This is a material halfway between sugar and starch, and is between 4 and 20 dextrose units long. Because of its complexity, it is unfermentable by brewer's yeast. It is present in quantity in finished beers, between 0–6 percent. Used as an additive especially in pale extract beers, it can supply some of the richness missing in that type, although crystal malt will add more flavor. Using 1/4 to 1/2 pound per 5 gallons of extract beer is typical.
HONEY	Somewhat slow	.1 .25 .5 .75 1 2 3 4 5 6	10042 10106 10212 10318 10424 10847 11271 11695 12118 12542	10008 10021 10042 10064 10085 10169 10252 10338 10424 10508	Honey is a complex mixture containing about 45 percent fructose, 35 percent dextrose, 13–20 percent water, and small amounts of maltose, sucrose, dextrins, gums, vitamins, enzymes, protein and other stuff, including flavor and color chemicals. Avoid strongly flavored honey, such as buckwheat, as it can be overpowering. Also, honey contains natural antibiotic compounds which can make fermentation difficult when used in large amounts, as in mead. Typically, 10–20 percent honey can be used in the kettle in place of malt, sugar, or extract. This has the effect of lightening up the beer; especially useful in high-gravity pale beers. Freshness is an important consideration with honey; use it within a few months of purchase. Honey is available in many interesting varietals, including orange blossom, cranberry, fireweed, snowberry, raspberry, mint, apple, eucalyptus. These are never strongly fruit flavored; rather, they have a sweetish perfumy character that can add a touch of class to the beers in which they're used.

INGREDIENT	BREWING STAGE	WHAT IT IS	WHAT IT DOES	TYPICAL USE	QUANTITY USED
ENZYMES	Mash, Secondary	Alpha amylase enzymes, from bacteria. *Bacillus subtilis.*	Breaks starch into fermentable sugars. Most active @ 155°F/68°C.	Pre-mash grain adjuncts. Cure for too-hot mash, up to 190°F/90°C.	1/2 tsp. per 5 gal.
ASCORBIC ACID	Bottling	Vitamin C, an oxygen-scavenger called a reductone.	Helps prevent oxidation of beer. Also as a chill-proofing agent.	Add to beer at bottling. Heat destroys. Of marginal value.	1/2 to 1 tsp. per 5 gal.
GELATIN	Secondary	Ordinary unflavored gelatin.	Clears yeast and other suspended matter from beer by adsorption.	Add to hot water, dissolve well. Add to secondary.	1 packet per 5 gal.
HEADING COMPOUND	Bottling	Prepared vegetable extracts, probably gums, mostly.	Artificially enhances head formation in beer.	Add to beer at bottling. Use in high-sugar, low-maltbeers.	1/2 tsp./5 gal. or as directed.
IRISH MOSS	End of Boil	*Chrondus crispus,* A dried marine algae.	Helps coagulates hop tannins and proteins in boil (hot break).	Add to last 10 minutes of the boil. Hastens and improves hot break.	1/2 tsp. per 5 gal.
ISINGLASS	Secondary	The prepared, dried swim bladder of certain fish.	Clears yeast and other suspended particulates from beer.	Finings are soaked in cold water, added to ales above 70°F/22°C.	As directed on package
KOJI ENZYMES	Pre-mash, Mash	Alpha amylase enzyme derived from a fungus, *Aspergillus oryzae.*	Breaks starch into sugars and dextrins. Used in sake brewing.	Pre-mash corn, rice, wheat. Remove starch haze in secondary.	1/2 to 1 tsp. per 5gal.
PECTIC ENZYMES	Primary, Secondary	Enzymes that dissolve pectin, a complex polysaccharide in fruit.	Breaks up fruit pectins so they cannot form haze in beer.	Add to fruit beers in primary to remove pectin, a haze source.	1/2 tsp. per 1 gal.
POLYCLAR	Secondary	Microscopic plastic beads that adsorb protein in beer.	Clears beer of yeast, by adsorption.	Add during lagering to pale all-malt beers, especially those with six-row.	1/2 ounce per 5 gal.
PROTEOLYTIC ENZYMES	Primary, Secondary	Cultured purified enzymes that dissolve protein.	Breaks-up proteins into smaller, soluble units.	Add to high %N beers (secondary) to remove haze.	1/2 tsp. per 5 gal.
YEAST NUTRIENT	Primary	Diammonium phosphate, vitamins, yeast extract, or a similar mix.	Provides nitrogen and other nutrients to yeast. Not needed in all-malt beer.	Add to boil. Use only on very low-gravity or beer made with sugar.	1/2 tsp./5 gal. Or as directed.
LACTOSE	Boil, Bottling	Milk sugar, an unfermentable disaccharide of galactose.	Adds sweetness. Not fermentable by yeast.	Add to boil or at priming to London stout, milk stout.	1/4–1 lbs. per 5 gal.

Brewing with fruit goes back to ancient Egypt, when many different types were being used. Today, only Belgium retains a tradition of fruit beer brewing, although some American micro-breweries are dabbling in it.

Brewing with fruit may sound intimidating, but it really isn't difficult. It does require patience, as it often takes much longer than regular beer.

Handling Fruit

Use fresh or frozen uncooked fruit. I usually freeze fresh fruit to help break down the cellular structure, making the sugars more available to the yeast. And though it doesn't actually sterilize it, freezing does reduce the quantity of microbes on the fruit that could affect your beer.

You can use a juice extractor to produce fermentable juice, provided you're confident you can thoroughly clean the juicer's inner working parts. Juicing makes dealing with the fruit far easier, but removing the skin, pits, and the like may lessen the beer's complexity.

Fruit and Fermentation

Always add the fruit to the secondary, after the yeast has had a chance to establish itself. The beer is much less vulnerable at this stage to the inevitable contaminating bugs. Also, the vigorous bubbling of the primary fermentation tends to drive off the volatile fruit aromas.

This secondary can be carried out in a plastic fermenter. Be sure there is plenty of headspace, as the fermentation can become quite vigorous for a while. I recommend flushing the fermenter with CO_2 to provide protection from the adverse effects of oxygen and keep mold and acetobacteria from growing. You can add pectic enzymes to help further break up the plant tissue.

Do not ferment fruit in a glass carboy, unless you have PLENTY of headspace. If you don't, fruit chunks can rise up and clog the blow-off hole,

FRUIT BEERS TO PONDER

Sour Cherry Wheat Cream Ale
Black Cherry Stout
Raspberry Apricot Brown Ale
Pomegranate Lambic
Black Raspberry Imperial Stout
Blueberry Porter
Peach Passionfruit Weizen
Cranberry Berliner Weisse
Passionfruit Märzen

then kablooey! Sticky, fruity, beery pulp all over the basement. It has happened!

The fruit should stay in the beer for a minimum of two weeks. A month or two is usually better. Let it go until the fruit is reduced to pulp, if you can tie up your fermenter that long. The Belgians used to let their cherries sit in the beer for a year, with the pits and everything.

At the end, rack the beer off the fruit into a carboy to allow it to clear. When doing this, use a piece of cheesecloth or fine mesh fastened over the end of your siphon tube inlet. There will be lots of gunk. Keep the tube end up high, or wherever you can keep the mass of fruit away from the tube. Siphoning may be frustratingly slow, but be patient.

Allow the beer to thoroughly clear in the carboy, and make sure all signs of fermentation have stopped before bottling. Fruit beers contain some complex sugars, which the yeast will slowly munch away on for months.

It is a good idea to prime fruit beers on the light side, to prevent overpriming. Allow plenty of conditioning time before drinking. Like wine, fruit beers are not at their prime until they have some age on them, and they'll hold up beautifully for years. There are few pleasures like tasting your own eight-year old cherry ale.

Fruit and Beer Flavor

Make sure you use enough fruit. Yes, it is expensive, unless you grow it yourself, but the end product will be as precious as fine wine. Check the farmers' markets at the peak of the season for bargains. You can use bruised or overripe fruit as long as it's not moldy. Fruits vary greatly in intensity, so refer to the chart to determine the minimum recommended quantity. A pound per gallon gives good results with most fruits.

Some fruits lack the acidity needed to bring out their best. Peaches, plums and blueberries can sometimes be bland, and benefit greatly from the addition of a small amount of citric acid or winemakers acid blend. You can add this after racking the beer off the fruit, when you have a chance to taste it. Acidity can be added with sour fruit as well. Lemons, cranberries, sour cherries, and others can be used this way.

Be sure you have enough malt to stand up to the fruit. It is important, especially if you're entering competitions, that you be able to taste some malt. Generally, the more fruit, the more malt, up to about 1060 OG/14°P. Conversely, low-gravity beers may be flavored with only a little fruit, and are best enjoyed rather quickly.

Hops are usually included but remain in the background as a subtle bitterness to balance the malt sweetness and fruit character.

Flavoring with Syrups and Liqueurs

Since at least the days of the ancient Egyptians, brewers have been flavoring their beers with fruits, herbs and spices. Almost any pleasant-tasting (and sometimes not-so-pleasant) seasoning has at one time been added to beer. Certain beer styles still require some spicing to be truly authentic.

Dealing with fruits and herbs can often be a messy and chancy affair. Herbs added to the boil will incorporate well, but can easily lose aromatic compounds essential to good flavor. Adding herbs or fruit to the primary may introduce infections at the beer's most vulnerable stage. Also, the vigorous yeast activity can "scrub" aromatics from the beer. Adding them to the secondary is safer, but necessitates the use of a third fermentation to allow the beer to settle clear after the flavoring material has been removed.

What is the creative brewer to do?

There is a simple solution that makes it very easy to add exotic flavors to your beers without any effort at all. Flavored liqueurs may be added to the beer before bottling for a range of flavors limited only by your imagination.

Liqueurs are perfect for this purpose. Their alcohol preserves and sterilizes any wayward microbes. They usually contain very high-quality flavoring material and if additional sugar has been added, they are perfect for priming. Besides, they are available in a variety of flavors.

One of the best is Orange Curaçao. It is made from an intensely flavored bitter orange, and the flavor stands up well in the finished beer. Orange peel is one of the two main spices in Belgian *Wit,* or white ale, the other being coriander seed.

Steeping spices in a liqueur also works extremely well. The alcohol actually helps many flavor chemicals dissolve. And, of course, it's sterile. Simply make a mixture of your favorite liqueur with whatever herbs and spices you wish to use and let them soak for at least a week. Longer certainly would not hurt.

Coriander seeds also work well in the boil, added 15 minutes before the end, like aromatic hops. They also may be steeped in the liqueur for a week, then strained and added to the beer at priming. For the best flavor, do both.

Other useful liqueur flavors include peach, blackberry, crême de cacao (the best source for chocolate flavor you can find), cherry, apricot, and anise. There are also herbed ones, such as

ALCOHOL CORRECTION FIGURES FOR LIQUEUR		
80 proof (without sugar = .914 SG) = Add 20° Plato to measured gravity		
60 proof (without sugar = .936 SG) = Add 15° Plato to measured gravity		
40 proof (without sugar = .957 SG) = Add 10° Plato to measured gravity		

Benedictine and Chartreuse, which may lend a certain medieval authenticity to a brew, but I'm not sure I would add a whole bottle.

A typical bottle of liqueur contains almost enough sugar to prime a five-gallon batch. I have found that adding two ounces of corn sugar to the Triple Sec before adding to the batch works well, but sugar content does vary with the kind of liqueur used. If a liqueur seems extraordinarily sweet, hold off on the corn sugar. Certain others, especially schnapps, are lower in sugar. With these liqueurs you should add more.

You can measure the sugar content of the liqueur with your hydrometer, and make a rough determination as to the quantity of sugar present. °Plato measures percent of sugar in solution, so it's pretty easy to figure out. The chart on the previous page shows how many degrees P to add to your readings to compensate for the amount of alcohol present, which distorts the numbers on sugar percentage. Once you determine the sugar percentage, it is a simple matter to calculate the quantity in a bottle. A 750 ml bottle of pure water weighs 26.7 ounces. If the liqueur is 10 percent sugar, then there are about 3 ounces of sugar in it. If it's 20 percent, then the bottle contains about 5½ ounces of sugar you can use for priming.

To use liqueur for priming, just add it to the batch at bottling time. There's no need to boil before adding, as it's already sterile. If you've soaked herbs or spices in the liqueur, run it through a coffee filter to get the floaters out.

This method will add a certain amount of alcohol to your beer. To find the amount, simply divide the proof by 50. This is the percentage of alcohol you will add to a 5-gallon batch of beer from one fifth (750 ml) bottle. So a 60-proof liqueur will add 1.2 percent alcohol. This is usually not a problem, as these beers can benefit from the added kick.

You can even create your own special priming liqueurs from vodka, sugar, or honey or malt extract, and whatever herbs or spices you like.

Just measure the normal amount of priming sugar into the vodka and herb mixture.

Coriander and orange peel work very well for white beer, but limit the soaking time for the orange, as it can become unpleasantly bitter; check on it every few days.

I have tried a few of the liqueur flavor concentrates, but some of them are strictly artificial and give flavors that are one-dimensional, to say the least. Some are high in oil, which can be disastrous for the head of your beer.

Fruit juice concentrates can be a good shortcut to making fruit beers. Bottles of concentrated juice are available at health food or gourmet markets. The flavor selection is sometimes limited, but the flavor is quite good. And, typically the concentrates contain nothing but pure fruit juice. I have had great success with a black cherry juice concentrate. One pint of the stuff is the equivalent of five pounds of cherries. The price is usually about the same as for the equivalent amount of cherries, so considering the convenience, it's a bargain. Add the concentrate to the secondary to allow the sugars present to ferment out.

The black cherry is a little bland and one-dimensional by itself. The beer is usually improved dramatically by the use of two pounds or more of frozen sour pie cherries. It is important to have enough acidity in fruit beers or meads. Otherwise, the fruit flavors are extremely flat and drab. The sour cherries provide that, but a winemaking acid blend might do the trick. There are also specialty fruit syrups, especially those from Eastern European countries, that are good in beers.

FRUIT TYPE	BREWING TRADITION	QUANTITY Lbs/Gallon	COMMENTS & DESCRIPTION
APPLES	Farm	Cider + malt	Cider fortified with malt.
APRICOTS	None	.5–2	As additive to peach beer. Fresh or dried.
BLACKBERRIES	None	.5–2.5	Good color and acid. Flavor strong, long-lasting.
BLACK CURRANTS	Lambic type: Cassis	.25–1	Distinctive. Hard to find in United States.
BLUEBERRIES	None	1–3	Kind of bland. Good red color.
CHERRIES	Used in kriek lambic and sometimes in sour brown ales. Whole fruit often fermented for long periods.	1–6	Sour cherries best. Black or Bing good for color. Ferment on pits for most complex flavor. Syrups and extracts available, work well.
DATES	Ancient Egypt/Mesopotamia	1–2	Bland, high in sugar.
GRAPES	Lambic type: Druiven	1–3	Raisins might do.
PASSIONFRUIT	None	.25–1 pint syrup	Distinct, intense taste. Would go well with peach, blueberry.
PEACHES	New lambic style; created at Lindeman's Farm Brewery, Belgium.	1–4	Hard to get good aroma. Not strongly flavored. Best to use large amounts.
PLUMS	Mirabelle, in lambic, brandy	.5–3	Good color. Somewhat delicate. Laxative. (Prunes come from plums, remember?)
POMEGRANATES	Egyptian	.2–.5 pint syrup	Fruit hard to deal with. Syrup or concentrate available, try Middle Eastern grocery. High acid and tannin.
RASPBERRIES	Lambic type: Framboise	.5–3	Fantastic! Long-lasting intense flavor. Good color. Keeps well.
STRAWBERRIES	Lambic type: Aardbien	2–5	Flavor and color fade quickly. Need a lot to cut through.

HOPS

8

HOP BOTANY

The hop plant is a flowering, climbing vine of the *Cannabicinae* family. Its flowers provide the bitterness and flowery aroma we expect to find in beer. The flowers are the only part that is useful in brewing.

There are actually three species of hops. Two are useful in brewing, and the third, *Humulus japonicus*, is strictly a decorative plant. The first two are closely related, and hybrids between the two have been bred with much success.

Humulus americanus is, as you would expect, the native American hop. Its usefulness in brewing has been mostly for crossbreeding with European species to develop new varieties.

Humulus lupulus is the European hop and has been cultivated for brewing purposes for at least a thousand years. There is some evidence that hops were grown in ancient Babylon, but the first documented use was in Germany. From there, they spread to the rest of Europe, and finally to England. Their use was opposed by every country into which they were introduced, for the hop allowed brewers to make a weaker beer. Since hops act as a preservative in beer, very high levels of alcohol were no longer needed to protect the beer from infection. Drinkers used to the astonishingly strong ales of the Middle Ages may have felt cheated, perhaps an early consumer's movement of sorts.

Before hops became the herb of choice, lots of other plant materials were employed. Balsam, betony, bog myrtle, yarrow, dandelion, mint, pennyroyal, rosemary, sage, tansy, and wormwood and many others were used. Herbs with strictly medicinal effects were often used to create tonics.

Hops are perennial. A fresh plant, or bine, arises from the rootstock every year. The bines grow to a length of 25 to 35 feet in commercial cultivation. The best soil is deep, with good drainage. A plant will typically last between five and fifteen years. They are climbing plants, coiling clockwise around any available support. In cultivation, they are trained up strings that are attached to horizontal supports overhead.

Hops are dioecious, meaning there are male and female plants. The male produces a pollen-producing structure. The pollen is carried by wind to fertilize the female, whose flowers will then produce seeds.

There are several problems with raising hops from seed, so propagation is by rootstock. Eliminating the uncertainties of windborne pollination by growing only female plants creates a more uniform, agriculturally controllable plant. This ensures a crop with uniform flavor, and which ripens all at the same time.

Most of the major hop-growing areas of the world are temperate, with good moisture and mild winters. Different hops prefer different types of weather. In Britain, Fuggles do well in wet years, while Goldings prosper in dry years. Alpha acid content can vary by a third or more from year to year.

Everywhere in the world except England, hops are grown as sterile female plants, with the male plants not being allowed in the hop-growing areas. Left unfertilized, the female plants produce flowers without seeds. Since the seeds have no brewing value, seedless hops have a higher content by weight of the oils and resins used in brewing. Seeds also contain some fat, which is potentially harmful to beer, and they can cause mechanical difficulties with pumps, valves, and the machinery of mechanized brewing. English hop growers claim that seeded hops have a higher resistance to disease.

Hops are picked at the end of the summer. Ripe hops begin to turn yellowish, some vari-

MAJOR HOP CATEGORIES	
TYPE	EXAMPLE
Central European	Hallertau
British Isles	Fuggles
North American	Cluster
Hybrid	Northern Brewer

eties (English and Belgian) more than others. The cones (flowers) are the only part picked for processing. At the time of picking, they have a 75 percent moisture content. Kilns are used for drying, typically 10 hours at 140°–167°F/60°–75°C, with a strong flow of air forced through. After being dried down to 7 percent moisture, the hops are compressed into bales for transportation and storage.

Hop Varieties

The 20th century has seen intense efforts to improve hops. Numerous new varieties have been developed which have improved characteristics in the areas of yield, disease resistance, alpha acid content, storage life, and so on. Very recently, varieties known as super-high alpha have been put into production. These hops have an alpha acid content over 10 percent, about double that of the traditional hop types. The most recent ones, such as Centennial, have pleasing aromas, in addition to intense bitterness, although it's still easy to overdo it, especially with lighter beers.

The most famous hop-growing areas in the world are Saaz, in the Czech Republic; the Spalt, Tettnang and Hallertau Mittelfrüeh regions in Germany; Kent, in England; and the Pacific Northwest, in the United States, and British Columbia in Canada.

In Germany, the finest hops have long been thought to come from the Hallertau region. Spalt and Tettnanger hops are also highly regarded, the latter reputedly having a milder flavor than Bavarian hops. Hersbrucker, or mountain hops, are considered to be of lower quality.

The English hop universe is divided into two big halves, the Fuggles and the Golding. The East Kent Golding is the monarch of British hops, suitable for adding aroma to the finest of pale ales. Traditionally, Fuggles is the hop of choice for dark ales.

As everywhere else, Belgium had a very large variety of different hop types in times past. Some varieties, such as Burrine and Groene Bel were commercially cultivated until quite recently, and may still be lurking in monastery gardens.

FACTORS AFFECTING HOP BITTERNESS IN BEER	
HOP VARIETY LOCALITY YEAR GROWN	All these can cause considerable variation in the flavor and bittering power of hops. There can be variation from year to year by as much as a factor of two. The best guide is an alpha acid analysis, which may be provided from your supplier.
PELLET vs. LEAF	Pellets are usually 1¼ to 1½ times as bitter as leaf hops of comparable origin. Pellet hops lose less during storage, and they are better assimilated into the wort during the boil.
WATER pH, CARBONATE TO SULFATE BALANCE	An excess of carbonate, and hence a high pH, hinders incorporation of hop resins into the wort. At the same time the harsh, rough qualities of hop flavor are exaggerated.
BEER STRENGTH	As the gravity of wort increases, incorporation of the hop resins becomes poorer.
STORAGE OF HOPS	Hops lose much of their aroma and some of their bittering powers upon prolonged storage. There is much variation according to hop type. Cold storage and the exclusion of air improve the survival of essential hop qualities.
AGE OF THE BEER	Beer seems to lose about half of its bitterness in the first six months after bottling.

Until recently, the main hop cultivated in the United States was the Cluster. Not the most flavorful of hops, it yields well and has good storage life. A number of more interesting hops are now being grown in the Pacific Northwest. We now have access to European types such as the Fuggles/Willamette, as well as the newly developed super-high alpha hops, such as Chinook. The Cascade is a uniquely American hop, having a distinctive, floral aroma. In Canada, the story is much the same, although through the years

Canadian brewers seem to have paid a bit more attention to hop flavor in beer than have the industrial brewers in the United States.

Hop Storage

Hops degrade rapidly in storage. The bitter alpha and beta acids are oxidized to form a wide range of new substances, some of them bitter, some not. Certain of these have considerable foam-stabilizing properties, which probably play a role in beer head retention. The aromatic oils suffer the most, evaporating into the air and simply vanishing.

Oxygen is the enemy of all that is good in hops, as far as storage is concerned. And heat speeds up the effects of oxygen. Therefore, the best place to store hops is in outer space! Closer to home, the next best thing is to pack the hops tightly in oxygen-barrier bags and store them in your freezer.

The bittering power of hops stored at room temperature noticeably decreases in just a few months. Hop aroma suffers even worse deterioration, so if your freezer space is limited, give preferential treatment to the aromatic varieties.

The Forms of Hops

After drying, hops may be processed in several ways. They may be used just as they are, providing mechanical action that speeds up coagulation of proteins in the boil, and serving as a filter bed holding the protein matter (trub) back when the kettle is drained.

HOP CONSTITUENTS	
Moisture	9–13%
Resins	10–20%
Oils	0.2–0.5%
Tannins	2–5%
Pectins	9–11%
Ash K_2O	18%
Ash P_2O_5	30%
Nitrogen	2–4%
Glucose, Fructose	2–4%

Whole hops may be chopped up finely and compressed into pellets. These pellets exclude oxygen better, and so have a longer storage life. At any given alpha acid content, ounce-for-ounce, pellets are more bitter. Some brewers feel that the pelletizing process allows chlorophyll and other materials to leak out of the ruptured cells, con-tributing "green" or "grassy" flavors to the finished beer.

A number of processes are used to manufacture hop extracts which simplify life for the brewer. Alpha acid is treated with alkali, or reacted with catalysts to isomerize, or to be transformed chemically to a form that is more bitter and more soluble in water than the original resin. Older extraction methods use petroleum products such as hexane. Newer technology uses liquid carbon dioxide as a solvent, and these CO_2 products seem to have a fresher, more-natural whole-hop character. Hop extracts may be added during conditioning to adjust bitterness to the desired level.

Some American brewers use specially treated hop extracts, with the precursor of methyl mercaptan (the skunkiness chemical) removed. These extracts are usually used in beers packaged in clear or green glass bottles, which would otherwise have problems with light-induced skunkiness.

Extracts of essential aromatic oils are produced by treating the hops with a solvent. These extracted oils keep very well and may be added during fermentation, or at bottling, as a replacement to dry-hopping, without biological contamination to the brew.

Hop Constituents

The flower cones of hops contain a variety of organic substances, as can be seen from the accompanying chart. Of all these, only three are important to the brewer. The resins provide bitter flavor to beer, the oils contribute most of the hop aroma, and the tannins (polyphenols) are important in the coagulation of protein during the wort boil and fermentation.

The resins and oils of hops are contained in the lupulin glands, small golden beads of waxy material concentrated at the base of the bracts that form the hop cone. Lupulin, the waxy resinous material extracted from them, is a mixture of substances, including various oils and resins.

Hop Resins

There are three types of hop resins: alpha, beta, and gamma. Alpha and beta are soft resins; gamma is a hard resin, a result of the various oxidation products of the first two types.

Alpha acids are the most important from a brewer's perspective, as they provide most, if not all, of the hop bitterness in beer. Alpha acid content is used to measure the bittering power of hops. Alpha acid (humulone), is about nine times as bitter as beta acid, and is actually a group of closely related compounds with similar effects on the brew. The beta acids are collectively known as lupulone.

It has been traditionally thought that hop resins contributed nothing but bitterness toward beer flavor. Recent studies suggest that at least some of the aromatic qualities long attributed to hop oils may, in fact, be derived from the resins and their degradation products.

Hop Bitterness

It is hop bitterness that complements the syrupy, sticky qualities of malt, and the counterpoint of maltiness to bitterness is known as balance in beer. Finding the correct balance is an important part of creating a recipe, being true to a particular style, and making the beer palatable. The **Hop Rate vs. Gravity chart, Section 3–2**, shows values for the major beer types.

Bitterness is measured in commercial breweries as the parts-per-million of dissolved iso-alpha acids present in the finished beer. It is expressed as International Bitterness Units, referred to in this book as IBUs. This value may be anywhere from 15 to 35 percent of the total amount of alpha acids present in the bittering hops added to the beer, and this value depends on many factors.

One widely used formula is ounces times alpha acid percentage, divided by the total gallons of

the batch. This is known as Homebrew Bitterness Units, or Alpha Acid Units, and is really a measure of how much alpha acid material gets added to a wort. Because of the wide variation in hop utilization, this number can actually be quite misleading, and may result in beers that are either too bitter, or not bitter enough. It is far better to attempt to calculate IBUs, which correlate to the amount of alpha acids actually present in finished beer.

To calculate IBUs, you multiply Homebrew Bitterness Units by a factor that depends on kettle utilization. But since wort gravity and boil length are the two most important factors in determining utilization, lumping everything together like this isn't a very accurate way to do it. Look at the **Hop Utilization charts, Sections 8–4** and **8–5**, which will give you more accurate results when calculating bitterness for your beers. You must calculate the bitterness for each individual hop addition to get a number that corresponds to IBUs, the generally accepted commercial measurement for hop bitterness in beer.

Hop Oils

Hops contain a rich spectrum of powerful aromatic oils that contribute the floral perfume to beer. There are several hundred individual components of this oil, mostly of a class of hydrocarbons known as terpenes, which are responsible for most of hop aroma. Also present are esters, aldehydes, ketones, acids, and higher alcohols. Much of the material in hop oils evaporates, oxidizes, and otherwise degrades after harvesting, so proper storage of hops intended for aromatic purposes is very important.

The class of chemicals known as terpenes are the soul of the hop. There are a number of very distinct ones, each with its own characteristic aroma. It is the types and quantities of these terpenes that largely determine the specific character of a hop variety, making a Cascade taste different in beer from a Fuggles, for example.

Hop aroma is one of the big contributors to the national character of beers. British varieties lend an authentic touch to bitter, pale ales, etc. German hops should dominate a fine Continental lager. You can't even think of brewing a Czech pilsner without Saaz hops. Traditional American beers are less distinct, hop levels being lower, but tend to be somewhat European in their hop flavor. U.S. premium beers often use Hallertau or other German hops. The classic American hop, Cluster, has a mildly disagreeable "catty" flavor, much despised by European brewers. Cascade is a uniquely American hop with a delightful aroma. It is essential for American pale ales of the micro-brewed variety, and seems to lend a Canadian character to lagers.

HOPS IN BREWING

The chemicals present in hops undergo numerous changes during the brewing process. Most significant is the isomerization, or chemical re-arrangement, of the alpha acids. When boiled, they become more bitter and much more soluble than in their original state. Oxidation also takes place, creating a range of nonbitter products that have strong foam-stabilizing properties. They may contribute to head retention in the finished beer.

Beta acids are also transformed in the boil, oxidized into bitter and non-bitter substances. Compared to alpha acid, beta acid is a minor player in beer.

In the boil, about half of the alpha and beta acids are incorporated into the wort. Further losses occur during fermentation, so the ultimate utilization of hop alpha acids is between 5 and 40 percent in finished beer.

Hop–Tannin Interactions

Tannins, or polyphenols, react with protein

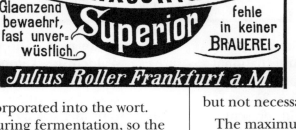

derived from malt to form insoluble compounds which clump together and precipitate to form the hot break. When the wort is chilled, more of the same material comes out of solution as the cold

VARIETIES FOR DRY HOPPING & HOP TEA	
SAAZ	Pilsners, pale lagers, Belgian ales.
CASCADE	American pale ales, barley wines
TETTNANGER HERSBRUCKER	European lagers, wheat ales
EAST KENT GOLDINGS	English pale ales
FUGGLES	Dark English ales, stouts, porters

break. This action is important, as it removes much of the proteinaceous material that would otherwise come out of solution later when the finished beer is chilled and pose haze problems.

Preservative Effects

Although in commercial pasteurized beers the this factor has lost its importance, in homebrewing, the antibiotic effects of hop resins do help fight unfriendly microbes. Most affected are lactic acid bacteria. Gram-negative bacteria are unaffected by hop resins, as are all types of wild yeasts.

Hops in the Boil

Leaf or pellet hops may be used, but ounce for ounce, pellets give a more bitter beer. Twenty minutes is the minimum time for extracting the bitter substances from hops and converting (isomerizing) them into compounds that are soluble in wort. One hour is more typical, but the usual rule is to put in half of the hops for the duration of the boil. Better hop character can be had by loading up the hops toward the end of the boil, where aroma and hop flavor but not necessarily bitterness can be extracted.

The maximum bitterness is achieved at about three hours, and does not increase much with additional boiling. See the **Hop Utilization charts, Sections 8–4** and **8–5**.

Aromatic hops are added toward the end of the boil. Typically, you add some aroma hops for 20 minutes of the boil, and the rest at or just before the end of the boil, so as not to lose the volatile aromatic oils that contribute so much.

At the end of the boil, breweries typically use the hops as a filter bed, trapping much of the protein trub precipitated as the hot break. Hot water is sometimes run through the spent hops to recover the last bit of extract and hop flavor. This is done in a straining vessel known as a hop back, or a whirlpool device.

As a homebrewer, there are a couple of ways you can do this. You can strain the whole boiled wort through your lauter tun. Pour the hot wort into the well-sterilized sparging vessel, allow to stand long enough for the hops to settle to the bottom, then open the tap and allow the wort to flow into the wort chiller. When the wort is drained, pour a quart or two of boiling water through the hop bed, allow to settle, then drain off the last bit of hop flavor and wort extract.

If you have a boiling kettle with a tap on the bottom (see **Section 15, Homebrew Equipment**), you can fit the kettle with a stainless steel screen in the bottom, which serves to hold back the spent hops and trub. As with the above technique, allow the hops to settle after the heat is turned off, and before draining into the wort chiller. Sparge with boiling water as above.

Dry-hopping

The addition of aromatic hops to the fermenting beer can be an effective way to add extra hop flavor and aroma. Aromatic hops are traditionally used in strong British pale ales

during maturation in the pub cellar. In home-brewing practice they are best added to the secondary. If you use whole hops in the secondary, be sure you have sufficient headspace in your carboy. More than one big sticky explosion has been caused by hops rising up and clogging the stopper hole, allowing too much pressure to build in the fragile glass carboy. Hops may be added dry, or steeped in boiling water a few minutes before they are added.

Hops also contain small amounts of diastase, and so dry-hopped beers will be slightly more attenuated than normal.

Hop Tea

Hop tea can be added to the beer in the secondary or at bottling to add hop aroma. Similar in effect to dry-hopping, this method is more sanitary and definitely less messy.

Technique

1. Boil 16 ounces of water. Add hops, same as for dry-hopping. Boil for about 3 minutes.

2. Strain through a coffee filter into either a sterilized container (if being added to secondary) or a saucepan for priming, along with priming sugar.

3. If using at bottling, proceed with priming as usual. If adding at secondary, allow to cool somewhat before adding.

4. Flavor will seem harsh at first if added at bottling. Let beer age to mellow out roughness.

A Note on Hops in Lambics

Lambic brewers don't want the flavor or bitterness other brewers crave. Their sole interest is in the preservative qualities. They use hops that have spent a few years in the rafters of the brewery, and have lost their aroma and bitterness. Caution must be exercised to be sure the hops have not picked up oxidized "cheesey" aromas, which are pretty offensive in beer.

Hops in Berliner Weisse

This lightly hopped wheat beer is a distant cousin to the lambic style. Berliner brewers have been known to use their hops in the mash. This extracts some bitterness, but more importantly, aids in the filtering of the mash, made gooey by the presence of a large proportion of wheat.

VARIETY	COUNTRY	APPLICATIONS	AROMA/BITTER	AVERAGE ALPHA %	STORAGE	DESCRIPTION	SUBSTITUTE
BREWER'S GOLD / BULLION	England, (Origin) U.S.	English ales, especially dark, strong, highly hopped ones. Sometimes used for aroma in ales.	Mostly bittering, some aroma	7–10	Poor	These two are interchangeable. English flavor. Pungent, heavy, very bitter. Can be overpowering as aromatic.	Comet, Chinook, Eroica, Galena.
CASCADE	U.S., Canada	American ales and other distinctly American beers. Inappropriate in German or British styles.	Aroma, rarely bittering	4.5–7	Poor	Unique aroma—floral, minty, herbal, spicy. Gives American or Canadian flavor to lagers.	Centennial, but use less due to its higher alpha acid.
CENTENNIAL (CFJ 90)	U.S.	American pale ales, other new U.S. styles.	Aroma and bittering	9.5–11.5	Good	New variety with some similarities to Cascade. Brewer's Gold parent.	Cascade, but use more. Other varieties for bittering.
CHINOOK	U.S.	Best for porters and stouts, but may be used in a wide variety of beers, with caution. Very strong.	Bittering	12–14	Good	New variety. Very bitter, with some noble aromatic character. Use caution.	Galena, Comet, Eroica, Bullion. Brewer's Gold.
CLUSTER	U.S.	The traditional American hop of choice. Used in American beers for many years.	Bittering	5.5–9	Very good	Pungent, medium-bitter. Long-rejected by British brewers for its "catty" aroma. Not very good.	Anything would be better. Hallertau, Spalt, or any high-alpha type.
CRYSTAL	U.S.	Primarily German-styled lagers.	Aroma	2–4.5	Poor	New variety resembling Hallertau, perhaps the best of these new varieties.	German Hallertau.
EROICA	U.S.	Bittering for all beers, especially dark, English ones.	Bittering	11–13	Poor	Pungent, very bitter. Derived from Brewer's Gold. English flavor.	Bullion, Brewer's Gold, or other high-alpha type.
FUGGLES	England	Classic English hop for bittering and aroma in English ales, especially dark ones.	Aroma and bittering	4–6	Fair	Mild, spicy. Recognizable English taste.	Willamette, Styrian Golding.

VARIETY	COUNTRY	APPLICATIONS	AROMA/ BITTER	AVERAGE ALPHA %	STORAGE	DESCRIPTION	SUBSTITUTE
GALENA	U.S.	Bittering for all types of beers, especially English ales.	Bittering	12–14	Very good	Pungent, heavy, very bitter. Definite English flavor. Brewer's Gold ancestry.	Chinook, Eroica, Comet, or other high-alpha type.
GOLDING	England	Aroma for all types of English ales, especially paler ones.	Bittering and aroma	3.5–5	Poor	Clean, spicy. British flavor "black currant" taste. Classic English hop.	Kent Golding, Fuggles.
HALLERTAU	Germany, U.S.	All types of German beers, American and Canadian premium lagers.	Aroma and bittering	3.5–7	Fair to poor	Clean, spicy. German flavor, almost neutral.	Crystal, Liberty, Perle.
HERSBRUCKER	Germany, U.S.	Aroma for German beers, especially lighter ones.	Aroma and bittering	3–6	Fair	Fresh, delicate, spicy. Somewhat flowery.	Saaz, Hallertau, Tettnanger. Possibly Spalt.
KENT GOLDING	England	Aroma for highest quality English pale ales, bitters, and other ales.	Aroma	4–6	Poor	Refined, aromatic, sweet, and spicy. Definite English flavor.	No real substitute. Try Fuggles, or Golding.
LIBERTY	U.S.	German-styles lagers, any beer where a Germanic hop character is called for.	Aroma and bittering	7–10	Poor	One of the spicier of the new varieties with Hallertau characteristics.	Mt. Hood, Crystal, Hallertau.
LUBLIN LUBELSKI	Poland	Czech-style pilsners, Belgian strong ales.	Aroma and bittering	3–5	Fair	Same variety as Saaz, but grown in Poland. Similar spicy character of Saaz.	Saaz.
MT. HOOD	U.S.	All types of European beers.	Bittering and aroma	12–14	Poor	One of the newer varieties similar to Hallertau.	Liberty, Crystal, Hallertau.
NORTHERN BREWER	Belgium, Germany, England, U.S.	Belgian ales, German lagers. California common beers.	Bittering and aroma	7–9	Good	Rich, aggressive, fragrant, distinctive. Neither German nor English.	Hallertau, Spalt. Possibly Styrian Golding.
NUGGET	U.S.	Bittering for all types of beers.	Bittering and aroma	12–14	Good	Bitter! Other high-alpha hops have better aroma.	Any other super-high-alpha type.

VARIETY	COUNTRY	APPLICATIONS	AROMA/BITTER	AVERAGE ALPHA %	STORAGE	DESCRIPTION	SUBSTITUTE
PERLE	Germany, U.S.	German lagers, premium American and Canadian lagers.	Aroma and bittering	7–9.5	Good	Very bitter, flavor similar to Hallertau. Germanic.	Hallertau. Liberty, Crystal, Mt. Hood.
PRIDE OF RINGWOOD	Australia	Bittering and aroma for Australian lagers. Not widely available in America.	Aroma and bittering	7–10	Poor	Created by crossing a Tasmanian wild hop with a Pride of Kent female plant. Sharp, spicy.	Any other super-high-alpha type.
SAAZ	Czech Republic	The classic hop of pilsners. Used in Belgian pale ales.	Aroma and bittering	3.5–6	Poor	Spicy, delicate, clean. A very refined and noble hop. Unique.	Lublin, Spalt, Hersbrucker, Tettnanger.
STYRIAN GOLDING	Yugoslavia	Pale ales, bittering mostly. Often used in Belgium.	Bittering	4.5–7.5	Good	Aromatic, sharp. Somewhat English. A seedless variety of Fuggles.	Fuggles, Golding. Maybe Northern Brewer.
SPALT	Germany, U.S.	German lagers and premium American beers. A fine hop.	Aroma	3.5–6.5	Fair to poor	Mild, delicate, clean. German-tasting. Very high quality.	Saaz, Hallertau, Hersbrucker.
TETTNANGER	Germany, U.S.	Aroma for German lagers and wheat ales. Also good in American lagers.	Aroma	4–5.5	Fair to poor	Very spicy, herbal. Unique flavor, delicate, flowery.	Saaz, Spalt, Hersbrucker.
WILLAMETTE	U.S.	British ales, all varieties.	Bittering and aroma	4–6	Good to fair	Mild, spicy, aromatic. English taste. A seedless variety of Fuggles.	Fuggles. Perhaps Styrian Golding.
WYE CHALLENGER	England	All British-styled ales.	Bittering and aroma	6.5–8.5	Good	Spicy high-alpha hop with good aroma properties.	Northern Brewer, Chinook.
WYE TARGET	England	All British-styled ales.	Bittering, possibly aroma	9.5–13	Poor	High-alpha hop with some British aromatic qualities. Best as bittering hop.	Galena, Brewer's Gold.

Use to figure hop quantity needed to get to a given bitterness level (approx only).

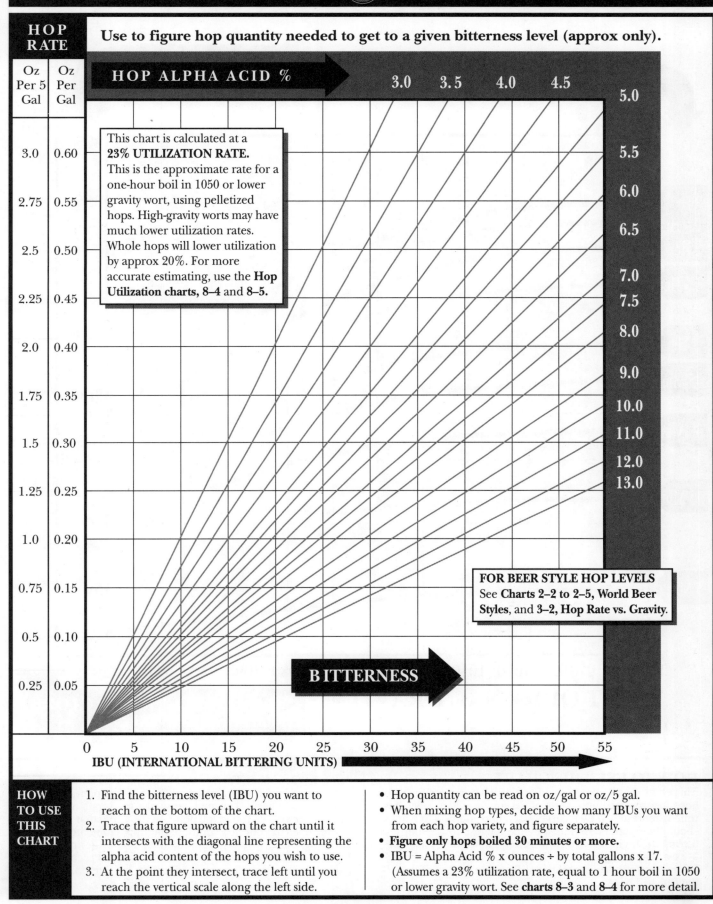

This chart is calculated at a **23% UTILIZATION RATE.** This is the approximate rate for a one-hour boil in 1050 or lower gravity wort, using pelletized hops. High-gravity worts may have much lower utilization rates. Whole hops will lower utilization by approx 20%. For more accurate estimating, use the **Hop Utilization charts, 8–4** and **8–5.**

FOR BEER STYLE HOP LEVELS See **Charts 2–2 to 2–5,** World Beer Styles, and **3–2, Hop Rate vs. Gravity.**

HOP RATE

Oz Per 5 Gal	Oz Per Gal
3.0	0.60
2.75	0.55
2.5	0.50
2.25	0.45
2.0	0.40
1.75	0.35
1.5	0.30
1.25	0.25
1.0	0.20
0.75	0.15
0.5	0.10
0.25	0.05

HOP ALPHA ACID %: 3.0 3.5 4.0 4.5 5.0 5.5 6.0 6.5 7.0 7.5 8.0 9.0 10.0 11.0 12.0 13.0

BITTERNESS

IBU (INTERNATIONAL BITTERING UNITS): 0 5 10 15 20 25 30 35 40 45 50 55

HOW TO USE THIS CHART

1. Find the bitterness level (IBU) you want to reach on the bottom of the chart.
2. Trace that figure upward on the chart until it intersects with the diagonal line representing the alpha acid content of the hops you wish to use.
3. At the point they intersect, trace left until you reach the vertical scale along the left side.

- Hop quantity can be read on oz/gal or oz/5 gal.
- When mixing hop types, decide how many IBUs you want from each hop variety, and figure separately.
- **Figure only hops boiled 30 minutes or more.**
- IBU = Alpha Acid % x ounces ÷ by total gallons x 17. (Assumes a 23% utilization rate, equal to 1 hour boil in 1050 or lower gravity wort. See **charts 8–3** and **8–4** for more detail.

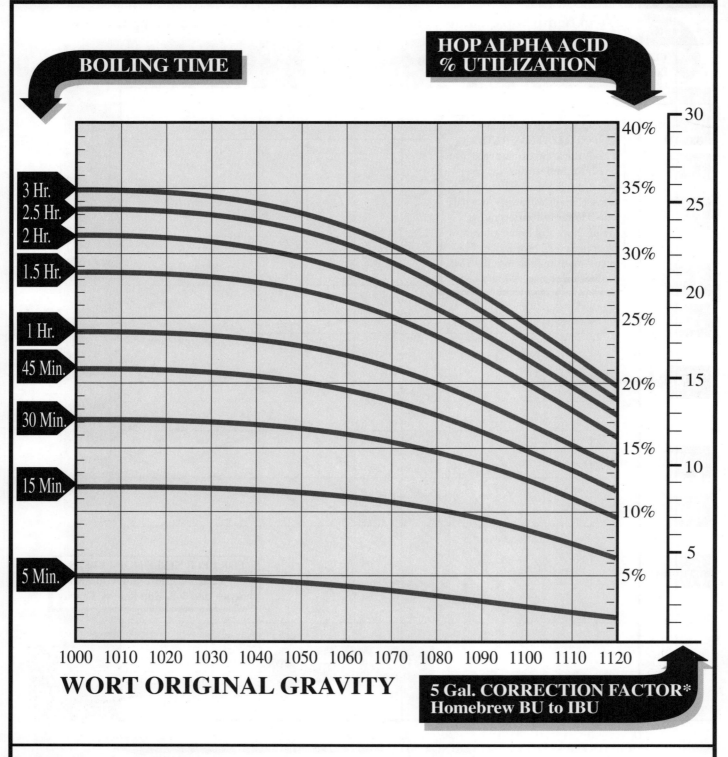

BOILING TIME

HOP ALPHA ACID % UTILIZATION

(Boiling time curves, from top to bottom: 3 Hr., 2.5 Hr., 2 Hr., 1.5 Hr., 1 Hr., 45 Min., 30 Min., 15 Min., 5 Min.)

Left vertical axis (% Utilization): 40%, 35%, 30%, 25%, 20%, 15%, 10%, 5%

Right vertical axis: 30, 25, 20, 15, 10, 5

WORT ORIGINAL GRAVITY: 1000, 1010, 1020, 1030, 1040, 1050, 1060, 1070, 1080, 1090, 1100, 1110, 1120

5 Gal. CORRECTION FACTOR*
Homebrew BU to IBU

HOW TO USE THIS CHART:
This chart shows approximate hop utilization rates for whole hops incorporated into worts of varying gravities. Each boil time is represented by a curve. Each hop addition to a brew should be figured individually—the longest boiling hops having the highest rate of utilization, the shortest ones, the lowest. The utilization rates from this chart can be used to figure approximate International Bittering Units (IBUs) in the finished beer.

*Use the Correction Factor number to convert Homebrew Bitterness Units (ozs x alpha acid %) to IBUs (ppm hop iso-alpha acids in beer). This number works for 5-gallon batches only. After you've found the point on the curve that corresponds to your hop addition, multiply Homebrew Bittering Units by it to get approximate Hop Bittering units. For larger batches, simply factor this correction accordingly (for example: 10-gallon = ÷ 2, 15-gallon = ÷ 3, etc.).

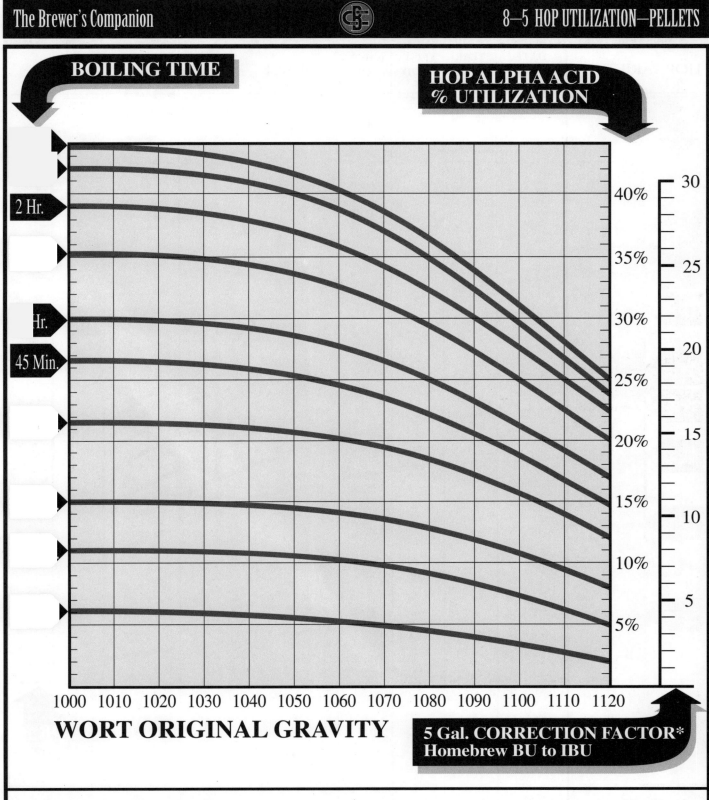

BOILING TIME

HOP ALPHA ACID % UTILIZATION

2 Hr.

Hr.

45 Min.

40%
35%
30%
25%
20%
15%
10%
5%

30
25
20
15
10
5

1000 1010 1020 1030 1040 1050 1060 1070 1080 1090 1100 1110 1120

WORT ORIGINAL GRAVITY

5 Gal. CORRECTION FACTOR*
Homebrew BU to IBU

HOW TO USE THIS CHART:

This chart shows approximate hop utilization rates for pellet hops incorporated into worts of varying gravities. Each boil time is represented by a curve. Each hop addition to a brew should be figured individually—the longest boiling hops having the highest rate of utilization, the shortest ones, the lowest. The utilization rates from this chart can be used to figure approximate International Bittering Units (IBU) in the finished beer.

*Use the Correction Factor number to convert Homebrew Bitterness Units (ozs x alpha acid %) to IBUs (ppm hop iso-alpha acids in beer). This number works for 5-gallon batches only. After you've found the point on the curve that corresponds to your hop addition, multiply Homebrew Bittering Units by it to get approximate Hop Bittering units. For larger batches, simply factor this correction accordingly (for example: 10-gallon = ÷ 2, 15-gallon = ÷ 3, etc.).

HOP VARIETY	DATE OF PURCHASE	YEAR OF CROP	ALPHA ACID %	WHOLE OR PELLET	SOURCE	NOTES

HOP VARIETY	DATE OF PURCHASE	YEAR OF CROP	ALPHA ACID %	WHOLE OR PELLET	SOURCE	NOTES

HOP VARIETY	DATE OF PURCHASE	YEAR OF CROP	ALPHA ACID %	WHOLE OR PELLET	SOURCE	NOTES

ION	CHEMICAL SYMBOL	TYPICAL PPM	AFFECTS MASH pH	WATER SOLUBLE?	PPM = MILLIVAL	EFFECT ON MASH	EFFECT ON BEER
CALCIUM	Ca	25–90	More acid	Yes	0.050	Acidifies. Precipitates phosphates. Enhances enzyme action. Improves runoff. Speeds proteolysis.	Enhances stability of finished beer. Improves clarification. Principle component of hardness.
MAGNESIUM	Mg	1–10	More acid	Yes	0.0833	Acidifies. Precipitates phosphates.	In excess, may contribute to unpleasant bitter flavor.
SODIUM	Na	2–12	No effect	Very	0.0435	Not really important in the mash.	Disagreeable in excess. In moderation, adds a fullness, especially to darker beers. Enhances sweetness.
POTASSIUM	K	0.5–2	No effect	Very	0.0256	Not really important in the mash.	Similar to sodium. Important in yeast nutrition.
NITRATE	NO_3	<1	No effect	Very	0.01613	No effect on mash.	No positive effects. Strictly a contaminant, from organic material. Toxic to yeast.
CHLORIDE	Cl	5–16	No effect	Very	0.02817	No effect on mash in normal quantities.	Increases hop bitterness. In limited amounts, gives fullness.
SULFATE	SO_4	5–70	More acid	Yes	0.02083	Acidifies. Best for pale, dry beers, especially pale ales.	Enhances clean hop flavor. Decreases hop bitterness. Lightens color.
BICARBONATE	HCO_3	10–300	Less acid	Yes	0.01639	Strongly alkaline, resists acidification of the mash. Hinders alpha amylase. Reddens pale beers. Impedes cold break.	Emphasizes bitterness, but harshly. Best for lightly hopped dark beers. Carbonate becomes soluble in water by combining with dissolved CO_2, changing to bicarbonate. May be removed by boiling.
CARBONATE	CO_3	—	No direct effect	Barely	0.03333		

MINERAL IONS	CHEM SYMBOL	MAX PPM	COMMENTS
ALUMINUM	Al	1.0	Involved in haze formation. May leach from cooking or storage vessels.
AMMONIA	NH_3	0.05	When present, a symptom of organic contamination of the water source. Highly undesirable.
CHLORINE (Free)	Cl		Added to municipal water supplies as an antiseptic agent. Highly toxic to yeast. Carbon filtration removes; reduced by boiling or allowing water to stand uncovered a few days.
COPPER	Cu	0.05–0.1	Important yeast nutrient, but may inhibit yeast growth in large quantities. Reduces sulfur compounds in fermentation.
FLUORIDE	Fl	1.5	Added to municipal water supplies as a dental cavity-preventing measure. Has no effect on yeast growth.
IRON	Fe	0.3	Causes yeast degeneration and haze formation. Often a real problem with well water. Removed in various ways, including sand filtration, oxygenation, and chemical treatment.
LEAD	Pb	0.1	Toxic to yeast, causes haze. May be leached from solder joints in equipment.
MANGANESE	Mn	0.05	Similar to iron. Often a problem in ground water.
NITRATE	NO_3	25	Over 10 ppm indicates polluted water. Degrades to toxic nitrite during fermentation. Highly undesirable.
NITRITE	NO_2	0.1	Found only in highly polluted water. So toxic to microorganisms, it is used as a preservative in meats.
SILICA	SiO_2	10	Relatively inert, but can create colloidal haze. Found in ground water, also leached from the husks of malt.
TIN	Sn	1.0	Powerful haze-former. May be leached out of solder joints— even the lead-free variety—in equipment.
ZINC	Zn	1.0	Needed in very small amounts for yeast nutrition, but harmful to yeast in larger amounts.
CADMIUM MERCURY SILVER	Cd Hg Ag	0.001 to 0.01	Extremely powerful yeast growth inhibitors. Not normally present in problem-causing quantities.
ARSENIC BERYLLIUM NICKEL	As Be Ni	0.05 to 0.1	Very powerful yeast growth inhibitors. Not quite as bad as the group immediately above.

MINERAL/Common Name	CHEM SYMBOL	DRY MEASURES		1 GRAM PER GALLON =			
		g/tsp	tsp/g	ppm		Millival	
CALCIUM SULFATE/Gypsum	CaSO$_4$	4.0	0.25	Ca	SO$_4$	Ca	SO4
				61.5	147	3.075	3.06
MAGNESIUM SULFATE/Epsom salts	MgSO$_4$	4.5	0.22	Mg	SO$_4$	Mg	SO4
				37	145	3.06	3.02
SODIUM CHLORIDE/Table salt	NaCl	6.5	0.17	Na	Cl	Na	Cl
				104	160	4.52	4.5
CALCIUM CHLORIDE	CaCl2	3.4	0.29	Ca	Cl	Ca	Cl
				140	124	6.99	3.48

TREATMENT	TECHNIQUE	EFFECT
BOIL & DECANT	Bring water to a boil. Turn off and allow to cool. Siphon off, leaving sediment in bottom of kettle.	Removes bicarbonate ions by precipitation, but only to the extent that there is calcium or magnesium to combine with (adding gypsum may help). Removes free chlorine, too.
CHARCOAL FILTER	Run water through activated charcoal filter. Slow flow rates best.	Removes free chlorine, which can create off-tasting chlorophenols. Also removes organic impurities.
STANDING	Allow water to stand, uncapped, for several days.	Allows some of the free chlorine to evaporate. Does not change mineral composition—bicarbonates, etc.

WATER TYPE		Ca	Mg	Na	HCO$_3$	SO$_4$	Cl
BURTON-ON-TRENT	Strong pale ales	268/13.4	62/5.2	30/1.3	141/4.7	638/14	36/1.0
LONDON	Sweet stout, porter	90/4.5	4.0/0.3	24/1.05	123/4.1	58/1.2	18/0.5
EDINBURGH	Malty amber, brown ales	140/7.0	36/3.0	92/4.0	270/9	231/4.8	60/1.7
DORTMUND	Pale lager	260/13	23/1.9	69/3.0	270/9	240/5.0	106/3.0
MUNICH/DUBLIN	Dark lager/dry stout	80/4.0	19/1.6	1.0/0.05	164/5.5	5.0/0.1	1.0 /0.05
PILSEN	Hoppy pale lager	7.0/0.35	0.8/0.07	3.2/0.14	9/0.3	5.8/1.2	5.0 /0.14
YORKSHIRE	Malty pale ale	105/5.3	17/1.4	23/1.0	153/2.5	66/1.4	30 /.85
PALE ALE		110/5.5	18/1.5	17/0.75	<70	350/8	50/1.5
MILD ALE/DARK LAGER		75/4.5	12/1.0	35/1.5	<120	120/2	100/3
STOUT/PORTER		50/2.5	12/1.0	60/2.5	<170	46/1	175/5
PALE LAGER		>20/1.0	<6/0.5	<24/1.05	<60	5.0/0.1	<18/5
OTHERS							

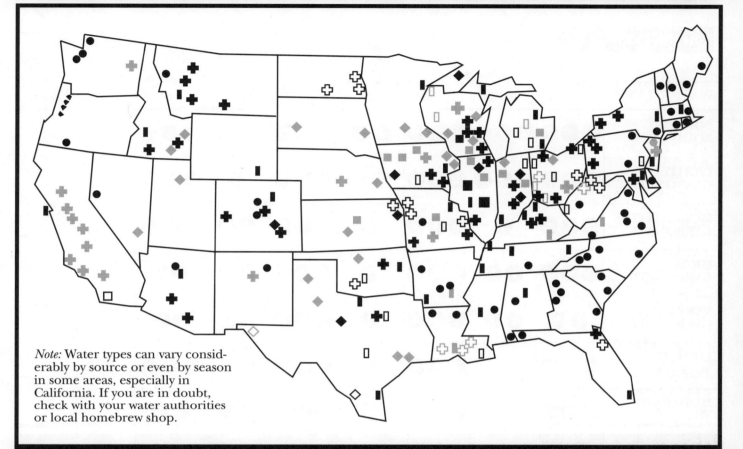

Note: Water types can vary considerably by source or even by season in some areas, especially in California. If you are in doubt, check with your water authorities or local homebrew shop.

WATER TYPES–Categorized by brewing type for easier treatment

Locate your area on the map and note the symbol nearest it. The water type is described below. If you live in a rural area and depend on a well, go for the closest gray symbol, usually harder than surface supplies. If in doubt, call the water company or a testing service.

The chart below is based on published water analyses of municipal water supplies. They have been grouped into broad categories, which makes determining treatment quite simple. Once you have found your water type, use the chart on **9–6** to decide on the appropriate treatment.

MAP SYMBOL Surface	Well	WATER TYPE	CARBONATE CONTENT IS	& SULFATE CONTENT IS	SODIUM (ppm)	BEST FOR BREWING THESE BEER TYPES
●	●	Soft	Under 40 ppm	Under 40 ppm	4	Classic pilsner
▌	▌	Light	40–100 ppm	The same or less than the carbonate ppm	7	Pale lager (pilsners after boiling)
✚	✚	Moderate	100–200 ppm		11	Dark lagers, stout, porter
◆	◆	High	200–325 ppm		11	Dark lager, stout, porter
■	■	Very high	Over 325 ppm		25	Brown & black ales, dark lager, bock
▯	▯	Light		40–100 ppm	10	Pale lagers, blond ales
✛	✛	Moderate	Half or less of the sulfate ppm	100–200 ppm	12	All ales, dark lagers
◇	◇	High		200–325 ppm	25	Pale ale, Dortmund lager
☐	☐	Very high		Over 325 ppm	25	Strong, and/or hoppy pale ales

WATER TYPE \ BEER TYPE	PALE ALES	SWEET STOUT	MILD, BROWN ALES	DARK LAGER, DRY STOUT	PALE LAGER	CLASSIC PILSNER	BURTON-ON-TRENT (Pale Ale)	NOTES
SOFT OR EQUIVOCAL	1 5 7	1 3 9	1 4 9	1 3	1 5 8	2	1 6 7	
LIGHTLY CARBONATE	1 5 7	1 3 9	1 4 8	1 3	1 5 8	2	1 6 7	
MODERATELY CARBONATE	2 5 7	1	1 4 8	1	1 5 8	2 11	1 6 7	
HIGH CARBONATE	2 5 7	1 9	1 4 8	1	1 5 8	2 12	1 6	
VERY HIGH CARBONATE	2 5	1 3	1 6 8	2	1 5 8	10	2 6	
LIGHTLY SULFATE	1 5 7	1	1 4 8	1	1 5 8	1 11	1 6 9	
MODERATELY SULFATE	1 5 7	1	1 3 8	1	1 4 8	1 12	1 6	
HIGH / VERY HIGH SULFATE	1	1 9 12	1 8 11	1 12	1 7	10	1	

CORRECTING YOUR WATER FOR BREWING VARIOUS BEER STYLES

1) First determine what kind of water you have. Call your water company for this information and log it at the bottom of 9–3, or check the map on 9–5.

2) Compare your numbers to the water types listed on 9–5, and determine which of the eight water types you have in your area. You can make notes about it in the space above, right.

3) Find the box on the chart above where your water type intersects with the type of beer you wish to brew.

4) Follow directions for each numbered water treatment shown in that box. Treat all brewing water, not just mashing water. If boiling is called for, add all ingredients beforehand. After boiling, siphon water off to allow carbonate to remain in bottom of kettle.

WATER TREATMENT SPECIFICS

1 Filter through activated charcoal.*

2 Boil and decant. Removes carbonate (and chlorine).

ADDITIVE TREATMENTS	Tsp/5Gal	Gm/Gal	ppm	ADDITIVE TREATMENT	Tsp/5Gal	Gm/Gal	ppm
3 Add Gypsum ($CaSO_4$)	1/5	0.15	22 SO_4	plus Epsom Salts ($MgSO_4$)	—	—	—
4 Add Gypsum ($CaSO_4$)	1/2	0.5	74 SO_4	plus Epsom Salts ($MgSO_4$)	1/8	0.1	1
5 Add Gypsum ($CaSO_4$)	2	1.5	221 SO_4	plus Epsom Salts ($MgSO_4$)	1/2	0.5	7
6 Add Gypsum ($CaSO_4$)	3	2.5	368 SO_4	plus Epsom Salts ($MgSO_4$)	1 3/4	1.5	21
7 Add Table Salt (NaCl)	1/4	0.2	32 Cl	**8** Add Table Salt (NaCl)	1/3	0.5	8
9 Add Table Salt (NaCl)	3/4	0.85	137 Cl	**10** Not Suitable. Use other water for this beer type.			

11 Dilute 1:1 with distilled water   **12** Dilute with distilled water—3 parts distilled to 1 part

*If filter is unavailable, draw water off and allow it to stand a few days, which reduces, but does not remove all free chlorine from water, but it is better than nothing. Unnecessary if boiling to remove carbonates.

WATER AND TREATMENT	QTY ADDED		MINERAL IONS—PPM					
	g/gal	g/5gal	Ca	Mg	Na	SO_4	Cl	HCO_3
YOUR WATER								
TO MATCH								
DIFFERENCE, PLUS OR MINUS								
BOILED—MINUS HCO_3 (to limit of Mg & Ca)								
PLUS NaCl (table salt) or $CaCl_2$ (calcium chloride)								
PLUS $MgSO_4$ (Epsom salts)								
PLUS $CaSO_4$ (gypsum)								
PLUS OTHER								
CORRECTED TO								
YOUR WATER								
TO MATCH								
DIFFERENCE, PLUS OR MINUS								
BOILED—MINUS HCO_3 (to limit of Mg & Ca)								
PLUS NaCl (table salt) or $CaCl_2$ (calcium chloride)								
PLUS $MgSO_4$ (Epsom salts)								
PLUS $CaSO_4$ (gypsum)								
PLUS OTHER								
CORRECTED TO								
YOUR WATER								
TO MATCH								
DIFFERENCE, PLUS OR MINUS								
BOILED—MINUS HCO_3 (to limit of Mg & Ca)								
PLUS NaCl (table salt) or $CaCl_2$ (calcium chloride								
PLUS $MgSO_4$ (Epsom salts)								
PLUS $CaSO_4$ (gypsum)								
PLUS OTHER								
CORRECTED TO								
YOUR WATER								
TO MATCH								
DIFFERENCE, PLUS OR MINUS								
BOILED—MINUS HCO_3 (to limit of Mg & Ca)								
PLUS NaCl (table salt) or $CaCl_2$ (calcium chloride)								
PLUS $MgSO_4$ (Epsom salts)								
PLUS $CaSO_4$ (gypsum)								
PLUS OTHER								
CORRECTED TO								

WATER AND TREATMENT	QTY ADDED		MINERAL IONS — PPM					
	g/gal	g/5gal	Ca	Mg	Na	SO$_4$	Cl	HCO$_3$
YOUR WATER								
TO MATCH								
DIFFERENCE, PLUS OR MINUS								
BOILED—MINUS HCO$_3$ (to limit of Mg & Ca)								
PLUS NaCl (table salt) or CaCl$_2$ (calcium chloride)								
PLUS MgSO$_4$ (Epsom salts)								
PLUS CaSO$_4$ (gypsum)								
PLUS OTHER								
CORRECTED TO								
YOUR WATER								
TO MATCH								
DIFFERENCE, PLUS OR MINUS								
BOILED—MINUS HCO$_3$ (to limit of Mg & Ca)								
PLUS NaCl (table salt) or CaCl$_2$ (calcium chloride)								
PLUS MgSO$_4$ (Epsom salts)								
PLUS CaSO$_4$ (gypsum)								
PLUS OTHER								
CORRECTED TO								
YOUR WATER								
TO MATCH								
DIFFERENCE, PLUS OR MINUS								
BOILED—MINUS HCO$_3$ (to limit of Mg & Ca)								
PLUS NaCl (table salt) or CaCl$_2$ (calcium chloride)								
PLUS MgSO$_4$ (Epsom salts)								
PLUS CaSO$_4$ (gypsum)								
PLUS OTHER								
CORRECTED TO								
YOUR WATER								
TO MATCH								
DIFFERENCE, PLUS OR MINUS								
BOILED—MINUS HCO$_3$ (to limit of Mg & Ca)								
PLUS NaCl (table salt) or CaCl$_2$ (calcium chloride)								
PLUS MgSO$_4$ (Epsom salts)								
PLUS CaSO$_4$ (gypsum)								
PLUS OTHER								

Carbohydrates in the Mash

Carbohydrates comprise a group of chemicals of different types of sugars and the compounds formed from their combination. Carbohydrates should be thought of as a continuous spectrum of differing length chains of sugar molecules.

Simple sugars, or monosaccharides, are five- or six-sided ring-shaped molecules. Most of the sugars encountered in brewing are six-sided, and are known collectively as hexose. Glucose, also known as dextrose, is the most omnipresent. It forms the basis for maltose, the main wort sugar; dextrins, the unfermentable wort sugars; and starch, present in the endosperm of barley and malt. Fructose is another common hexose sugar, but is not a factor in brewing. Other hexoses include galactose and mannose, which are weakly fermentable and occur in wort only in small quantities.

Some five-sided sugars, or pentoses, also occur in brewing. Arabinose, xylose, and their polymers are present. None are fermentable by brewer's yeast, and they are most important in brewing as gums and other longer molecules. Polymers of pentose are collectively known as pentosans.

Oligosaccharides are two, three, or four simple sugars, joined, called di-, tri-, or tetrasaccharides. Longer chains of 5 to 20 units are dextrins, which are largely tasteless.

Starch comes in two forms and may be several hundred sugar units long. There are two types of chemical bonds in carbohydrates—a straight one and another that forms branching structures.

Cellulose is similar in structure to starch, but its chemical bonds make it more difficult to render into its component parts. It is present in barley and malt, but plays no role in brewing, except as structural material, making the husks a good filtering bed for the mash.

Beta glucans are a carbohydrate containing yet another type of chemical bond, giving them a viscous, gummy consistency. Only partially soluble, they may precipitate in the mash or during fermentation as a jelly, causing numerous problems. Rarely a problem for homebrewers, fortunately.

Sugars

The simple sugars are the most fermentable, as well as the sweetest. The predominant sugar in wort is maltose, a disaccharide formed from two molecules of glucose, joined. Yeast metabolizes these sugars with the greatest of ease.

Fructose, or fruit sugar, is a monosaccharide with the same chemical formula as glucose/dextrose, but a different arrangement. Fructose is a more difficult sugar for yeast to ferment, but it will choke it down once it's eaten all the good stuff. Also present in small quantities are galactose and mannose, which are not fermentable by brewer's yeast.

Sucrose, or cane sugar, is a disaccharide formed of one molecule each of glucose and fructose. Yeast likes it even less. Fortunately, malt contains little of either sucrose or fructose. Sucrose is readily available in any kitchen, of course, and may be used for priming, if you're desperate. It is used in some English and Belgian ales, but is not recommended as a regular brewing ingredient.

Maltotriose and maltotetraose exist as minority sugars in the wort. They are formed of three and four molecules of glucose, respectively. The slow period when the yeast eats these sugars is the secondary fermentation.

DEXTRIN TYPES

Alpha-limit dextrins: These are larger, random chunks than beta-limit dextrins, left over from the action of alpha amylase.

Beta-limit dextrins: These are y-shaped chunks, the branching points from amylopectin, left over because enzymes cannot break them up easily.

Dextrins and Starches

In size, dextrins are between sugars and starches. They are created by the enzymatic destruction of starches during malting and mashing. They are mostly stubby ends and branching points that starch-converting enzymes cannot, or will not, break apart.

Two forms of starch are present in malt: amylose, and amylopectin. Both are formed from glucose molecules hooked in chains about 20 units long. In amylose these subunits hook together end-to-end in straight chains. In amylopectin, the subunits connect end-to-middle, forming treelike structures (see **Section 7–1, Carbohydrates**).

Most of the carbohydrate present in barley is in the form of starch, enclosed in tiny granules. When the barley is malted, the enzymes are activated and begin to attack the protein walls of these granules, as well as the starch inside. The result is that malt has a crumbly texture and a larger amount of simpler sugars and dextrins. The lack of these changes makes unmalted grain unsuitable for beer production, except as an adjunct.

The main object of mashing is to break up the large starch molecules into dextrins and sugars through enzyme action. Two enzymes, collectively called diastase, accomplish this. Alpha amylase and beta amylase both attack the two kinds of starch, but their specifics differ.

Alpha amylase chops the starch chains into hunks at random locations, producing residue of widely varying lengths. Beta amylase attacks the starches and dextrins from one end of the molecules only, producing molecules of the disaccharide maltose. Every time alpha amylase strikes, it creates another place for the beta amylase to work, so they complement each other (see also **Section 4–6, Brewing Enzymes**).

Released by proteolytic enzymes during malting, alpha and beta amylase produce a small amount of sugar in the finished malt. Drying the malt keeps the enzymes from producing sugars during storage.

When the malt is wetted at the beginning of the mash, enzyme activity resumes. At the low temperatures of proteolysis, 122°F/50°C, this activity is quite slow. At higher temperatures, the rate of starch conversion by the enzymes increases to a maximum at about 155°F/68°C. As the temperature is raised, the enzymes begin to degrade, and soon stop working.

Further, the two enzymes do not share the same optimum temperature. Alpha amylase has a higher optimum temperature than beta amylase. This means that a mash at a lower temperature favors the production of simple maltose sugar by beta amylase, while at a higher temperature the mash favors alpha amylase, which tends to produce mostly dextrins.

The balance between these two enzymes, which

MASH TYPES IN COMMERCIAL PRODUCTION

Infusion: Hot water is added to the malt and allowed to stand. Classic English style. Used by most homebrewers.

Step: Mash is started with hot water as above, but at a lower temperature (122°F/50°C) for protein degradation to take place. Heat (or hot water) is applied to raise the mash to starch conversion temperatures.

Decoction: Mash is started with hot water, then some of the mash is removed (one-quarter to one-third) and slowly raised to a boil. This is then added back to the mash to raise the temperature. There can be as many as three of these decoctions. The classic lager beer mash in Germany.

Step with Boiled Adjunct: Mash is begun at protein rest temperatures. Cereal adjuncts are boiled after enzyme treatment, to gelatinize the starch, to make it soluble and available to the enzymes. This is added to the mash to raise the temperature up to starch-conversion temperatures.

controls the ratio of fermentable (sugars) to unfermentable (dextrins) material in the wort, is affected by many factors:

Temperature—High temperature favors dextrin production; low temperature, maltose.

Dilution—Thin mash favors maltose, thick favors dextrins.

Time—Short time favors dextrins; long time, maltose.

pH (acidity—Lower pH (more acid)favors production of maltose.

Starch Conversion—Practice

In the mash, hot water is mixed with the crushed malted barley, and enzyme activity converts starch into smaller components, most of which are fermentable.

Proteins and Nitrogen

Proteins are complex organic molecules containing nitrogen that occur widely in all living things. They are made of amino acids strung together into coiled, twisted chains containing thousands of atoms. Proteins function in many ways both chemically and structurally.

The amount of nitrogen in malt and other grains varies from one type to the next. Some types, such as rice, have little. Other types, such as six-row malt, have lots. The % Nitrogen measurement reflects the protein content. Simply multiply the %N by 6.25 to calculate the approximate percentage of protein.

The percentage of nitrogen in malt is measured in two ways: total %N, and % permanently soluble N (% PSN). The latter is an indicator of the amount of very simple nitrogen compounds present before mashing begins. These compounds have been degraded by enzymes during malting and will remain in solution even when the beer is chilled.

In brewing, protein is important for the following reasons:

• After enzyme attack, proteins yield amino acids and other smaller breakdown products, which are vital nutrients to the yeast.

• Proteins that remain in the finished beer contribute greatly to the richness, body, and mouthfeel.

• Protein gives beer the ability to form and retain a head.

• Enzymes are proteins, so the protein content is indicative the enzyme content

PROTEINS AND OTHER FORMS OF NITROGEN

FORM OF NITROGEN	MOLEC. WEIGHT	COMMENTS
ALBUMIN	210,000	Class of water-soluble proteins that may be coagulated by boiling. Most easily split when pH is 5.5–7.5.
GLOBULIN	210,000	Group of salt-soluble proteins (dissolves in 5 percent K_2SO_4). The most important protein group in haze formation, responsible for much of the chill-haze in beer. Most easily split at pH 4.7–5.0.
GLUTELIN	<100,000	Group of structural proteins found only in plants. Insoluble except in dilute caustic soda solutions. Attacked by proteolytic enzymes during malting and partially degraded.
HORDEIN	<100,000	The primary storage proteins in barley, and a major haze former. Alcohol soluble. Attacked by enzymes during malting and partially degraded.
PEPTONES, PROTEOSES		Water-soluble protein breakdown products. Not coagulated by heat. Important in head retention.
AMINO ACIDS		Class of 22 different subunits that form the basis of proteins. Each has a negative carboxyl group on one end and a positive amino group at the other, allowing them to form chains. All are metabolized by yeast except proline, which remains in beer. All combine with carbohydrates in browning reactions in malt kilning and wort boiling forming color and flavor compounds.

• Nitrogen products, especially amino acids, combine with carbohydrates during browning, forming many types of flavor and color chemicals.

• Excess proteins can cause chill-haze in the finished beer.

Proteins in beer may be categorized according to their solubility into four groups: albumin, globulin, glutelin, and hordein. These protein groups have various roles in barley, brewing, and beer. Albumin is largely responsible for head retention. Globulin is the prime culprit involved in chill-haze (see the chart above for more details).

Chill-haze

Proteins are less soluble in beer at colder temperatures, which cause them to precipitate out of a chilled solution in the form of a whitish haze. Chill-haze disappears when the beer is warmed slightly. Over time, proteins combine with tannins and become even less soluble. Chill-haze is also aggravated by other factors, such as lead, tin, iron, and other metals, excess tannins from the husks, and repeated cycles of warming and chilling.

Chill-haze is flavorless and harmless. But because of the extreme importance of beer clarity to the beer-drinking public, commercial breweries take pains to chill the beer, then filter out the haze. This kind of ultrafiltration is not available to the homebrewer.

Preventing Chill-haze

With proper technique, chill-haze can easily be minimized. The protein rest is the most important way of limiting the amount of chill haze in your beer, but not the only one. Other techniques include:

• Limit mash and wort contact with metals, especially iron, lead, tin, and copper. Solder is potentially very troublesome.

• Do not use spargings of very low gravity, because they contain a large amount of tannins.

• Keep the fermenting and finished beer at a constant temperature. Especially avoid chilling and warming cycles. Once you put it in the refrigerator, leave it there. After two weeks in the fridge, the haze will settle out and leave the beer clear. It will stay that way as long as it stays cold.

• Avoid introducing oxygen during later stages of fermentation.

Splashing during transferring and bottling are the main opportunities for inadvertently adding oxygen.

Protein Rest

This is a rest, during mashing, of 30 to 60 minutes at 122°F/50°C. The purpose of the rest is to break the long chains of protein molecules into smaller hunks.

A protein rest is needed when you are brewing pale beer that you will serve chilled, or when you are using lager or pilsner malt. These malts, being less well modified, have a higher %N than English-style pale ale malt. The chart on this page shows this to be true for two-row, and more true for six-row.

MALT NITROGEN CONTENT		
MALT TYPES	%N	%PSN
English 2-row pale ale	1.34	.51
English 2-row mild ale	1.47	.49
Pilsner/Munich	1.82	—
Wisconsin 6-row lager	2.37	.68

Lack of a protein rest can cause these problems:

• A temporary haze, which forms when the finished beer is chilled. This is caused when proteins and tannins combine, becoming insoluble.

• Lack of amino acids, which are essential to yeast nutrition. This may result in a sluggish fermentation, and worse, increased vulnerability to infections by bacteria that are not as picky in their eating habits. This is only a problem in lighter-gravity beers, or those made with a large proportion of rice, corn, sugar, or honey.

Any all-malt beer will develop some amount of chill-haze, but a protein rest will make a noticeable difference.

Proteolytic Enzymes—Theory

Two important enzyme groups are involved in the degradation of protein—proteinase, and peptidase. The details of their mechanisms differ.

Proteinase chops the very large protein molecules at random locations, splitting them into smaller chains of amino acids, and is most active at 122°F/50°C; it is destroyed by temperatures above 150°F/65°C. Proteinase is the most active type of proteolytic enzyme in the mash. Optimum pH is about 4.6–5.0, lower than for diastatic enzymes. In brewing practice, this difference is not a problem, as it works fine at normal mash levels of pH 5.2–5.8.

Peptidase attacks the proteins and fragments produced by the action of proteinase, from the end of the chains only. The result is the liberation of amino acids, the building blocks of proteins. This enzyme is most active in malting, and destroyed by heat when the the malt is dried. For more information, see **Section 4–6, Brewing Enzymes.**

Proteins—Brewing Practice

Lager beers traditionally use a protein rest—a pause of 30 minutes at 122°F/50°C—during the mash. When doing a decoction mash, be sure the first decoction is allowed to stand at 122°F/50°C for at least 15 minutes on its way to higher temperatures of starch conversion and boiling.

In practice, there is proteolytic enzyme activity between 100°–140°F/38°–60°C. As the temperature rises, the activity increases, but the enzyme soon quits, deactivated by the heat.

English ales do not normally require a protein rest for the following reasons:

• Low to medium nitrogen barley varieties are selected for malting.

• Malting is carried out so malt is fully modified. Longer sprouting time allows proteolytic enzymes present in the malt to break up proteins to a certain extent.

• Normally they are not drunk chilled.

• Amber to deep-brown color of traditional ales hides haze pretty well.

If you like to drink your ales chilled, or use malt other than English pale ale malt, a protein rest stage is a good idea. Just make your initial rest temperature lower than normal, then after the rest, add more water to bring it up to saccharification temperature.

VARIABLE	RANGE	EFFECT	% VARIATION	COMMENTS
TEMPERA-TURE	122°F 82°C	122°F/82°C is optimum for protein digestion. Elimination of this step is not advisable, except with English pale and mild malts.	Depends on malt type	Protein rest is essential for brewing with lager malt types, which are undermodified and contain less-soluble protein.
	145°F to 165°F 62.5°C to 74°C	During saccharification, higher temperatures speed up activity but shorten the life of both diastatic enzymes, and also shift the balance between the two.	10%–15% variation in fermentability	Temperature is the main way to control the fermentability of the mash. Combined with control of the mashing time, long mashes are used with lower temps, short mashes with high temps. Malt type important: mash highly modified malt at low temps, undermodified malt at high temps.
	140-9°F	Maximum beta amylase activity.		
	149°F	Most fermentable wort.		
	158°F	Maximum alpha amylase activity.		
DILUTION	0.8 qt per gal	Less stability of enzymes (shorter life). Dilutes enzymes. Aids enzyme mobility, speeds reactions. Creates more fermentable worts. Protease enzymes stable only to 140°F/60°C. Contributes more soluble nitrogen to wort. Creates a less fermentable wort. Slows reactions of enzymes. Protease stable up to 150°F/65.5°C.	2% variation in fermentability	Not an easy or effective way to vary the mash constitution. It's best to use the recommended dilutions for the specific mash type. Adding hot or cold water to the mash to fine-tune the mash temperature won't mess things up, because the effects of dilution are relatively minor.
	2.1 qt per gal			
DURATION	20 min 90 min	In general, the longer the mash, the more complete the conversion of dextrins to simpler sugars, giving a more fermentable wort. At high temperatures, the enzymes are destroyed more quickly, so extra time isn't needed. Low temperature mashes need more time to complete starch conversion, since enzyme activity is slowed.	Can be a big factor. Depends on temperature	Most of the action at normal mashing temperatures occurs in the first 30 or 45 minutes. It's best to coordinate this control with the mash temperature. You have greater control when the two are used together. There is no need for a main mash to last longer than a couple of hours.
pH (Acidity & Alkalinity)	5.3 to 5.9	This is the optimal range for pH in the mash. The low end of this range slightly favors the action of beta amylase, creating a more fermentable wort. Infusion mashes should fall at the lower end of this scale, if possible.	Slight (pH is more important for other reasons: efficiency, flavor, etc.)	pH is often a problem with hard water, due to carbonate. Adjust by removing the carbonate by boiling prior to mashing and then adding calcium sulfate, which is acidic, to the brewing water. Dark malts in the mash tend to make it more acidic (lower pH).
	4.6–5.0	Optimum for proteinase enzyme activity.		
	5.3–5.4	Most fermentable wort.		

The Right Setup

Having the right equipment is pretty important. In addition to the tubs, spargers, faucets and so on, you'll need some way of arranging them into the three-tiered stack of sparge-water vessel, sparger, and wort receiver. This setup allows gravity to do most of the work, freeing you from having to be constantly scooping water into the sparge.

It will probably take you a few batches after you start mashing to feel comfortable with all this shuffling of water and grain and wort all over the place. Think of it as the Buddhist tea ceremony on steroids—and go with the flow.

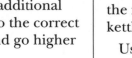

Some Tips

• Set up all vessels to connect with the same size hose, preferably with compression fittings.

• Calibrate all the vessels in gallon or quart gradations. Use a permanent marker or tape on the outside, or take a dowel rod and make marks on it to serve as a dipstick (the best method with larger stainless steel vessels).

The Strike

This is when the mash begins. Hot water is added to grain and mixed until all the grain is thoroughly wet and temperature has stabilized.

The resting temperature is often critical and sometimes it's difficult to predict how much heat will be taken up by the grain and how much will be lost to the mash tun and to the air. The **Strike Water Guide, 10–9,** can serve as a starting point. Heat more water than is called for, then add 3/4 of the listed amount of water, mix well, let it stabilize and check the temperature. Add additional water and mix to bring the mash up to the correct temperature. It's better to start low and go higher than the other way around.

Strike Tips

• Adding the crushed grain to water already in the mash tun seems to mix more completely.

• Watch out for lumps—they are generally totally dry inside. Smash them with your spoon and mix until no lumps are present. Check especially the outside edges of the mash, right at the bottom.

• Never use strike water over 185°F/85°C as it can dissolve undesirable stuff and damage enzymes. 185°F is plenty hot.

The Stand

Insulate your mash tun in some way—lots of different approaches will work:

• Make a jacket around the mash vessel from cut-up styrofoam building insulation.

• Use two tubs, one larger than the other with a blanket in between. Cover the lid with a second blanket (sleeping bags or moving pads work even better).

• Many people mash in a cooler—this can be used for sparging too, if it is fitted with a false bottom or other drainage device, such as a network of copper tubing with slits cut in it. Don't use a cheap styrofoam cooler, as the chemicals present can flavor the beer.

For the most part, the mash should be covered and left alone for the stand periods. Take the temperature no more than every half-hour.

Decoction

This is an old traditional method of brewing still widely used in Europe. Virtually all Continental lagers are produced this way. Decoction technique varies in detail from one type to the next, but the actual process is quite simple:

A portion (usually one-quarter to one-third) of the mash is removed from the standing mash and heated slowly to boiling, held there for a few minutes, and then returned to the mash. For more detailed description of different decoction types, see **Mash Charts 10–5, 10–6,** and **10–7.** Besides the mash tun, you need a second vessel—a mash kettle.

Using a decoction has the following effects:

• More fully gelatinizes the malt. Lager malts are less completely modified than English ale malts. Consequently, they have a firmer, less crumbly texture, which requires extra effort to make accessible to enzyme action. The starch in barley and malt gelatinizes (in the absence of enzyme activity) at temperatures above the mash range, but well below the boiling point. The decoction has a profound effect on the ease of starch conversion of the lightly modified lager malt.

• Boiling destroys the enzymes present in the decocted portion. This is why the usual method is to boil only the thick portion of the mash. Sometimes a thin portion is boiled, but only for the last decoction, when enzyme activity is pretty well finished anyway.

• When added back to the mash, the boiled decoction raises the mash to a temperature appropriate for each stage. There is some inaccuracy in this method of control, at least for the homebrewer. Commercial breweries have worked everything out through experience. I've found the temperatures achieved to be quite close to those desired. But as these specific mashing temperatures can be critical, it is sometimes necessary to make adjustments to the resting temperatures.

Decoction Quantity

• One-third is the typical amount, but sometimes can be one-quarter or one-half—see the chart for your mash type. The more mash boiled, the greater the temperature rise when the decoction is added back to the main mash. Also, the greater the temperature difference between the decoction and the main mash, the greater the temperature rise when the decoction is returned to the mash.

Doing the Decoction Shuffle

After dough-in, or strike, and a suitable rest, you're ready to begin the decoction. See your mash chart for specifics of time and temperature.

Use a large measuring cup, scoop, or small saucepan to remove the mash to be decocted. Dip down deep into the mash tun to get the thick portion—the grain. Hold your scooper against the mash tun side when full to drain excess liquid. Keep scooping until you have the required amount in your mash boiling pot.

The next step is to bring the decoction up to boiling, raising the temperature slowly and stopping (usually) at a number of rest points along the way. The malt will scorch quite easily, so it requires your attention to monitor the temperature and to stir the malt to prevent it from sticking to the bottom and burning.

On a gas stove, you can adjust the flame to heat at the perfect rate. An electric stove is either on full-blast or off, so stirring is especially critical. Always take a temperature reading immediately after a good stirring. When you get it where you want it for a rest, take the pot off the burner.

No matter what kind of heat source you're using, adding a couple of quarts of water to the decoction will loosen up the mash to make stirring easier and scorching less probable.

When boiling finally happens, remember to stir often. Check the bottom of the pot by scraping with your spoon—don't allow gunk to build up. Keep scraping to keep the bottom clear.

After boiling the specified time, add the decoction back to the mash—hold back one-third of the decoction at first. Stir the rest in, wait a minute or two, then check the temperature. If it's low, add the rest of the decoction. Stir and check temperature. If it's still low, add some hot (180°F/82° C) water to raise the temperature to where it should be. If it's at the right temperature, wait for the remainder of the decoction to cool to the correct mash temperature. If it's high, mix cool or cold water with the remainder and add it to the mash. Fiddle with it until it's as close as you think you can get it.

Repeat decoction per instructions for the particular mash type you're brewing with.

BRITISH-STYLE INFUSION MASH

Grains are ground and simply mixed well with water, then allowed to stand. Temperature is raised slightly by adding more hot water. This is the simplest mashing method, and requires less equipment in the brewhouse than other types.

MALT TYPES:

Best suited for use with highly modified malts, such as pale ale malt. Less than 10 percent adjuncts OK. Lightly modified lager malt are not best suited for this method.

BOIL LENGTH

• 1 hour for pale ales, bitters, etc.
• 1-1/2 hours for strong ales, etc.
• 2–3 hours for stouts, brown ales.

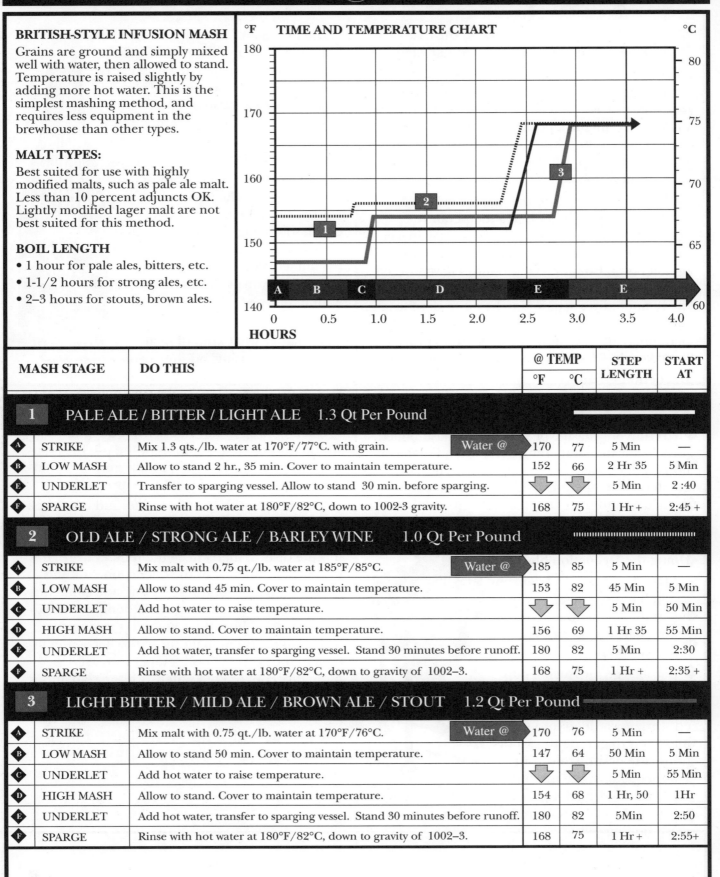

TIME AND TEMPERATURE CHART

MASH STAGE	DO THIS	@ TEMP °F	@ TEMP °C	STEP LENGTH	START AT

1 — PALE ALE / BITTER / LIGHT ALE   1.3 Qt Per Pound

	MASH STAGE	DO THIS	@ TEMP °F	@ TEMP °C	STEP LENGTH	START AT
A	STRIKE	Mix 1.3 qts./lb. water at 170°F/77°C. with grain. *Water @*	170	77	5 Min	—
B	LOW MASH	Allow to stand 2 hr., 35 min. Cover to maintain temperature.	152	66	2 Hr 35	5 Min
E	UNDERLET	Transfer to sparging vessel. Allow to stand 30 min. before sparging.	⬇	⬇	5 Min	2 :40
F	SPARGE	Rinse with hot water at 180°F/82°C, down to 1002-3 gravity.	168	75	1 Hr +	2:45 +

2 — OLD ALE / STRONG ALE / BARLEY WINE   1.0 Qt Per Pound

	MASH STAGE	DO THIS	@ TEMP °F	@ TEMP °C	STEP LENGTH	START AT
A	STRIKE	Mix malt with 0.75 qt./lb. water at 185°F/85°C. *Water @*	185	85	5 Min	—
B	LOW MASH	Allow to stand 45 min. Cover to maintain temperature.	153	82	45 Min	5 Min
C	UNDERLET	Add hot water to raise temperature.	⬇	⬇	5 Min	50 Min
D	HIGH MASH	Allow to stand. Cover to maintain temperature.	156	69	1 Hr 35	55 Min
E	UNDERLET	Add hot water, transfer to sparging vessel. Stand 30 minutes before runoff.	180	82	5 Min	2:30
F	SPARGE	Rinse with hot water at 180°F/82°C, down to gravity of 1002–3.	168	75	1 Hr +	2:35 +

3 — LIGHT BITTER / MILD ALE / BROWN ALE / STOUT   1.2 Qt Per Pound

	MASH STAGE	DO THIS	@ TEMP °F	@ TEMP °C	STEP LENGTH	START AT
A	STRIKE	Mix malt with 0.75 qt./lb. water at 170°F/76°C. *Water @*	170	76	5 Min	—
B	LOW MASH	Allow to stand 50 min. Cover to maintain temperature.	147	64	50 Min	5 Min
C	UNDERLET	Add hot water to raise temperature.	⬇	⬇	5 Min	55 Min
D	HIGH MASH	Allow to stand. Cover to maintain temperature.	154	68	1 Hr, 50	1Hr
E	UNDERLET	Add hot water, transfer to sparging vessel. Stand 30 minutes before runoff.	180	82	5Min	2:50
F	SPARGE	Rinse with hot water at 180°F/82°C, down to gravity of 1002–3.	168	75	1 Hr +	2:55+

GERMAN 2-MASH DECOCTION
Zweimaischverfahren

This is the most common German mash, perfect for brewing Continental lagers, especially pale ones such as pils.

FOR BEER TYPES
All lager beers, especially light-colored ones. Also altbiers.

MASH DILUTION
1.5 qts./lb.

WORT BOIL LENGTH
• 2–3 hours for dark beers.
• 1 to 1-1/2 hours for light beers.

USE MALT TYPES Best suited for use with highly diastatic, lightly modified European lager or pilsner malts. Two-row is traditional, but six-row is OK. Wheat, up to 60% is fine. Rice or corn should be precooked, and kept to 10% or less of the batch.

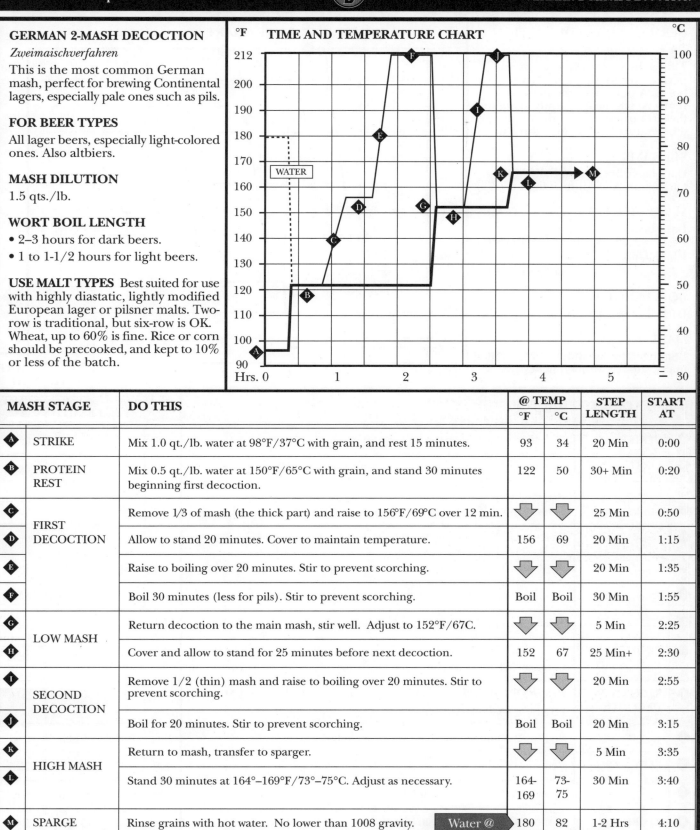

TIME AND TEMPERATURE CHART

	MASH STAGE	DO THIS	@ TEMP °F	@ TEMP °C	STEP LENGTH	START AT
A	STRIKE	Mix 1.0 qt./lb. water at 98°F/37°C with grain, and rest 15 minutes.	93	34	20 Min	0:00
B	PROTEIN REST	Mix 0.5 qt./lb. water at 150°F/65°C with grain, and stand 30 minutes beginning first decoction.	122	50	30+ Min	0:20
C	FIRST DECOCTION	Remove 1/3 of mash (the thick part) and raise to 156°F/69°C over 12 min.	⬇	⬇	25 Min	0:50
D	FIRST DECOCTION	Allow to stand 20 minutes. Cover to maintain temperature.	156	69	20 Min	1:15
E	FIRST DECOCTION	Raise to boiling over 20 minutes. Stir to prevent scorching.	⬇	⬇	20 Min	1:35
F	FIRST DECOCTION	Boil 30 minutes (less for pils). Stir to prevent scorching.	Boil	Boil	30 Min	1:55
G	LOW MASH	Return decoction to the main mash, stir well. Adjust to 152°F/67C.	⬇	⬇	5 Min	2:25
H	LOW MASH	Cover and allow to stand for 25 minutes before next decoction.	152	67	25 Min+	2:30
I	SECOND DECOCTION	Remove 1/2 (thin) mash and raise to boiling over 20 minutes. Stir to prevent scorching.	⬇	⬇	20 Min	2:55
J	SECOND DECOCTION	Boil for 20 minutes. Stir to prevent scorching.	Boil	Boil	20 Min	3:15
K	HIGH MASH	Return to mash, transfer to sparger.	⬇	⬇	5 Min	3:35
L	HIGH MASH	Stand 30 minutes at 164°–169°F/73°–75°C. Adjust as necessary.	164-169	73-75	30 Min	3:40
M	SPARGE	Rinse grains with hot water. No lower than 1008 gravity. Water @	180	82	1-2 Hrs	4:10

GERMAN 3-MASH DECOCTION

Dreimaischverfahren

This is the classic Bavarian mash, perfect for brewing dark lagers and bocks. A portion of the mash is removed and heated slowly to boiling, then returned to raise the mash temperature. This is done three times.

BEER TYPES

Dark lager beers, especially Munich dark beers. Also Munich light (*Helles*).

MASH DILUTION/STRIKE TEMP

Dark beer
    1.25 qts./lb. @ 101°F/38°C.
Pale beer
    1.75 qts./lb. @ 100°F/38°C.

BOIL LENGTH

Dark, 2–3 hours. Light, 1 to 1-1/2 hours.

MALT TYPES

Best suited for use with highly modified malts, such as Munich malt.

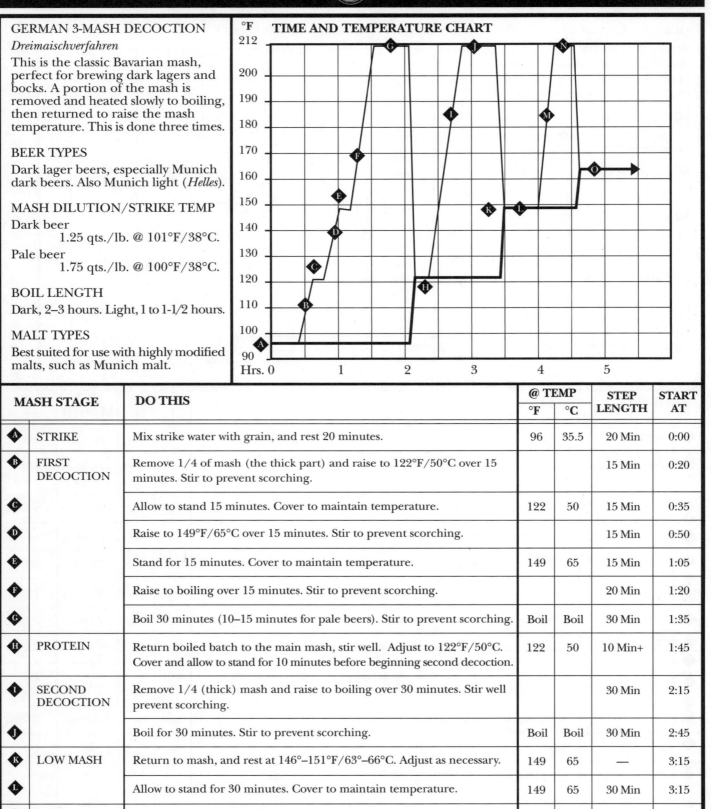

TIME AND TEMPERATURE CHART

	MASH STAGE	DO THIS	@ TEMP °F	@ TEMP °C	STEP LENGTH	START AT
A	STRIKE	Mix strike water with grain, and rest 20 minutes.	96	35.5	20 Min	0:00
B	FIRST DECOCTION	Remove 1/4 of mash (the thick part) and raise to 122°F/50°C over 15 minutes. Stir to prevent scorching.			15 Min	0:20
C		Allow to stand 15 minutes. Cover to maintain temperature.	122	50	15 Min	0:35
D		Raise to 149°F/65°C over 15 minutes. Stir to prevent scorching.			15 Min	0:50
E		Stand for 15 minutes. Cover to maintain temperature.	149	65	15 Min	1:05
F		Raise to boiling over 15 minutes. Stir to prevent scorching.			20 Min	1:20
G		Boil 30 minutes (10–15 minutes for pale beers). Stir to prevent scorching.	Boil	Boil	30 Min	1:35
H	PROTEIN	Return boiled batch to the main mash, stir well. Adjust to 122°F/50°C. Cover and allow to stand for 10 minutes before beginning second decoction.	122	50	10 Min+	1:45
I	SECOND DECOCTION	Remove 1/4 (thick) mash and raise to boiling over 30 minutes. Stir well prevent scorching.			30 Min	2:15
J		Boil for 30 minutes. Stir to prevent scorching.	Boil	Boil	30 Min	2:45
K	LOW MASH	Return to mash, and rest at 146°–151°F/63°–66°C. Adjust as necessary.	149	65	—	3:15
L		Allow to stand for 30 minutes. Cover to maintain temperature.	149	65	30 Min	3:15
M	THIRD DECOCTION	Remove 1/3 (thin) of mash, heat to boiling in 15 minutes.			15 Min	2:45
N		Boil 15 minutes. Stir to prevent scorching.	Boil	Boil	15 Min	3:00
O	SPARGE	Return to mash. Transfer to sparger, stand 30 minutes before beginning sparge.	164	73	30 Min+	3:15

AUTHENTIC CZECHOSLOVAKIAN PILSNER 3-MASH

FOR BEER TYPES
Czech Pilsners. Produces a darker, more caramelly beer than German pils.

MASH DILUTION
2.1 qts./lb.

WORT BOIL LENGTH
1-1/2 to 2-1/2 hours (or longer).

MALT TYPES:
Best suited for use with highly diastatic, lightly modified pilsner-type lager malts. Two-row is traditional, even essential. Use the palest malt available. European malts give fuller, richer flavor. Up to 10% adjuncts will lighten up the beer, but will produce a less authentic beer.

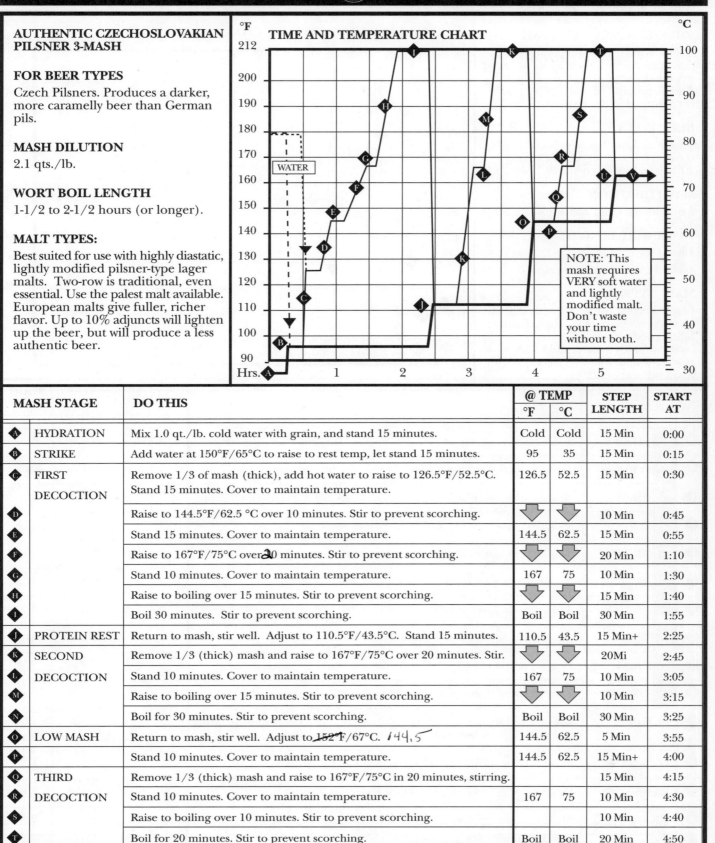

TIME AND TEMPERATURE CHART

NOTE: This mash requires VERY soft water and lightly modified malt. Don't waste your time without both.

	MASH STAGE	DO THIS	@ TEMP °F	@ TEMP °C	STEP LENGTH	START AT
A	HYDRATION	Mix 1.0 qt./lb. cold water with grain, and stand 15 minutes.	Cold	Cold	15 Min	0:00
B	STRIKE	Add water at 150°F/65°C to raise to rest temp, let stand 15 minutes.	95	35	15 Min	0:15
C	FIRST DECOCTION	Remove 1/3 of mash (thick), add hot water to raise to 126.5°F/52.5°C. Stand 15 minutes. Cover to maintain temperature.	126.5	52.5	15 Min	0:30
D		Raise to 144.5°F/62.5 °C over 10 minutes. Stir to prevent scorching.	⬇	⬇	10 Min	0:45
E		Stand 15 minutes. Cover to maintain temperature.	144.5	62.5	15 Min	0:55
F		Raise to 167°F/75°C over 20 minutes. Stir to prevent scorching.	⬇	⬇	20 Min	1:10
G		Stand 10 minutes. Cover to maintain temperature.	167	75	10 Min	1:30
H		Raise to boiling over 15 minutes. Stir to prevent scorching.	⬇	⬇	15 Min	1:40
I		Boil 30 minutes. Stir to prevent scorching.	Boil	Boil	30 Min	1:55
J	PROTEIN REST	Return to mash, stir well. Adjust to 110.5°F/43.5°C. Stand 15 minutes.	110.5	43.5	15 Min+	2:25
K	SECOND DECOCTION	Remove 1/3 (thick) mash and raise to 167°F/75°C over 20 minutes. Stir.	⬇	⬇	20Mi	2:45
L		Stand 10 minutes. Cover to maintain temperature.	167	75	10 Min	3:05
M		Raise to boiling over 15 minutes. Stir to prevent scorching.	⬇	⬇	10 Min	3:15
N		Boil for 30 minutes. Stir to prevent scorching.	Boil	Boil	30 Min	3:25
O	LOW MASH	Return to mash, stir well. Adjust to ~~152°F/67°C.~~ 144.5	144.5	62.5	5 Min	3:55
P		Stand 10 minutes. Cover to maintain temperature.	144.5	62.5	15 Min+	4:00
Q	THIRD DECOCTION	Remove 1/3 (thick) mash and raise to 167°F/75°C in 20 minutes, stirring.			15 Min	4:15
R		Stand 10 minutes. Cover to maintain temperature.	167	75	10 Min	4:30
S		Raise to boiling over 10 minutes. Stir to prevent scorching.			10 Min	4:40
T		Boil for 20 minutes. Stir to prevent scorching.	Boil	Boil	20 Min	4:50
U	HIGH MASH	Return to mash, transfer to sparger, stir well. Adjust to ~~152°F/67°C.~~ 162.5	162.5	72.5	5 Min	5:10
V	SPARGE	Stand 30 minutes before sparging with water @ 180°F/82°C. Water @	180	82	30 Min+	5:15

AMERICAN ADJUNCT MASH

Adjuncts are mashed separately with diastatic enzymes, then added to main mash to raise temperature to mashing. A small amount of malt (10%) can be used instead of the enzymes.

BEER TYPES

American lager beers, especially light-colored ones. Designed for typical 10%–30% rice or corn U.S. beers.

MASH DILUTION

2 qts./lb. for main and adjunct mashes.

WORT BOIL LENGTH

1 hour for light beers.
1-1/2 hours for dark beers.

MALT TYPES

Best suited for use with highly diastatic U.S. six-row lager malt. High diastatic action needed for adjuncts, high nitrogen content needs to be diluted. U.S. two-row lager malt will work, too, but with fewer adjuncts (<25%).

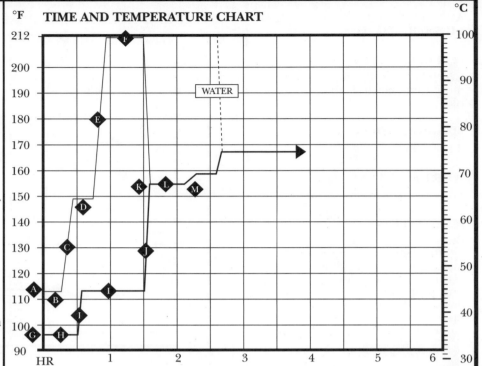

TIME AND TEMPERATURE CHART

MASH STAGE		DO THIS	@ TEMP °F	@ TEMP °C	STEP LENGTH	START AT
A	STRIKE	Add 2 qts./lb. water at 113°F/45°C to grain, stir, add diastatic enzymes.	⬇	⬇	5 Min	0:00
B	STAND	Allow to stand 10 minutes. Cover to maintain temperature.	113	45	10 Min	0:05
C	HEAT	Heat on stove to 149°F/65°C over 10 minutes. Stir to prevent scorching.	⬇	⬇	10Min	0:15
D	STAND	Stand 30 minutes at 149°F/65°C. Adjust as necessary.	149	65	20 Min	0:25
E	HEAT	Heat to boiling over 20 minutes. Stir to prevent scorching.	⬇	⬇	10 Min	0:45
F	BOIL	Boil gently 35 minutes. Stir frequently to avoid scorching.	Boil	Boil	35 Min	0:55
G	STRIKE	Add 2 qts./lb. water at 98°F/36°C to malt, stir well, stabilize at 95°F/35°C.	⬇	⬇	5 Min	0:00
H	STAND	Cover and allow to stand for 25 minutes.	95	35	25 Min	0:05
I	HEAT	Heat on stove to 113°F/45°C in 5 minutes. Stir to prevent scorching.	⬇	⬇	5 Min	0:30
J	STAND	Allow to stand 10 minutes. Cover to maintain temperature.	113	45	50 Min	0:35
K	RETURN	Mix malt and adjuncts together in mash vessel. Temperature should stabilize at 154°F/67°C. Adjust with hot or cold water as needed.	⬇	⬇	5 Min	1:30
L	LOW MASH	Allow to stand 35 minutes. Cover to maintain temperature.	154	67	35 Min	1:35
M	RAISE	Heat to 159°F/70°C. Stir to prevent scorching.	⬇	⬇	10 Min	2:10
N	HIGH	Allow to stand 20 minutes. Cover to maintain temperature.	159	70	20 Min	2:20
O	SPARGE	Transfer mash to sparging vessel, liquid first. Stand without draining for 30 minutes. Sparge no lower than 1008 original gravity. Water @	167 180	75 82	30+ Min	2:40

ADJUNCT MASH (A–F), MAIN MASH (G–J)

REST TEMPERATURES APPEAR IN THE BOXES BELOW:

STRIKE TEMPERATURE

	0.5 Quart per Pound	0.75 Quart per Pound	1.0 Quart per Pound	1.25 Quarts per Pound	1.5 Quarts per Pound
180°F 82°C	145°F 62.5°C	150°F 65.3°C	154°F 67.7°C	158.5°F 70.2°C	160°F 71°C
170°F 76.5°C	139°F 54.3°C	144°F 62.2°C	148°F 64.3°C	151.5°F 50.3°C	154°F 67.7°C
160°F 71°C	134°F 56.5°C	138°F 58.8°C	142°F 61°C	145.5°F 63°C	148°F 64.3°C
150°F 65.3°C	129°F 54°C	133°F 56°C	136°F 55.6°C	139°F 59.3°C	140.5°F 60.3°C
140°F 60°C	125°F 51.5°C	128°F 53.2°C	131°F 55°C	132°F 55.3°C	133°F 56°C
130°F 54.3°C	120°F 48.7°C	123°F 50.5°C	124.5°F 51.3°C	125.5°F 52°C	126°F 52.2°C

MASH DILUTION

Use this chart to figure out the temperature of the mash after adding hot water. The temperature is shown along the left, the dilution of the mash, in quarts per pound, is shown across the bottom. The resting temperatures of the mash are shown in the blocks in the center of the chart. These charts were based on small-scale tests and homebrew experience. Your results may vary depending on your setup. These figures were calculated/ measured based on adding hot water to malt in a nonpre-heated container. Having the mash tun preheated will give a smaller temperature drop.

TEMPERATURE DROP CHART

This chart shows the expected temperature drop after adding the strike water.

Use this to figure strike temperature other than the ones on the big chart above.

Be conservative when adding the strike water. Mix in 3/4 of the water, mix, wait, and add the rest if the temperature is still low.

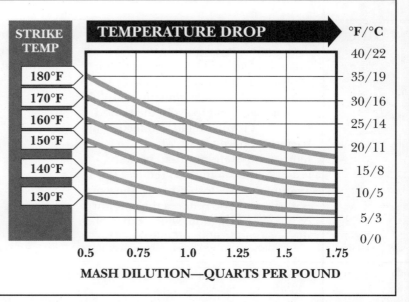

STRIKE TEMP — TEMPERATURE DROP — °F/°C

40/22, 35/19, 30/16, 25/14, 20/11, 15/8, 10/5, 5/3, 0/0

180°F, 170°F, 160°F, 150°F, 140°F, 130°F

MASH DILUTION—QUARTS PER POUND: 0.5, 0.75, 1.0, 1.25, 1.5, 1.75

STAGE	GENERAL INFORMATION	CARBOHYDRATES	PROTEINS, ETC.
SPARGE	Water, at 167°–176°F/75°–80°C, is gently sprayed on the surface of the goods, allowing it to trickle through the bed of grains, which forms a natural filter. Enzymes are inactivated. pH rises toward the end, as the runoff becomes weaker, and more tannins and silicates, detrimental to beer quality, are leached into the wort.	At first, enzymes continue to break up starch and dextrins. As amylase enzymes are destroyed by heat, this stops. Some starch remains, and sparge water that is too hot will allow starch to dissolve in wort where it will cause a permanent haze.	A gray, gunky sludge of proteins, called *teig*, can accumulate on top of the mash, making sparging difficult. Let mash partially drain, and carefully scoop off the goo. A problem sometimes in wheat beers and brews with lots of six-row malt.
BOIL	Wort is vigorously boiled for 1 to 3 hours. Hop alpha acids are isomerized (change shape) and become soluble. Hop tannins combine with protein and coagulate as the hot break. Wort darkens with the formation of melanoidins and other complex caramelly flavors develop in the beer. Mechanical action of a vigorous boil helps to coagulate proteins. Boil it as hard as you can. Watch for boilovers when bringing wort up to boiling point.	Various sugars combine with amino acids and other protein breakdown products to form melanoidins. These are the chemicals that form the color of caramel, and they darken the wort in proportion to the length of the boil. Many specific varieties are formed from combinations of the specific types of sugars and protein breakdown products.	Various nitrogenous compounds combine with carbohydrates to form melanoidins. Also combine with hop tannins and precipitates in large flakes as the hot break, removing haze-forming material from the wort. Vigorous boiling is needed to make the hot break form. Trub is the sludgy material that precipitates out.
CHILL	Wort is run through a heat-exchange device and cooled quickly to yeast pitching temperature. The more rapid the cooling the better. The objectives are to cause a cold break, eliminating insoluble protein haze, and to avoid the period when wort is vulnerable to infection by bacteria and wild yeast, which are less temperature-sensitive than brewer's yeast. Rapid cooling also reduces the amount of DMS formed while the wort is warm, and also reduces the amount of hot wort oxidation, which can darken the beer and lead to off-flavors.	Carbohydrates pass through the cooling stage without changing.	A small amount of protein, one-tenth the amount of the hot break, is precipitated out as the cold break. These protein fractions become insoluble as the temperature is lowered. Rapid chilling makes the cold break more pronounced, and results in a cleaner-tasting beer.

Table embedded in SPARGE row:

Sparge Stage	Germany	U.S.	Britain
First Runnings	1090	1080	1100
Last Runnings	1004	1008	1001

Table embedded in BOIL row:

Beer Types	Boil Length
Pale Lager	1–1.5 hours
Dark Lager	2–3 hours
Pale Ales	1 hour
Dark Ales	2–3 hours
Strong Ales	1.5 hours

**YEAST &
FERMENTATION**

11

Yeast is a microscopic single-celled fungus. There are thousands of species of yeasts, adapted to a huge range of habitats, nutritional opportunities, and environmental conditions.

Only two yeasts are commonly used for brewing: *Saccharomyces cerevesiae*, ale yeast, and *Saccharomyces uvarum* (formerly *S. carlsbergensis*), lager yeast. They are so closely related that scientists have decided they both belong to *S. cerevesiae* after all, but in brewing practice the distinction between the two is still strongly made. In addition to "normal" brewing yeast, a few other species are cultivated for specialty beers, such as weizens and certain Belgian types. *Brettanomyces bruxellensis* and *B. lambicus* are two of the wild yeasts used to produce lambic beers.

ALE YEAST	Top-fermenting, forms foamy mass on top of wort during active fermentation. Best at temperatures between 59°–68°F/15°–20°C, but functions over a wider range. Ferments only one-third of raffinose molecule.
LAGER YEAST	Bottom-fermenting. Sinks to bottom during active fermentation. Primary at 39°–54°F/4°–12°C. Lager, or secondary, as low as 33°F/1°C. When fermented warm, like ale, it is used to produce California common beer. Completely ferments raffinose, which ale yeast cannot do.

Other genera of yeast will grow in wort or beer causing infections in the brewery. These "wild yeasts" include *Pichia, Candida, Hansenula* and others, as well as mutated brewing strains. (See also **Section 11–3, Wild Yeast.**)

Yeast Metabolism

Brewing yeast consumes sugar in its main fermentation cycle, producing ethyl alcohol and carbon dioxide. Maltose, glucose, maltotriose, and other sugars are metabolized. Vitamins, minerals and other chemicals are needed for growth. The particulars of this process are quite complex.

Yeast Growth

During the growth stage, yeast reproduces by budding, building up the crop of yeast that will

---

YEAST LIKES AND DISLIKES

YEAST LIKES
- Steady temperatures.
- Plenty of oxygen, especially at the start.
- Amino acids, and other protein fragments.
- Maltose, glucose, fructose, maltotriose, and matotetraose, in that order of preference.
- Moderation in all things.
- Certain vitamins.
- A very clean environment.

YEAST HATES
- Rapid temperature changes.
- Heavy metals, such as lead and tin, even in very small amounts. See **Section 9–2, Trace Minerals**.
- Chlorine, as in disinfectants.
- High alcohol content, over 10–12 percent.
- Competition from other organisms.
- Temperatures that are too low or too high.

YEAST IS AMBIVALENT ABOUT
- Dextrins   • Hop rate
- Beer color   • CO_2 (carbonation)

---

turn the wort into beer. Oxygen is consumed in addition to nutrients in the wort.

The yeast's ability to grow is strictly limited by the amount of available oxygen dissolved in the wort. This is of critical importance for the brewer. Lack of sufficient oxygen can cause a fermentation to conk out suddenly, leaving the wort vulnerable to the ubiquitous wild yeast present in every brewing environment, no matter how clean.

Be sure to spray, sprinkle, or splash the chilled wort thoroughly before or immediately after pitching, to aerate the wort. Do not splash when hot, however. Doing so will speed up browning and other oxidation reactions, and cause the beer to taste stale long before its time.

Yeast and Beer Flavor

Yeast is a key player in beer flavor. Important groups of flavor chemicals produced by yeast include esters, aldehydes, fusel oils (higher alcohols), sulfur compounds, and diacetyl. (For more information on yeast's role in beer flavor, see **Section 3–5, Beer Flavors.**)

These chemicals are produced in greater abundance at high temperatures. This is the main reason for the vastly different flavor profile of lagers versus ales. And also why beers made with lager yeasts at higher temperatures (>50°F/10°C) taste more like ales than lagers. The one chemical that contradicts this somewhat is diacetyl, which is also produced at lagering temperatures (< 40°F/4°C), and may be reduced by a couple of days at a higher temperature (56°F/13°C), a process known as a diacetyl rest.

Selection Characteristics for Brewing Yeast

Brewers are very choosy about their yeast. To ensure consistently high-quality yeast, cultures are periodically regrown from a single cell. A yeast slurry is diluted and streaked on petri dishes and grown into colonies, each formed from a single cell. Tests are run on a number of colonies to determine the one with the best characteristics for brewing a particular beer. The following are among the most important:

Flocculation: The speed at which yeast links into chains and drops to the bottom after fermentation has ceased. The nonflocculent, powdery types tend to give more completely attenuated beers than the flocculent types, which settle out of suspension sooner. Flocculation is a characteristic that is easily changed by minor mutations that occur under normal brewing conditions.

Attenuation Limit: How completely yeast ferments the sugars in wort. Related to flocculence. Strains used for Bavarian lagers are not very attenuative, resulting in sweet, rich-tasting beers. Altbiers attenuate much more completely, creating crisp, dry beers. Certain wild yeasts are superattenuative, containing an enzyme that breaks down dextrins and complex sugars, in a fermentation that never seems to end.

Beer Flavor: Yeast affects the taste of beer to a very great degree. Each strain of yeast has a unique flavor profile. Some enhance malt character, some are very estery, some nutty, some appley, some simple and clean. Some, like Belgian Trappist yeasts, have a spiciness or other flavor that is a signature for the beer style.

Speed of Growth/Viability of the Yeast: This is a very important factor in the commercial brewery, but a little difficult for the average homebrewer to

evaluate. Some yeasts are more sensitive to growing conditions—temperature, alcohol, etc. Ask people who have brewed with the strain you plan to use.

YEAST HANDLING TECHNIQUES

It is important to treat the yeast correctly to avoid infections and produce delicious beer. These guidelines should be followed as nearly as possible in the home environment.

Cleaning and Sanitation

Cleanliness and sanitation are absolutely critical to brewing. Thoroughly clean and sanitize everything that comes in contact with chilled wort or fermenting beer. Chlorine cleaner or bleach work perfectly. Use in cold water, at the rate of 1/2 ounce per gallon. Anything more is overkill, and could be difficult to get off the equipment. Be sure to rinse your equipment well, as residual chlorine can harm yeast. If your tap water is questionable, sanitize with large amounts of a weaker chlorine solution (1 ounce per 10 gallons), use a 20-minute soak, and allow the equipment to air-dry before using. You can also use commercial solutions of iodine, such as those used in the dairy and health care industries. These solutions do not need to be rinsed off, are less toxic and far less corrosive to such metals as brass and stainless steel; the negative is that some people are allergic to them. BUT, any commercial brewer worth his wort will tell you that all the sanitation in the world is wasted unless the surfaces in question aren't physically clean. Hot water, lots of elbow grease, and an occasional pinch of TSP are the best cleaning agents to use. Commercial breweries use sodium hydroxide, a dangerously corrosive substance. If you decide to use this caustic, take thorough precautions to protect your skin and eyes.

Protected Fermentation

If a wort is chilled quickly, pitched with a sufficient quantity of actively fermenting yeast, and provided with an adequate supply of oxygen and nutrients, it will be very difficult for contaminating organisms to get a foothold. The yeast will quickly usurp the nutrients and raise the pH and alcohol levels to the point where competing bacteria and yeasts can't survive. Surgical standards of cleanliness are not required if you maintain a protected fermentation.

Use a yeast starter if possible, as this is the only way to get the required quantity of active yeast. A pint to a quart of starter does a pretty good job, but commercial breweries pitch at the rate of 20 million cells/ml, 1–1.5 lb/bbl, equivalent to .5–.75 oz/gallon. Starters are equally important with dry and liquid yeast. You should do starters of at least a pint in size to get good results. Pour off the clear liquid and add the sludge to your beer. Breweries add massive amounts of yeast to high-gravity beers, and you should pitch as large a starter as you can. A quart of thick yeast slurry wouldn't be too much for a barley wine or doppelbock!

Yeast Rehydration

With dry yeast, it is important to rehydrate the yeast before pitching. Simply add the yeast to 1/2 cup sterile (boiled and cooled) water at about body temperature (100°F/37°C). Allow to stand for a few minutes before pitching. Do not use sugar or malt extract for this purpose, as either may cause osmotic shock, which can damage cell membranes.

Yeast and Freshness

Pay close attention to the storage instructions and code dates on yeast; all packaged yeast deteriorates during storage. Cells die for various reasons, greatly reducing the number of active cells available to start fermentation, another very good reason for using a starter.

Dry *vs.* Liquid Yeasts

On average, liquid yeasts make cleaner-tasting beers than dried yeast. In addition, liquid yeasts offer much better variety, and usually a clear pedigree as well, which is especially important if

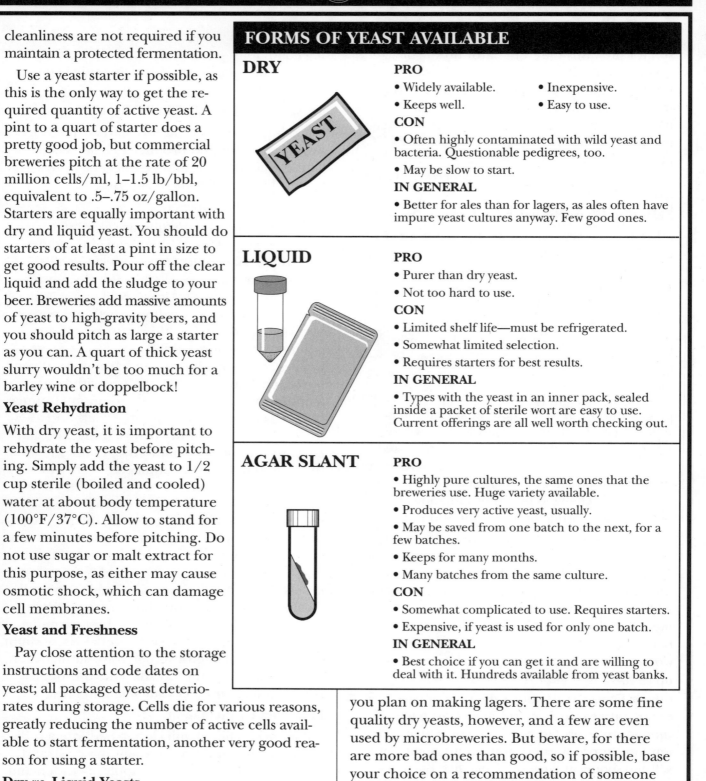

FORMS OF YEAST AVAILABLE

DRY

PRO
- Widely available.
- Keeps well.
- Inexpensive.
- Easy to use.

CON
- Often highly contaminated with wild yeast and bacteria. Questionable pedigrees, too.
- May be slow to start.

IN GENERAL
- Better for ales than for lagers, as ales often have impure yeast cultures anyway. Few good ones.

LIQUID

PRO
- Purer than dry yeast.
- Not too hard to use.

CON
- Limited shelf life—must be refrigerated.
- Somewhat limited selection.
- Requires starters for best results.

IN GENERAL
- Types with the yeast in an inner pack, sealed inside a packet of sterile wort are easy to use. Current offerings are all well worth checking out.

AGAR SLANT

PRO
- Highly pure cultures, the same ones that the breweries use. Huge variety available.
- Produces very active yeast, usually.
- May be saved from one batch to the next, for a few batches.
- Keeps for many months.
- Many batches from the same culture.

CON
- Somewhat complicated to use. Requires starters.
- Expensive, if yeast is used for only one batch.

IN GENERAL
- Best choice if you can get it and are willing to deal with it. Hundreds available from yeast banks.

you plan on making lagers. There are some fine quality dry yeasts, however, and a few are even used by microbreweries. But beware, for there are more bad ones than good, so if possible, base your choice on a recommendation of someone who has had a recent positive experience.

Yeast Nutrient Additives

This material is used in some kinds of wine-making and in the baking industry. The only real use for it in brewing would be very low-gravity beers, made with a large proportion of adjuncts—light beers. Some extract brands contain a high proportion of nonmalt additives, such as corn syrup, and are consequently deficient in the free amino nitrogen needed for proper yeast nutrition.

Oxygen Management

This is somewhat paradoxical. In the early stages yeast requires at least 8 mg/liter of dissolved oxygen—more for lagers and strong ales. This is really more than can be gotten by simply splashing the wort around, but for five-gallon batches, long, vigorous splashing delivers acceptable yeast growth. This becomes more of a problem with larger batches. The higher the starting gravity, the more important this is. You need a lot of oxygen to grow up enough yeast to ferment a high-gravity beer.

One way to increase aeration is to make a sprayer from a piece of stainless steel tubing to spray the wort into the primary fermenter (see **Section 15–1, Homebrew Equipment**). To use, attach to the outlet of your wort chiller and let the cooled wort spray into your fermenter.

An aquarium pump is also an effective aeration tool. Simply connect it, via a length of tubing, to a fishtank aeration stone. (Place a disposable medical air or syringe filter inline to exclude airborne microbes.) Sink the stone in your chilled wort and allow the pump to run until beer foams up to the top of your fermenter. Let it settle, then repeat. You'll want to run it for two to four hours for maximum effect. Do not aerate hot, or even warm, wort. Doing so will cause many unpleasant problems with oxidation, and you will hate yourself later. Make sure the wort is cooled to pitching temperature before aerating.

Commercial breweries often use medical oxygen to achieve proper oxygen levels. However, with this method it is possible to add too much, causing oxidation problems later on.

HOW TO MAKE A YEAST STARTER

1. Obtain a 500 or 1,000 ml Pyrex flask, with a stopper drilled to accept a fermentation lock. Now you can feel like a real scientist.

2. Sterilize and fill half full with spring water or dechlorinated water.

3. Add about 1/2 cup of malt extract. Put a ball of sterile cotton into the neck of the flask, and cover tightly with a double layer of foil.

4. Swirl around until extract is dissolved.

5. Bring to a boil on the stove, making sure the bottom doesn't burn. Boil gently for 30 minutes.

6. Turn off heat and allow to cool. DO NOT put in refrigerator (it's full of germs). Use a cold water bath to speed things up if you like.

7. When cooled to 90°F/32°C, remove foil and cotton (don't put cotton down on unsterilized surface). Have sterilized lock and stopper ready to go.

8. Add yeast. If from a packet, sterilize the packet before opening.

9. Put in the stopper and lock. Shake vigorously to aerate and dissolve.

10. Allow to ferment for 12 hours or more at the desired fermentation temperature.

11. After thick head has developed, you can add starter to the main batch.

12. Use starter when visibly active. If it has gone flat, add more malt extract and wait until fermentation is active.

13. This yeast may be used to start an additional starter at the same time you pitch into your chilled wort.

Aluminum foil
Cotton wad
500 or 1000ml Pyrex® flask
Wort, about 1/2 full

After primary fermentation, exclusion of oxygen from the fermented beer is critical. To exclude oxygen: (1) Transfer the beer only when absolutely necessary: once from primary to secondary, and once at bottling. Some people bottle from a pressurized keg, letting CO_2-filled foam top off the bottles and push out any air. (2) Avoid splashing when siphoning. Put the end of the siphon tube under the liquid. Don't let beer splash on the bottom. (3) Fill bottles to within 1/2" of the top.

Reusing yeast

Breweries reuse yeast from batch to batch. Some use the same yeast for dozens, or even hundreds of batches. This is an attractive option for homebrewers as well, because it eliminates the necessity of growing a new starter every time you brew.

Scooping up the yeast from the bottom of the fermenter can be a challenge. The yeast forms a thin layer, and includes lots of other gunk, some of it not very pleasant-tasting. Yeast saved this way only lasts a week or two, and after that it needs to be grown up into a starter again. There is also the ever-present danger of contamination. Breweries and yeast labs "wash" their yeast in a bath of mild acid, which reduces the bacteria present. Washing is a tricky procedure that can do more harm than good, and is usually best left to the professionals.

If you do wish to harvest and reuse yeast, pour off the dregs of primary fermentation into a sterilized jar and refrigerate. Allow the yeast to settle, then scoop off the top layer; only use the yeast from the middle of the jar. Dead yeast cells and trub will either sink or float, leaving the most viable cells in a clean, creamy layer in the center.

Culturing from Bottles

Homebrew and some commercial beers contain live yeast that can be cultured with good success. Chimay, an unpasteurized Belgian ale, works well. The bottles are dated on the corks, so use the freshest bottle you can find. If you have a choice, use a normal-gravity beer. (High amounts of alcohol can cause the yeast to mutate, possibly producing beers high in diacetyl.) Other good beers to culture are Belgian ales, such as Duvel and Westmalle (if they're fresh). Some success has been had with Orval; its mixed cultures make it tricky, but worth the effort. German hefe weizens usually use lager yeast in the bottle, rather than the distinctive weizen yeast. Sierra Nevada ales culture well, too.

Pour off most of the beer and enjoy. Then, flame the top of the beer bottle with a propane torch and quickly pour the sludge into a freshly prepared starter wort of about 1045 OG. This technique works best if the starter is grown up in several increasing size starters, beginning with about 50 ml, and moving up to the pint or so needed for pitching.

Making and Using Slants

Slants allow you to preserve and share yeast samples with other brewers. A malt agar medium is used as a base for growing a small amount of yeast that can then be maintained for a few months in a refrigerator, ready for use. Consult a microbiology lab textbook for the detailed procedure used to create slants.

To grow up yeast from a slant, prepare a 50 ml starter as described on the previous page. Use a flamed sterile inoculating loop to scoop up a small amount of the yeast culture from the agar, and swish it around in the starter. Replace the cotton and foil, and wait for fermentation to begin. This small culture can be used to start a 250 ml starter, which can then be used to inoculate a full-sized starter.

Fermentation Temperatures

Fermenting beer needs an environment that maintains a constant temperature. Basements are great if they're not dirty or damp. Maintain the temperature as close as possible to the ideal temperature for the beer type (ale or lager).

Be especially careful to prevent rapid temperature drops of 10°F/6°C or more. Such drops can cause the yeast to shut down or mutate, causing stuck fermentations.

Lager beers require low temperatures. This means a refrigerator is essential. You can pick up a used one for a few bucks. Many people fit a second thermostat to allow use at higher temperatures than the built-in one allows. Programmable air conditioner add-on thermostats are a good choice for this purpose.

One-stage *vs.* Two-stage Fermentation

Leave the beer in a fermenter until it has stopped fermenting and dropped clear, which can take from two weeks to six months. If the beer sits on the dregs of the primary fermentation longer than a week or two, it may pick up unpleasant flavors from dead yeast, hop tannins, and any remaining cold break. Also, beer in a tub has a large surface area exposed to air, making it a breeding ground for molds and certain bacteria (like *Acetobacteria*), which would be no problem otherwise.

Many brewing kits recommend a single-stage fermentation, usually in a plastic tub. A tub can be used to produce good beer, but there are a few problems. Most tubs don't seal well and offer easy access for bacteria. Additionally, the plastic material quickly develops small scratches where bacteria can snuggle into, making them resistant to efforts to kill or remove them, even with powerful chlorine sanitizer.

The solution is to ferment in two stages. The primary can be done in plastic, or better, glass. The large 6½-gallon glass carboys make excellent primary fermenters, with enough headspace to make a blow-off arrangement unnecessary. The ubiquitous 5-gallon glass carboys are highly recommended for secondary fermenters.

Various Yeasty Tips

• Make two starters from a batch of liquid yeast. This allows you to use one to start a batch of beer, and the other to start two more starters, keeping the process up indefinitely (sort of). If you're using the sterile starter technique described here, it can be safer and cleaner than pitching from the dregs.

• Build a "cooler box" out of foam building insulation. Simply build a box to place over your carboys with the open end at the bottom. Be sure to make it large enough for the lock to fit inside, too. Size it to fit one or many carboys, as you like. Cut the stuff with a kitchen knife or razor blade and tape it together with duct tape. This really works, and can minimize daily temperature fluctuations when beer is kept in an area where temperature does vary. In a basement, the box keeps the beer cooler than the air, by insulating it from everything but the cool floor.

• Fill the fermentation lock with cheap vodka to help maintain sterility. A chlorine solution would work, but if some gets sucked into the carboy (as happens when the beer cools), the chlorine could be harmful to fermentation. However, the small amount of vodka that could get into the beer won't harm it. This technique is especially useful during the primary fermentation, when the beer often bubbles its way out of the fermenter, creating the potential for infection in the lock.

• Use a common propane torch for flaming the mouths of flasks and bottles whenever you are transferring starters.

• Use a commercially available media for detecting the presence of bacteria and wild yeast in your beer. They are used by commercial breweries on a regular basis to check their product. The two most widely used are:

HLP (Hsu's Lactobacillus/Pediococcus) inhibits the growth of all yeast and bacteria other than those it is designed to detect. Breweries use HLP to measure the levels of *Lactobacillus* and *Pediococcus* contamination at each stage of fermentation.

Lynn's Wild Yeast Media is designed to inhibit the growth of everything but a variety of wild yeast, and so is used to detect wild yeast.

Prepare according to instructions, then add to culture tubes or petri dishes, and heat-sterilize (preferably in an autoclave or pressure cooker). A measured amount of beer (typically 10 ml), often taken at various stages of fermentation, is added to the media, then incubated. After a specific period of time, the tubes or plates can be visually checked. Each colony visible to the naked eye represents a single bacteria or yeast. The count determines the extent of contamination of the sample. Breweries expect some contamination and it's rarely zero. But these tests are directionally important, and an increase is viewed as significant.

• If you have a tank of CO_2 for a draft system, fill your carboy with the gas prior to transferring beer into it. Sterilize the carboy and the gas line, insert the gas line into the carboy, and turn on the gas until you can smell it strongly coming out of the top. CO_2 is heavier than air, so it will push the air out the top as it fills. This reduces the amount of oxygen that can be taken up by the beer. It will also allow you to keep a less-than-full carboy of beer without danger of contamination by aerobic bacteria and mold. This is especially useful in fermenting fruit beer when the fruit is added during the secondary, and a full carboy would be foolhardy. (See also **Section 7–4, Brewing with Fruit.**)

BOTTOM FERMENTATION

Lager beer
Saccharomyces uvarum

- Low temperature fermentation 33°–54°F/1°–12°C.
- Yeast pitched @ 45°F/7°C.
- Slow fermentation.
- Primary complete in 9–14 days.
- Requires long secondary, lager period of 2–6 months at 33°F/1°C.
- Usually more unfermentables than ales of similar gravity.
- Flavors (esters, etc.) generated by yeast at lower levels than ales.
- Breweries typically use single-cell culture.

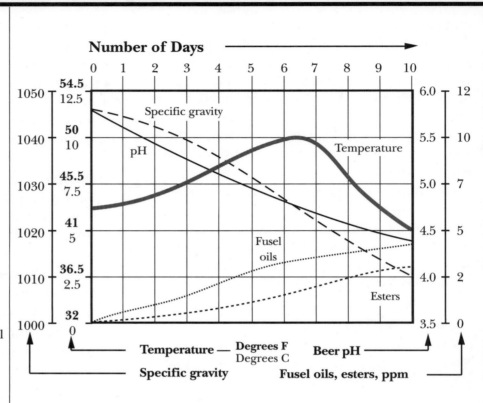

TOP FERMENTATION

Ale, Altbier
Saccharomyces cerevesiae

- High temperature fermentation.
- Yeast pitched at 59°–61°F/15°–16°C, or higher.
- Rapid fermentation.
- Primary complete in 3–5 days.
- Secondary in 2–6 weeks.
- Longer for high-gravity ales.
- More complete attenuation than lagers; less unfermented material.
- Typically mixed yeast strains, with (in U.K.) measurable bacterial population, which contributes to flavor.
- Larger amounts of yeast-generated flavors (esters, etc.) than lager, due to higher temperatures.

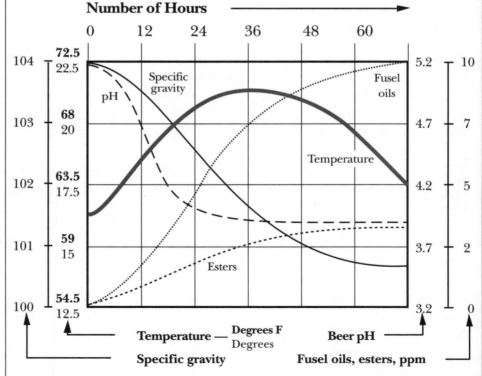

YEAST TYPE	ASCO-SPORE	PELLI-CLE	FERMENTS	CELL SHAPE	DISCUSSION
SACCHAROMYCES CEREVESIAE	○	●	Gl, Ga, S, Ma, 1/3 R	Roundish to elliptical 2–10 x 5–20 μ	The common ale, or top-fermenting yeast. Considered a contaminant when a strain other than that desired is present. Harmful strains can cause haze and off-flavors, especially strong phenolic flavors. Var. *diastaticus* can ferment dextrins and maltotetraose, causing superattenuation. Sometimes evidenced by fermentation that won't stop. Some wild strains are resistant to pasteurization, and can cause trouble at extremely low concentrations. Var. *bayanus* used in wine and sherry fermentation. It can cause harsh, smoky flavors. Pitching lots of active yeast into well-aerated wort is best preventative measure. Wild strains not as picky about oxygen requirements as brewing cultures.
var. BAYANUS formerly *PASTORIANUS*	●	○		Oval, elongate, to sausage-shaped	
var. DIASTATICUS	●	—	Above + Dextrin	Same as *S.C.*	
var. TURBIDANS	●	●		Same as *S.C.*, also sausage-shaped	
var. WILLIANUS	●	●		Same as *S.C.*, also elongate	
SACCHAROMYCES UVARUM formerly *S. CARLSBERGENSIS*	●	—	Gl, Ga, Ma, Me, all R, S	Roundish to elongate 2.5–9.5 x 5–25 μ	Lager, or bottom-fermenting, yeast. Found as a contaminant in ale breweries.
HANSENULA ANOMALA	●	●	Gl, Ga, Ma, S, 1/3 R	Roundish to long 2–4.8 x 2.6–5.2 μ, or up to 30μ long	Needs air to grow rapidly. Forms film. Produces esters, oxidizes organic acids and esters. Some species produce slime.
PICHIA MEMBRANAFACIENS	●	●	Gl (Slow)	Oval to cylindrical 2–5.5 x 4.5–20 μ	Forms film. Needs air to grow rapidly. Oxidizes alcohol, may create spicy aromas.
BRETTANOMYCES BRUXELLENSIS B. LAMBICUS	—	●	Gl, Ma, R, S	Oval to elongate 2–6.5 x 4–22 μ	Wild yeasts used in lambic production. Slow-growing, takes six weeks to become evident. Aerobic, causes off-flavors. Oxidizes alcohol and acetic acid, forms esters.
CANDIDA NORVIGENSIS formerly *C. MYCODERMA*	—	●	Gl (Slow)	Long-oval to cylindrical 2–8 x 5–13 μ	Forms film. Needs air to grow rapidly. A common contaminant in half-empty British ale casks. Oxidizes alcohol to acetic acid.
KLOECKERA APICULATA	—	○	Gl	Lemon-shaped, oval, or elongate 1.4–5.3 x 2.6–12.2 μ	Found on fruits and in soil. Present in early stages of lambic fermentations. Sometimes a contaminant in British draught beer.
RHODOTORULA RUBRA formerly *R. MUCILAGINOSA*	—	—	No ferment	Short-oval to elongate 2–5.5 x 2.5–14 μ	Common in milk and cheese, less common in beer. A pink or salmon color in culture. Aerobic.
TORULOPSIS INCONSPICUA	—	●	No ferment	Ovoid 1.5–5.5 x 3–7.5 μ	Some species can give beer a "meady" aroma and a spicy taste. Aerobic. Commonly a contaminant in pitching yeast.

● **Definite and well-defined**   ○ **Indefinite, not well-defined**

Gl=Glucose, Ga=Galactose, Ma=Maltose
S=Sucrose, R=Raffinose

BACTERIA VARIETY	DESCRIPTION & OCCURRENCE	OPTIMAL TEMP	pH	SYMPTOMS & EFFECT
LACTOBACILLUS **Lactic acid bacteria**	Ferments simple sugars into lactic acid. Alcohol-sensitive, so only a problem in early stages. Complex nutritional requirements. Gram positive. Inhibited by 50–60 ppm SO_2.	95° to 112°F 30° to 45°C	4.0 to 5.0	All strains can cause acidity, off-flavors, and turbidity. *L. pastorianus* forms ropey slime. *L. diastaticus* can break down and metabolize starch. Important in certain beer styles—Berliner weisse, lambic, sour brown and old ales.
PEDIOCOCCUS **Lactic acid bacteria**	Very similar to *Lactobacillus*. More common in lager breweries than *Lactobacillus*. A serious problem, difficult to eradicate. *P. damnosis* important in lambic production. Gram positive. Produces lactic acid.	70° to 77°F 25° to 30°C	4.0 to 6.0	All strains cause acidity (lactic and acetic), turbidity, and off-flavors, especially diacetyl. *P. damnosis* creates ropey slime. Goaty "sweat socks" aroma a giveaway. Difficult to eradicate once established.
ACETOMONAS **Acetic acid bacteria**	Oxidizes ethanol to acetic acid. Somewhat alcohol-sensitive, above 6 percent. Forms a tough pellicle on surface. Tolerant of low pH levels of beer. Gram negative.	77° to 86°F 25° to 30°C	3.2 to 4.5	Causes acidity, vinegariness. May produce ropiness with only a small amount of oxygen.
ACETOBACTERIA **Acetic acid bacteria**	Oxidizes ethyl alcohol to acetic acid (vinegar). Aerobic or microaerobic (must have some air). Tolerant of hop resins and low pH. Forms tough pellicle. Most common in draft beers.	86°F 30°C	Low	Causes acidity, turbidity, ropiness. Forms a greasy-looking pellicle on the surface of infected beer. Easily prevented by excluding air—keep carboys full, or flush with CO.
ZYMOMONAS and *PSEUDOMONAS*	Relatively rare. Produces acetaldehyde and hydrogen sulphide from fructose and glucose (not maltose). Anaerobic, inhibited by >6 percent alcohol. Tolerant of hop resins. Gram negative.	86°F 30°C	3.5 to 7.5	Known as "Burton stench," this one's a stinker. Rotten egg odor most common. Also DMS, and other vegetable odors (cabbage, parsnips, etc.). Can spoil beer in a few hours.
OBESUM-BACTERIUM	Grows in competition with active yeast cells. Anaerobic. Metabolizes simple sugars, and grows mostly in first 24 hours. Inhibited by alcohol over 1 percent Commonly found in pitching yeasts. Insensitive to hop resins. Gram negative.	89°F 32°C	4.4 to 6.0	Only one species, *Proteus*. Produces DMS, and the odor of parsnips, celery. Most dangerous in sluggish fermentations. Prevented by getting fermentation going as quickly as possible—wort chiller + starter.
COLIFORM BACTERIA *KLEBSIELLA ESCHERICHIA AEROBACTER CITROBACTER*	Anaerobic. Can multiply a million-fold in 7 hours. Able to metabolize lactose. Uninhibited by hop resins. Inhibited by yeast growth, over 2 percent alcohol, when it stops growing, but may survive for weeks. A problem only in early stage of fermentation. Involved in early stages of lambic fermentations. Inhibited by 60–80 ppm SO_2. Gram negative.	<103° F <40°C	5.0 to 7.5	Wide range of metabolic by-products create a range of strange tastes from these types of infections. May be sweet, fruity, celery-like, or cabbagy aromas. Also may cause acid flavors, ropiness, DMS, and gas production. Fairly uncommon. Easily prevented by getting yeast started as quickly as possible.

The Brewer's Companion

Many different cleaners are available, but chlorine cleaner should be the homebrewer's first line of defense. Caustic is useful, but requires special handling. Observe all precautions listed here and on manufacturers' labels. Get yourself a pair of goggles and long industrial rubber gloves. Be careful.

COMPATIBILITY

- ◆ Good. Useful for cleaning these materials.
- ◇ Not recommended for cleaning purposes. Won't hurt material.
- ✳ Useful, but corrosive. Be cautious, and limit exposure. Don't soak.
- ✖ Do not use. Will corrode or damage these materials.

PRODUCT	TYPE	PRODUCT	PRODUCT (notes)	Qty/Gal	Copper, brass	Glass, enamel	Stainless steel	Polyethylene	Vinyl tubing	Aluminum
CHLORINE Bleach or proprietary sterilizer (sodium hypochlorite)	Sterilizer	Very powerful disinfectant. Use in cold water to sterilize equipment in contact with cooled wort or fermenting beer. Powdered cleaners have good dissolving power.	Never combine with other cleaners, especially ammonia! (Mustard gas!) Rinse well—three clearwater rinses—after sterilizing. Limit exposure to skin.	1.5 oz liquid, 1 oz. dry	✳	◆	✳	◆	◆	✖
CAMPDEN TABLETS Potassium metabisulfate (Active ingr: sulfur dioxide)	Anti-fermentive	Slows growth of bacteria and yeast. Mainly used in winemaking to slow or stop fermentation. Does not actually disinfect.	Some people are violently allergic to this chemical. Not necessary for beer-making, but useful for mead, cider, etc.	1 oz. sodium bisulfite	◇	◇	◇	◇	◇	◇
TRISODIUM PHOSPHATE TSP	Detergent, scale remover	Use to remove dirt and scale on brewing kettle and really dirty equipment. Fairly effective on crusty carboys.	Be sure to rinse thoroughly to remove residual film. Residues harmful to beer. Safest detergent to use on beer gear.	1 oz. (5%)	◆	◆	◆	◆	◆	◆
SODIUM HYDROXIDE Lye	Strong caustic (alkali) cleaner	Powerful alkali. Dissolves most organic material. Only effective when used with very hot water. Best on glass, stainless.	DANGEROUS! Causes skin burns and SEVERE eye damage. Don't mix with other chemicals. Always wear long gloves and goggles when using.	.5 oz. (2%)	✖	◆	◆	◆	✖	✖
SODIUM BICARBONATE Baking soda	Sweetener, deodorizer	Sweetener, deodorizer for plastic tubs and tubing. Apply as paste. Stand. Rinse.	Very safe. Rinse well.	Make paste	◇	◆	◇	◆	◇	◇
PHOSPHORIC ACID Dairy acid rinse	Acid cleaner	Removes beerstone on kettles, etc. Available in form of dairy equipment acid rinse.	DANGEROUS! When diluting, add acid to water, not water to acid.	.5 oz. (2%)	◆	◇	✳	◇	◇	✳
SODIUM CARBONATE Washing soda	Mild cleanser	Gentle cleaning action. Dissolves organic matter, but slowly.	Very safe. Rinse well.	1–2 ozs.	◆	◇	◇	◇	◇	◇
DETERGENTS	Cleaner, degreaser	Use only on really dirty or greasy vessels and utensils.	Very safe. Rinse extremely well. Residue causes head problems.	Dilute well	◇	◆	◇	◇	✖	◇
VODKA, EVERCLEAR Ethyl alcohol + water	Sterilant	Fill fermentation locks with vodka. Use everclear to swab yeast starter flask necks.	Very safe. Harmless to beer in moderate quantities. Cheap vodka works fine.	Full strength	◆	◆	◆	◆	◆	◆

YEAST	DATE	SOURCE	NOTES

YEAST	DATE	SOURCE	NOTES

YEAST	DATE	SOURCE	NOTES

BOTTLING & CONDITIONING

12

BOTTLING PROCEDURE

1. After fermentation has stopped, rack from carboy to pot or plastic vessel. Put 2–4 cups in a saucepan.
2. Add priming sugar or dry malt extract based on the chart below. Heat beer in saucepan. Stir well.
3. Bring to a boil. Keep stirring until thoroughly dissolved.
4. Boil 5 minutes. Turn off heat.
5. Add slowly back to main part of batch. Stir to mix, but be extremely careful not to splash, which causes oxidation and associated off-flavors.
6. Make sure that all chlorine has been rinsed off, then siphon into sterilized bottles.
7. Fill to within 1" of the top, using a bottle, if necessary. Absolutely no more than 1½", no less than 1/2", from top.
8. Cap bottles with sterilized caps.
9. Rinse and dry before putting away in basement to pressurize.
10. Write batch number on caps with permanent marker. Tip: A two-letter abbreviation of beer type helps the beer-addled brain when searching the cellar (e.g., PA = Pale Ale).
11. Store at a constant temperature for two weeks before drinking.

	LOW	MEDIUM LOW	MEDIUM HIGH	VERY HIGH
BEER TYPE	**MOST ENGLISH ALES** Bitter Ale Special Bitter Ale/ESB Mild Ale Porter London/Irish Stout Imperial Stout Scotch Ale—all strengths Mild Ale **STRONG ALES** Old Ale Barley Wine **FRUIT ALES** Cherry Ales, etc.	**ENGLISH ALES** Pale Ale India Pale Ale Brown Ales **BELGIAN ALES** Saison Witbier/White Beer Pale Ales **STRONG LAGERS** Bock Doppelbock	**MOST LAGERS** Pilsner/Pils Munich Light or Dark Dortmunder Märzen/Oktoberfest Canadian California Common Beer **ALES (CHILLED)** Cream Ales Canadian Ales Altbiers **BELGIAN ALES** Abbey Doubles, Triples Sour Browns Strong Pale Ales	**VERY LIGHT LAGERS** American Regular and Light Japanese Australian **GERMAN ALES** Dusseldorfer Alt Kölsch Berliner Weisse Weizen/Weissbier **BELGIAN ALES** Lambics (except fruit)

BOTTLE PRESSURE lb/sq. in.

77°F/25°C   68°F/21°C   59°F/15°C   50°F/10°C   40°F/4°C

OZ/ GAL	0.55	0.	0.65	0.7	0.75	0.8	0.85	0.9	0.95	1.0	1.05	1.1	1.15	1.2	1.25
OZ/ 5 GAL	2.75	3.0	3.25	3.5	3.75	4.0	4.25	4.5	4.75	5.0	5.25	5.5	5.75	6.0	6.25
CUP/ 5 GAL	0.4	0.45	0.5	0.55	0.6	0.65	0.7	0.75	0.80		0.85		0.90		0.95

PRIMING SUGAR QUANTITY—DEXTROSE OR MALT EXTRACT

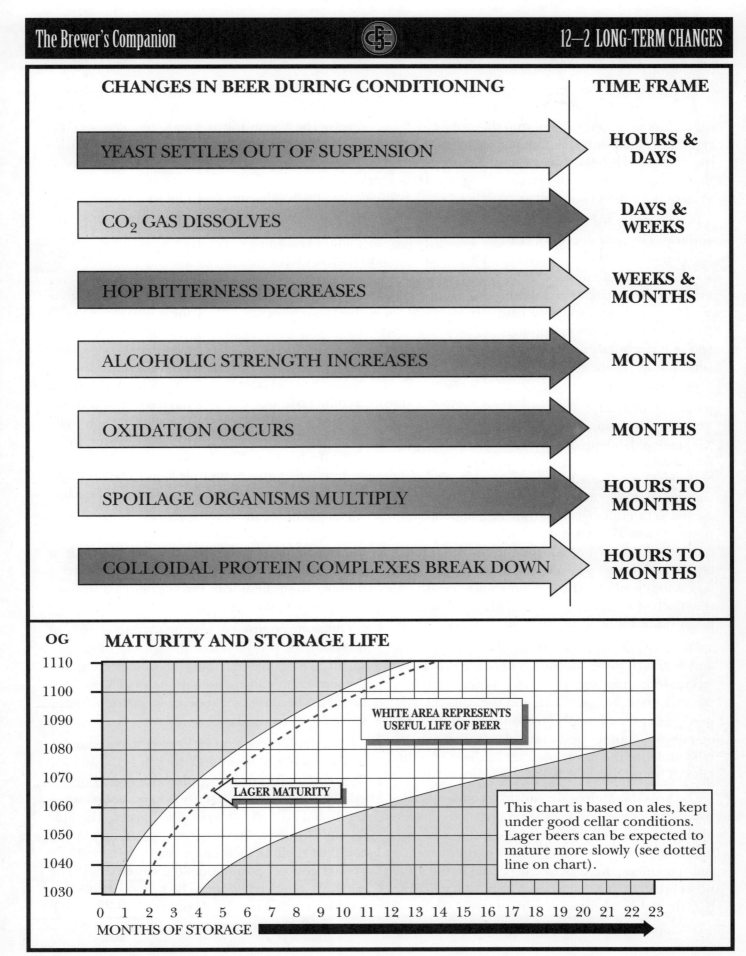

Having beer on draft frees you from the seemingly endless drudgery of bottle-washing. (That's not why you got into this hobby, right?) And not only that, but just like commercial beer, draft homebrew seems smoother and creamier than its bottled counterpart.

Draft systems are easy to set up and use. The only drawback is a high initial investment—up to about $200 if you buy everything new. But these systems are assembled from common soda-fountain parts, which are always popping (no pun intended) up at flea markets and other salvage sources.

The heart of the homebrew system is the five-gallon soda keg. These are tall, straight-sided, stainless steel tanks about 30 inches tall, usually with thick rubber bumpers top and bottom. They are made by various companies—Champion, Cornelius, etc., but they may be viewed as interchangeable from a functional point of view. There are three fittings on top: two quick-disconnects, one for gas and the other for liquid, and a large pop-out hatch that allows access for cleaning. There is a pressure-release on the hatch of some models which blows off at 90 psi or more.

The quick-disconnect fittings allow lines for CO_2 and beer taps to be attached. There are two different, incompatible systems in general use: the pin-lock, used by Coca-Cola, and the ball-lock, used by Pepsi and nearly everyone else. Both work equally well, but it's best to standardize on one kind and save the hassle of never having the right kind of fitting handy.

The kegs themselves are easy to scrounge. Once you start looking, you see them everywhere. Pick up a few tanks, and then build the rest of your system around whatever kind of fittings they have. But remember, there are likely people in the local homebrew club willing to swap kegs, so if you find the "wrong" kind cheap, don't pass 'em by.

If you do get used kegs, it's a good idea to throw

DRAFT HOMEBREW PARTS LIST

MINIMUM SETUP:
- CO_2 gas cylinder: 5- to 20-lb capacity
- Pressure regulator, with shut-off valve
- 5-gallon soda kegs (2 at least)
- Serving tap, with liquid keg-fitting
- Gas line, with gas keg-fitting

ADDITIONAL GOODIES:
- Small CO_2 tank for parties (2.5–5 lbs)
- Manifold for multiple gas lines
- 3-gallon soda kegs
- Additional serving taps
- Liquid transfer line
- Counter-pressure bottle filler
- Heads to fit commercial beer kegs
- Gas-line quick-disconnects
- Jockey box (quick-chill serving cooler)

away all the rubber washers and poppets (spring-loaded doohickies inside the quick-disconnect fittings). These wear out and leak, and also become contaminated with very un-beerlike flavors, such as grape and root beer. Many homebrew shops sell reconditioned kegs to which this has already been done.

The pressure regulator is the device that attaches to the CO_2 cylinder and drops the pressure down from 800 psi to 0–100 psi. It has a screw or a knob that allows you to set the low pressure to whatever level you like. It may be fitted with a manifold that allows multiple kegs to be hooked up simultaneously, with an on-off valve for each.

The gas hoses and serving taps are hooked up to fittings that clip onto the quick-disconnects on the kegs. Make sure you get ones that match. If in doubt, get the manufacturer's name and model number from the side of the keg, and ask whomever you're buying them from.

This same equipment may be used to serve commercial beer, provided that the correct valve or "head" is available to connect to the beer keg. By the way, I don't advise homebrewers to ferment in beer kegs because they require specialized equipment for cleaning.

Gas cylinders come in various sizes, measured by the pounds of liquid CO_2 they hold; 5-, 10-, and 20-pound tanks are all popular with homebrewers. The 20-pounders last the longest between refills, but are a chore to haul to parties. The little 2½- and 5-pound ones are great for parties, but you'll be refilling them more often, usually at greater cost per pound than the larger tanks. The tanks are required by law to be hydrostatically tested every five years, so if you are buying a used one, check the last test date, and figure the $25 (or more) test fee into the price you're willing to pay, if it's due for retesting soon.

Using Draft Systems

In my experience, the best way to use kegs is to put the beer through a normal two-stage fermentation and allow it to drop clear in the secondary. (If you do the secondary in the keg, you'll be pulling up a lot of yeast, as it settles right around the pickup tube for the beer.) Then, transfer the beer into a sanitized soda keg. *Note:* Do not leave chlorine cleaner or bleach sitting in kegs longer than an hour or so, as it can eat through the thin metal sides. After racking, put the lid back on and tighten down the quick-disconnects, making sure you include the poppets and the dip tubes for gas and liquid connections. If you don't want to drink the beer for a couple of weeks (yuk yuk), just put it on the gas, and set the pressure for about 12 psi. At the end of the fortnight, the beer will be perfectly carbonated. For a quicker turnaround, set the pressure higher (25–45 psi) and check it every day. Remember to vent the pressure and turn the regulator down before drawing beer, or you'll be cleaning beer off the ceiling. The quickest method is to jam the pressure up to 90 psi, hook up the gas line, then lay the keg on its side on the floor, and roll it back and forth briskly for 10 minutes. This agitation helps the gas dissolve. The colder the beer, the quicker the gas will dissolve in it. Experiment with pressure settings to find what you like: 8–12 psi is normal. For a "real ale" effect, try the pressure around 3–5 psi, and serve at cellar temperature.

Bottling from Draft Systems

You can bottle beer right from your draft system, making it easier to take beer to parties, enter competitions, and so on. The simplest method is just to fill bottles right from the tap. You lose some pressure, but it works just fine for parties and picnics. You may want to jam a length of hose onto the spout of your tap to minimize splashing and foaming. Getting the beer and the bottle as cold as possible before filling will help, too.

More elaborate fillers are available from homebrew sources. They have gas and liquid connec-

tions, and allow the bottle to be purged with CO_2 before the beer is introduced. This minimizes air, which can cause oxidation. The bottles are filled under pressure, which prevents carbonation loss in the process. Beers filled this way remain stable as long as bottle-conditioned beers.

Serving Draft Homebrew

There's not much to it. The small picnic or "cobra" taps work well, although some prefer the showiness of real beer taps coming out the side of the wall or refrigerator door.

For outdoor events, you may want to look into building or buying a device called a jockey box. This is essentially a heat exchanger for beer. A cooler is fitted with a coil of copper or stainless steel, or an aluminum plate, and loaded with ice. As the room-temperature beer flows through the coils, it is cooled to serving temperature. You can regulate the temperature by how much ice and water you put inside the cooler, thus making it possible to serve beers warmer than ice-cold.

Jockey boxes are very easy to make. The simplest form is a one- or two-gallon picnic cooler with a 10-foot length of 1/4" O.D. copper tube coiled up inside it. The ends of the tube are pushed through holes drilled in the sides or lid of the cooler, and the serving lines are attached to it. The tube can be sealed to the cooler with silicone bathtub caulk. More complex models have multiple lines in one cooler, and use the commercially made aluminum plates, which are expensive, and chill all beer to lip-numbing temperatures.

Real (Homebrewed) Ale

Devotees of real ale can have it their way also. The beer can be naturally carbonated by priming lightly, as for bottled beer. But when the keg is assembled, the gas and liquid dip tubes are switched with each other. (This is impossible on some keg models.) For serving, the keg is laid on its side, liquid fitting toward the bottom. The bottom end of the keg is propped up by a two-inch block of wood, or whatever is handy. A gas fitting with no hose attached is clipped onto the gas side, and a tap is attached to the liquid side. Gravity does the job of dispensing the beer.

YEAR	BREWER	LOCATION

JANUARY

1 2 3 4 5 6 7 8 9 10 11 12 13 14 15 16 17 18 19 20 21 22 23 24 25 26 27 28 29 30 31

FEBRUARY

1 2 3 4 5 6 7 8 9 10 11 12 13 14 15 16 17 18 19 20 21 22 23 24 25 26 27 28

MARCH

1 2 3 4 5 6 7 8 9 10 11 12 13 14 15 16 17 18 19 20 21 22 23 24 25 26 27 28 29 30 31

APRIL

1 2 3 4 5 6 7 8 9 10 11 12 13 14 15 16 17 18 19 20 21 22 23 24 25 26 27 28 29 30

MAY

1 2 3 4 5 6 7 8 9 10 11 12 13 14 15 16 17 18 19 20 21 22 23 24 25 26 27 28 29 30 31

JUNE

1 2 3 4 5 6 7 8 9 10 11 12 13 14 15 16 17 18 19 20 21 22 23 24 25 26 27 28 29 30

JULY

1 2 3 4 5 6 7 8 9 10 11 12 13 14 15 16 17 18 19 20 21 22 23 24 25 26 27 28 29 30 31

AUGUST

1 2 3 4 5 6 7 8 9 10 11 12 13 14 15 16 17 18 19 20 21 22 23 24 25 26 27 28 29 30 31

SEPTEMBER

1 2 3 4 5 6 7 8 9 10 11 12 13 14 15 16 17 18 19 20 21 22 23 24 25 26 27 28 29 30

OCTOBER

1 2 3 4 5 6 7 8 9 10 11 12 13 14 15 16 17 18 19 20 21 22 23 24 25 26 27 28 29 30 31

NOVEMBER

1 2 3 4 5 6 7 8 9 10 11 12 13 14 15 16 17 18 19 20 21 22 23 24 25 26 27 28 29 30

DECEMBER

1 2 3 4 5 6 7 8 9 10 11 12 13 14 15 16 17 18 19 20 21 22 23 24 25 26 27 28 29 30 31

Record your cellar or storage area temperatures every week or so throughout the year. Use different-colored pens to code for different years or locations.

BATCH	CAP CODE	BEER NAME	BEER STYLE	DATE BRWD	DATE BOTTLED

The Brewer's Companion

BATCH	CAP CODE	BEER NAME	BEER STYLE	DATE BRWD	DATE BOTTLED

BEER DESIGN

13

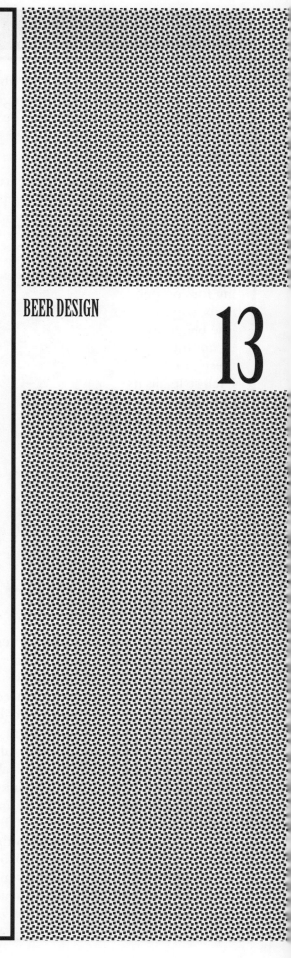

As a homebrewer, you have an almost infinite range of beer styles at your fingertips. Ales, lagers, light, dark, strong, weak. You can make any kind of beer you want.

THE BIG THREE

Gravity, color, bitterness. These are the most important variables in the brewing process. Controlling them is basic beer knowledge. With these three and the proper yeast, you can come very close to any beer style.

If you're brewing for competitions, you can lose big points by not hitting these just right. Each style has its own definite limit for each of these variables.

Gravity

Gravity is the amount of fermentables in the wort when fermentation begins. The more material dissolved, the higher the grav-

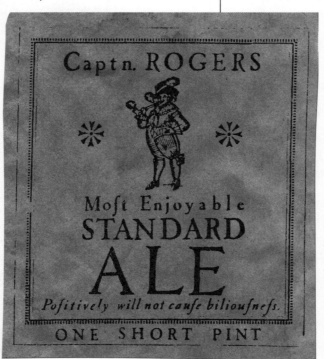

ity. Higher-gravity worts make higher-alcohol beers. A strong beer will take longer to ferment and condition, often considerably so. *Note:* When manipulating original gravity figures, ignore the "1" at the left, or you'll have a horrible mess of a number. As an example, pale ale malt yields 10075 gravity per pound per five gallons. If you start with six pounds, the theoretical yield is 1045 (75 x 6 = 450). But since you usually end up with about 80 percent, you'll end up with a gravity more like 1036 (450 x 80% = 360). In practice, it is more useful to calculate from the other direction. To reach a gravity of 1045, six pounds are theoretically required, but given the inefficiency of the brewing process, you actually require 1.25 times this number, or 7.5, figured at

an efficiency of 80 percent (80% x 1.25 = 100%). Yields of various malts and grains can be found in **Section 6–2, Grain Reference**, and the **Quick Reference Charts 5–2** and **5–3** can even eliminate some of the calculator work.

After brewing a few batches, you'll know where you stand on efficiency, but most homebrewers get between 75 and 85 percent of the laboratory maximum Hot Water Extract (HWE).

Doctor Bob Technical's Amazing Wheel of Beer is a circular slide rule with three discs, specially set up to deal directly in pounds of grain, gallons of wort, and various types of malts and extracts. It is also set up to give you gravity predictions at various mash efficiencies.

Color

Color is due to melanoidins formed in the malt during roasting, plus additional coloration from further browning during boiling of the mash and wort (see **Section 3–1, Beer Color & Gravity**.)

Calculating beer color is either impossibly difficult (the experts say impossible) or not terribly accurate. I, for one, opt for the easy yet inexact method—Homebrew Color Units. It works in a similar way that Homebrew Bittering Units do with hops. Grain color in °Lovibond is multiplied by pounds for each grain in the batch. These are added up and the total is divided by the total number of gallons of wort produced. This number does not add up in a linear fashion, so the resulting number must be translated to SRM numbers; see the scales at the bottom of **Section 3–1, Beer Color & Gravity** for this.

There is a considerable amount of controversy about the use of predictive methods for beer color, and there are a number of methods for getting there. And while it is true that beer color is impossible to predict exactly, it is possible to predict it in an inaccurate, but still useful way. I've brewed more than 50 batches using this method, and have found it to be predictable enough to get into the appropriate range for any given beer style.

Bitterness

Bitterness comes from isomerized hop resins that are dissolved during the boil. Commercial breweries measure bitterness directly, as parts-per-million of hop iso-alpha acids. The formulas used in this book to estimate IBUs approximate these units.

Bitterness is played against maltiness. Balance in beer is the interplay between these two characteristics. When determining bittering levels, take into account the strength of the beer. Refer to **Section 3–2, Hop Rate *vs.* Gravity** to see how beers compare.

To calculate hop bitterness, add up the alpha acid times the ounces for each hop addition in your beer (1 hour, 30 minutes, 15 minutes, etc.). Look up the HBU to IBU factor on the **Hop Utilization charts 8–4** and **8–5.** Multiply these numbers by the appropriate factor for each hop addition, then total them up. This is an approximation of IBUs, ppm of dissolved iso-alpha acids in the finished beer.

National Style

On top of the basic parameters of color, gravity, and bitterness is an overlay of national style. This is a whole group of things, including materials and techniques. Without this traditional framework, a mild ale would be much the same as a Munich dark. It is the fermentation method, ingredients, and mash techniques that really determine an individual beer style. All parts of the process work together. The lightly modified malt used for lager brewing really benefits from a decoction mash. The highly modified and mellow malt used for British ales is perfectly suited to infusion mashing. American six-row malt is strong stuff and really needs to be diluted with adjuncts, such as corn or rice. They, in turn, create a need for certain mashing techniques.

As much as possible, keep your malt selection appropriate for the type of beer you are brewing. Use pale ale for English ale styles and lager malts for lager beers. These malts are carefully processed to work best with a particular brewing style. You can certainly use them any way you like, but the results will be less authentic.

Hop character is a really important part of beer style. Hops fall into a few large categories. English hops, the classic Fuggles and Goldings combo, are essential to a true English-tasting ale. German hop types, exemplified by Hallertau, lend a Continental touch to any lager. Saaz is for pilsners and certain Belgian ales. In my book, Cascade is the true American hop, although American beers tend to go the Euro-route in hop flavor. Everything else is somewhere between these extremes, except high-alpha hops, which are on a weird plane of their own.

Hints for Recipe Formulation

• Using a range of roasted malts in a beer rather than just one type will give the beer a richer, more complex flavor. The chemical compounds responsible for roasted flavor and color  are created in a wide range of varieties according to time and temperature of roasting, as well as the materials being roasted. A wide selection of roasted grains equals a wide variety of flavor chemicals, giving the beer a better flavor. Typically, a recipe will include small amounts of the most darkly roasted types, and larger amounts of more lightly roasted grain types. In fact, recipes seem to be most successful when a good portion of the color is derived from a malt that is not the darkest one in the brew. For example, rather than using lager malt with a little chocolate malt to make a München, a better plan would be to use a large amount of Munich malt, perhaps half the batch or more. Then add some brown or copper-colored malt. A dash of chocolate malt serves as a roasty accent. Such a recipe will be bursting with rich malty flavors, far more complex than the simpler recipe.

• Even the palest beers are improved by the addition of a small amount of lightly colored malt, such as Vienna or Munich.

• Even the darkest beers benefit by the addition of 10 to 20 percent of a lightly roasted malt, such as Münich or amber.

• When formulating recipes, start with the medium-colored malts. Then add enough dark malts to reach the color level you like. Lastly, add pale malt to make it up to desired gravity.

• I highly recommend roasting malt in an oven to obtain malt types not available commercially. Roasting at home will give you a truly striking malty-toasty-roasty flavor complement. Let them mellow a couple of weeks before brewing with them (see **Sections 6–4** and **6–5**). The aromatic components of roasted malt are highly volatile and so dissipate in a short time.

LE GRAND BUFFOON

SAISON
S P E C I A L E

*"UN BLONDE
VACANT"*

GRAVITIE ORIGINALE — 1 0 8 0
TOTALMENT MALT PUR

Produit de Brasserie Maison SpangMo

• When using ingredients other than barley malt—corn, rice, wheat malt—use some six-row malt for its high protein content and for the filtering action of its plentiful husks.

• Stronger beers require higher hop rates for three reasons: to balance against more intense maltiness; to allow both hop bitterness and aroma to diminish over time, as these beers will be stored for a longer time; and finally, strong worts do not absorb hop resins to the extent that weaker ones do. With very strong worts this effect is dramatic (see **Sections 8–4** and **8–5**).

• Freshness and proper storage of hops have a great influence on their flavor. It's probably better to use fresh hops of the wrong variety than stale hops of the correct variety—especially when using aroma hops.

• Split batches can be a way to add variety to your brewing—make one high-gravity brew and dilute it to make two different batches. These can be fermented with different types of yeast, have different dry-hopping fruit added, or other variations (see **Section 13–2, Parti-Gyle Brewing**).

• A half-mash, half-extract beer is especially useful for large parties. A five-gallon boiling capacity can be used to make 15 gallons of beer. Brew a strong high-dextrin beer around 1080 gravity. Add a couple of cans of extract to the boil to bring the gravity up even farther. Hop at one-and-one-half times the normal rate. Add this syrupy wort to fermenters and top up with sterile water to make 5½ gallons each, or more if fewer batches are being made. Dilute at different rates for different gravities, if desired.

NOTES ON BEER STYLES AND RECIPE FORMULATION

This purpose of this book is to give you the tools to come up with recipes that make great beers, no matter what styles you brew. The point is for you to create your own recipes, suited to *your* brewery and *your* taste. That said, there are tidbits that may give you extra insight into particular styles. There are about a hundred ways to brew a stout, but only one Guinness. Traditional approaches are useful for authenticity as well as a starting point for your brews. So, in the same order that they are listed in **Sections 2–2 to 2–5, Beer Styles** (which you should check for vital stats), here are my tips and tidbits:

Bitter—Tricky beers to brew. High-quality pale malt is a must, as with all British pale ales. Many commercial brands use up to 15 percent sugar, but the best ones don't. Serving at very low carbonation levels is essential for authentic taste and texture. Crystal malts add complexity. Some small amount of oddball sugar or molasses may do the same. Using 5 percent wheat as an aid to head retention is not unheard of. Hop flavor is important, and bitters are often quite bitter, with Goldings being the variety of choice. Dry-hopping is recommended. Nonalkaline water is extremely important for pale hoppy beers.

Pale Ale—Ditto, but with more gusto. Hop character is often more pronounced in stronger bottled ones.

India Pale Ale—For some reason IPAs seem to be paler than equal gravity pale ales. Dry-hopped character is essential for this style. Please don't make the mistake of adding oak chips in an effort to create an authentic IPA. It simply is not the right effect.

Mild Ale—Very low-gravity beer, but rich and round, nonetheless. Malt of choice is mild ale malt, slightly darker than pale ale, more like Munich, which is a good substitute. Crystal malt adds richness. Smoothest dark flavor comes from black patent rather than chocolate. Toasted amber malt adds a nice toasty edge to this style. Fuggles is the hop of choice, but it should be very much in the background. Moderate to high carbonate water is OK for this style.

Brown Ale—Same as above. Higher gravity allows true voluptuousness. Complex malt profile is important, and amber malt is essential for the proper "brown" character. Hops are still secondary to malt. Traditionally, lightly attenuated.

Scotch Ales—Generally darker and sweeter than their English pale ale counterparts. Also fermented at lower temperatures for smoother, maltier taste and less fruitiness. Very dark crystal malt seems to be a touchstone for these beers, which have a toffeelike malt character. Hop character is secondary or just breaking even.

Porter—Which century? Vastly different approaches over time make this elusive, but fun.

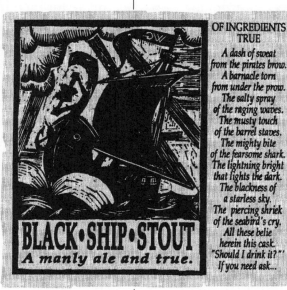

OF INGREDIENTS TRUE

*A dash of sweat
from the pirates brow.
A barnacle torn
from under the prow.
The salty spray
of the raging waves.
The musty touch
of the barrel staves.
The mighty bite
of the fearsome shark.
The lightning bright
that lights the dark.
The blackness of
a starless sky.
The piercing shriek
of the seabird's cry.
All these belie
herein this cask.
"Should I drink it?"'
If you need ask...*

BLACK·SHIP·STOUT
A manly ale and true.

In the beginning, recipes based on brown and amber malts were used. After 1820, black "patent" malt became popular and eventually replaced the less efficient brown and amber malts. Strength varied widely—1080 down to 1055—during its heyday. Porter and stout were one and the same until less than 100 years ago. If you have one of each in front of you, the stronger, darker one is the stout. Otherwise, you can't tell. In the current American porter revival, anything goes. Anchor's version has a ton of crystal in it; many others are quite burly. Hops balance is all over the lot, but aroma is usually not a big thing. Fuggles are traditional. Wheat or oats add a nice touch. Smoked grains work wonderfully well in porter, adding tremendous complexity. High-carbonate brewing water works fine for all dark beers.

Sweet Stout—Black patent malt is the signature for this style. Sweetness can be achieved by limited attenuation or by adding lactose (milk sugar). Crystal malt also does the trick in sufficient quantities—10–20 percent. Hopping very light, aroma unimportant.

Irish Stout—Velvety smoothness with a crisp roast barley bite defines this style. A pound of roast barley per five gallons is the usual amount. Gravity varies a little. Sweetness should be low. Very low carbonation important for true Guinness character. Sometimes made with the addition of soured beer for a slight acidic bite, especially in the stronger bottled versions. Hops are important for bitterness and little else.

Tropical Stout—We're talking extra-extra Guinness here. All of the above applies. Acidic character, originally derived from oak-barrel aging, is even more prominent.

Other Stouts—Oatmeal is quite popular, and lends a softness like nothing else. Oat aroma will be much more wonderful if the oats are toasted before brewing. Oatmeal preferred, steel-cut OK, too. Other forms may need precooking before use.

The narrow definitions of traditional stouts are cast aside on the U.S. micro scene, with some very big and characterful beers being brewed. Dry-hopping is sometimes used. Anything goes, really.

Old Ale/Strong Ale/Winter Warmers—Alas, these beers have also gradually diminished over the years. Old ale should be a barrel-aged product, acquiring a similar (but less intense) acidic character to the sour brown ales of Belgium, to whom they are cousins. The only British ale I know of with this acidity is Gale's Prize Old Ale, although they must have all been like this before stainless steel was invented. Strong ales or winter warmers are of-ten not all that strong, but do have a very rich taste. Color is usually sort of a mahogany, with a light tan head. Amber malt is very useful in imparting a toasty character. Some mild or Munich malt is also advisable. Hops rarely get above an even balance with the malt sweetness and toastiness.

Barley Wine—Essentially a very high-gravity pale ale. High-quality pale malt essential. Some crystal and amber useful. Alcohol-tolerant yeast strain needed to attenuate well, and prevent off-flavors like diacetyl. Must be highly hopped as age wears away the hop bite. Best to let it age a year or more before drinking, if your friends will let you. Divine at five years old. Brew some for your kids and wait for them to grow up.

Russian Imperial Stout—As much inky stuff as you can cram into a bottle. Ridiculously high hopping levels crucial for many reasons. Almost impossible to overhop. Long aging is crucial.

Czech Pilsner—Very complicated to make if you want to be authentic. The finest, palest malt should be used. Soft water is important to prevent high hop rate from creating a harsh astrin-gent aftertaste. Decoction mash and a long boil create caramelly richness. Saaz hops only should be used, liberally, especially toward the end of the boil. As with all lagers, accurate temperature control during fermentation is a must.

German Pils—Paler, drier, and more one-dimensional than their Czech cousins. Very bitter and refreshing. Saaz hops still recommended, but others, like Hallertau, are OK. Water chemistry is important. Nonalkaline water prevents harsh hop aftertaste and reddish color.

Dortmunder/Export—Hops-to-malt balance is in between pils and Munich helles, and suggestions for these beers apply. This beer is higher gravity than other mainstream pale lagers.

Munich Helles/Light—Malt-accentuated balance is the cornerstone of this beer. Using a good, malt-accentuating yeast at proper temperatures will assist. Also, European malts seem to have a richer taste than the Klages and other U.S. malts. A little Vienna or pale Munich malt will add sweetness and aroma. Cara-Pils malt is sometimes used, but there are better ways to achieve that kind of thickness. Tradition-ally, it is not very attenuated. Decoction mash also contributes to sweet malt profile. Hopping should be light, just enough to balance the malt.

Munich Dunkel—Malt, malt, malt! The use of a large proportion of Munich malt seems critical to this style: 25–75 percent. But be aware that Due to high kilning temperatures, Munich malt is deficient in beta glucanase. Give the mash a rest at 90°F/32°C to help get rid of these gummy nasties. Color should be just barely brown, not too deep. Flavor should be rich and toasty, never sharp or roasted. Avoid chocolate malt especial-ly. Black patent may be used in small quantities, if needed. Malt-accentuating yeast strain is rec-ommended, and low fermentation temperatures are needed to allow malt to express itself fully. Dark lagers are fermented a little warmer than their pale cousins. Decoction mash and a long boil will add to the caramelly effect. Hops are present only to prevent the beer from being too cloying. Hop aroma is undesirable.

Vienna, Märzen, Oktoberfest—These beers all started out the same, but eventually drifted slightly apart. Of the three, the Vienna is slightly weaker; the others are interchangeable. All share a beautiful amber color, rich malt character, and an even hop balance. Large proportion of Munich and/or Vienna malt is indispensable; use 100 percent Vienna, if you like. Coloring a pale lager with a little black or chocolate malt will not cut it. Decoction mashes are helpful in bringing out malt richness. Low fermentation temperatures and lager yeast must be used, but fermented a little warmer than pale lagers. German hops are essential.

Kulmbacher—These are black lagers, nearly as dark as porter sometimes. Similar recipes to Munich dunkel, but stronger and darker. Black patent should be used to create dark color and roasty edge. Hops can be more prominent than Munich beers.

Maibock/Pale Bock—Think of these as simply stronger versions of Munich helles or Dortmunders. Hop balance ranges from medium-malty to medium-hoppy. German hops are crucial, and hop aroma is OK.

Dark Bock—Strong, dark lager. Very much like strong version of Munich dunkel. Large quantity of Munich malt important for correct flavor. Hopping can be higher than Munich dunkel.

Doppelbock—Very high-gravity lagers. Color is deep gold to medium amber. Some Munich or Vienna malt will add richness. Alcohol-tolerant yeast strain is essential. Higher fermentation temperatures are used than for pale light lagers. Balance is generally quite malty.

Gesundheit

Altbäperische Weitzenbock

Ein gut Bier. Ein strong Bier. Maken fur you in mein Hausbräuerei mit qualitäts-ingredientsch. You will drink dies Bier. You will liken dies Bier. You will all fast becomen Gedrunken. Prosit!

Brauerei Spangma.r Fein Bier since 1984

Düsseldorfer Alt—Mahogany-colored German ale. Highly attenuated, crisp and dry. Color comes from small amount of black patent malt. Low mash temperatures should be used to produce a highly fermentable wort. Should be moderate to extremely bitter. After high-temperature primary fermentation, cold-conditioning should be used.

Kölsch—Pale German ale. Dry, crisp, refreshing. Delicate beers brewed with 10 percent wheat. Just a touch of acidity. Hop balance ranges around the middle. Fermented warm, then lagered cold. Similar to American cream ales.

Weizen/Wheat Beer—Bavarian wheat beers, fermented with unique ale yeast strains that lend a clove-y character to the beer. The 40–75 percent wheat makes sparging difficult. Some six-row malt is advisable, along with a dash of pale crystal. Absolutely necessary to use weizen yeast to get authentic German taste. U.S. West Coast wheat beers use ordinary ale yeast and lack the clove character. Hops used for balance, rarely detectable except a little bitterness.

Dunkel Weizen—Same as above, but with the addition of some crystal malt to create an amber color, rarely brown.

Weizenbock—Strong version of dunkel weizen. Color may be much deeper, into the brown range. Hopping rates may also be higher. Same clove character as other weizens.

Berliner Weisse—Very different than Bavarian weizens, these are extremely pale low-gravity beers. Fermented with ale yeast and *Lactobacillus*, which imparts a sharp acidity. Hard for the homebrewer to manage and to keep other beers free of the *Lactobacillus* contamination.

Abbey Double (Dubbel)—Generally, light-brown ales from Belgium and the Netherlands. Unique yeast strains produce characteristic spicy flavor. Sometimes medium-brown. Only moderately hoppy—Northern Brewer, Hallertau hops often used. Sugar, sometimes caramelized, may be used in small (10 percent) quantities. Corked bottles are traditional, and this does add a unique quality to all the abbey beers. Culturing yeast from fresh bottles often gives good results.

Abbey Special—Usually the middle beer in an abbey's range of products. Typically amber color, but this varies. Should be well-aged in the bottle. Alcohol-tolerant strains important to use.

Abbey Triple (Trippel)—Top beer in the range, and usually the palest, ranging from medium gold to pale amber. Alcohol-tolerant yeast strains are essential. Candy sugar—crystallized, partially refined beet sugar—is often used to thin down the otherwise syrupy taste of these massive beers. Look for these in Middle Eastern markets.

Amber Ale (Palm)—A rich, lightly hopped pale-amber ale. Similar to Märzen, but top-fermented.

Strong Pale Ale— Similar in concept to abbey triple. Extremely pale for its strength, it's made entirely from very lightly kilned pilsner malt. Saaz and Styrian Goldings hops are used. Abbey yeast can be used.

Brabant White/ Witte/Witbier— Uniquely seasoned beers made from malt (40 percent), unmalted wheat (50 percent), and oats (10 percent). They have an opalescent starch haze which gives them their name. This haze may be created by adding a handful of flour to the boil. Flavored with coriander seed and orange Curaçao (orange peel). Limited *Lactobacillus* fermentation gives this beer a little snap. Possibly done as a side fermentation, and pasteurized before adding to the main batch.

Strong White Beer—Higher-gravity versions of the above, usually darker. Some versions made with 100 percent malt. Spicing can be more complex than the lighter versions.

Saisons/Sezoens—Summer ales from the French part of Belgium. Gold to pale amber color, they are traditionally only lightly attenuated. Crystal malt is useful, as is Vienna or Munich. Authentic versions have a slight acidic tang, perhaps from wooden barrel aging. Hop rate relatively high, with Hallertau, Northern Brewer, and Styrian Goldings all being used.

Saisons Speciale—Same as above, but stronger. Higher-gravity beers need longer aging to mature, perhaps a year or more. Corked bottles are traditional.

Lambic Styles—These are ancient and maybe even bizarre beers created in and around Brussels. Fermented with a menagerie of wild and exotic microbes, nearly impossible to duplicate at home. Cross-contamination to your other beers can also be a problem. "Serial-killer yeast" approach from pure cultures sometimes produces passable imitations, but best results seem to be had from inoculated barrels, as wood provides a better home for the bugs than test tubes. Worts are 30–40 percent wheat, the balance malt. Long (three-hour) boil. Hops are purposely staled to diminish flavor, and are used for preservative value only. Patience is a must, as these beers require three summers to mature; the wait is even longer for fruit versions.

Trappist (Orval)—Idiosyncratic beer from a Belgium abbey. Pale gold color. Dry-hopped with Hallertau and Styrian Goldings. Unique yeast mixture creates unmistakable flavor. Some success has been had culturing yeast from a bottle.

American Lager—Adjunct-laden lagers. Rice offers cleaner taste than corn. Very lightly hopped, German varieties, such as Hallertau, are

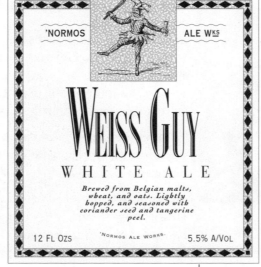

'NORMOS   ALE WKS

WEISS GUY
WHITE ALE

Brewed from Belgian malts, wheat, and oats. Lightly hopped, and seasoned with coriander seed and tangerine peel.

12 FL OZS   'NORMOS ALE WORKS·   5.5% A/VOL

best. Highly carbonated. Proper lager fermentation temperatures is a must.

American Light Lager—Same as above, but lower-gravity and more fully attenuated. Long, low-temperature mash should be used to create fermentable wort.

Cream Ale—Light, refreshing ale. Sometimes fermented with lager yeast at higher temperatures. Higher hopping rate than U.S. lagers. Hop aroma important. Very similar to Kölsch.

California Common—Fermented with lager yeast at ale temperatures. Open fermenters and deep gold color traditional. Fairly highly hopped, typically with Northern Brewer.

American Pale Ale—Revival style emerging from the micro scene. Characterized by full malt taste and generally high hop rate. Hop character often very individualistic. Cascades are widely used and dry-hopping is common. High-alpha hops used sometimes for dry-hopping, with varieties like Chinook imparting a citric/grapefruit nose. Color varies from pale gold to deep amber. Ales from Seattle are generally malty; those from California are generally hoppy, but exceptions abound.

Kentucky Common Beer—Brown, top-fermented beer once popular on the Ohio River. Sharp lactic tang, similar to Berliner weisse, but less sour.

ODDBALL BEERS

Wheat Porter—50 percent (or so) wheat gives this style incredible softness and smoothness, even at very high gravities.

Smoked Imperial Stout—Immense richness gives a good place for the smokiness to hide. Hard to overdo the smokiness (but watch out for oak), which shows up mainly in the finish. Actually, smoke is good in all black beer.

Christmas Ale—There are innumerable variations on these spiced brown ales. Common

spices are nutmeg, coriander, cinnamon (takes a lot), ginger (sharp flavor takes over easily), cardamom (very distinctive astringent taste), orange peel, cloves, allspice.

Gruit Beer—Authentic herbed ale from pre-hop Europe. Yarrow, wild rosemary, and bog myrtle are the three main herbs. Plus other stuff.

Honey Beer—Honey imparts subtle spiciness and a crisp character. Sounds more exotic than it is. Honey lightens the body.

Triple and Quadruple Bock— Yes, it's true. What could I add, except to remind you that you need a very alcohol-tolerant yeast.

Basil Beer—Delicate herbal taste that blends nicely with honey, woodruff, heather, and other green herbs.

Chocolate Porter or Stout—May be made with chocolate, cocoa, or creme de cacao liqueur. The chocolate taste does come through. Creme de cacao very good in Christmas ales, too, along with orange peel and coriander seed.

Gonzo—Ultra-high-gravity version of Belgian witte, spiced with orange peel, coriander, and other stuff, sometimes a little chocolate, too.

Swankey—An authentic historical style from Pennsylvania, a brown, low-gravity ale flavored with aniseed.

Pumpkin Ale—Easily accomplished by mashing in two to four cans of pumpkin along with the grist. Pumpkin pie spice defines the style.

Cherry Stout—Sharpness of the fruit works nicely with the roasted grain.

Potato Beer—If it has starch, you can make beer from it. Precook the spuds and add them to the mash. Strange Irish-famine novelty.

Oatmeal Cream Ale—Oats add a soft, round character and a tremendous head to this otherwise unremarkable beer style. Be sure to use plenty of aroma hops. The oat flavor is improved greatly by lightly toasting before using.

Apple Beer—Apple juice does incredible things to the head (of the beer). I recommend adding two gallons of apple juice to three gallons of water + extract, but you could use more.

Maple Syrup Beer—Those who know say the best stuff is made with straight unboiled sap, which is used as a base for regular beer ingredients. Maple stout is especially tasty!

Adulterated Stout—Sort of a pirate ale, usually made with some molasses, incautiously spiced with things like black pepper, ginger, hot pepper, bay leaves, nutmeg, rum, raisins, and other stuff. Most notorious ingredient is "grains of paradise,"

'NORMOS ALE WORKS INC., CHICAGO, IL
CONTINUING THE NEARLY 400 YEAR-OLD
MAKERS OF FINE ALES, PORTERS &T.C.

NIRVANA

A STRONG ALE MADE FROM PALE AND CARAMEL MALTS. SEASONED WITH CHANTRELLE MUSHROOMS.

"Setting Brewing Back at Least 100 Years"

TRADITION OF ALE BREWING IN AMERICA

a peppery West African cardamom relative with pinelike aroma and hot white pepper flavor; aka guinea pepper, alligator pepper.

Chanterelle Ale—Delicately flavored chanterelle mushrooms give this strong, simple pale ale a transcendent perfumy taste that reminds one of apricots as much as anything else. Soak a pound of chopped chanterelle mushrooms in a fifth of vodka for two weeks, then add to beer at bottling. Hedgehog mushrooms would be nice, too.

Pepper Beer—Various types of hot and mild peppers can be used to give these beers a tickle or a full-fledged kick. The longer you leave the peppers in the beer, the hotter it gets. Pale ales work nicely as a base. Oddly, smoked malts work well in pepper beers, smoothing out the prickliness of the pepper, and giving the beer some balance.

Whiskey Stout—Mad homebrewers have been known to pool several batches into one 50-gallon bourbon barrel for fermentation. Black lightning!

It so often happens that we find out that the old traditional methods turn out to be surprisingly sophisticated and practical.

A technique that has fallen into almost complete disuse in the world of commercial brewing is parti-gyle brewing. This is the practice of drawing off the first part of the mash and using it to make strong ale or barley wine, then remashing the grain, and drawing off the second runnings for a more ordinary brew. The third runnings were then used to brew an exceptionally weak and watery concoction called small beer, the light beer of its day.

When brewing changed from a craft to an industry in 18th century England, a new method of brewing, called entire, was developed. In this system, all the runoff was collected and boiled together to create a single large batch of consistent gravity. Porter was the first beer to be brewed this way. This is the method most homebrewers use, especially in five-gallon batches.

With somewhat larger batches it is possible to get more than one batch per brew, and to structure the strength of the two or three parts any way you like.

The technique is simple. The first runnings are drawn off the mash as usual, but instead of being all mixed up with later runnings, this first wort is boiled separately. The sparging process continues as normal until the desired amount of wort is collected. If needed, some of the first wort may be traded for the lighter wort, and thus it is possible to get whatever strengths you like in both parts.

In homebrewing practice it is generally best to do two runnings rather than three. You have the option of splitting the batch in one of two ways: 1/2–1/2 split, and a 1/3–2/3 split. The rule is the first third of the wort contains half the extract. This means that with a 1/3–2/3 split, the first runnings will be exactly twice as strong as the second. With a 1/2–1/2 split things are a little different, and the ratios are not nearly so tidy (see the chart on the right for details). Either way, you can get a strong beer and a normal-strength one every time you brew.

It is best to work in multiples of five gallons, as that is the most common fermenter size. Ten-gallon batch size is better suited to a 1/2–1/2 split, and 15 gallons are better suited to 1/3–2/3 split.

Naturally this makes calculation of the recipe a

TOTAL BATCH	1/3 • 2/3 SPLIT		1/2 • 1/2 SPLIT	
	1/3	2/3	1/2–#1	1/2–#2
10500	10750	10375	10666	10333
10510	10765	10383	10680	10340
10520	10780	10390	10693	10347
10530	10795	10398	10707	10353
10540	10810	10400	10720	10360
10550	10825	10413	10733	10367
10560	10840	10420	10747	10373
10570	10855	10428	10760	10380
10580	10870	10435	10773	10387
10590	10885	10443	10787	10393
10600	10900	10450	10800	10400
10610	10915	10458	10813	10407
10620	10930	10465	10827	10413
10630	10945	10473	10840	10420
10640	10960	10480	10853	10427
10650	10975	10488	10867	10433
10660	10990	10495	10880	10440
10670	11050	10503	10894	10447
10680	11020	10510	10907	10453
10690	11035	10518	10920	10460
10700	11050	10525	10933	10467
10710	11065	10533	10947	10473
10720	11080	10540	10960	10480
10730	11095	10548	10973	10487
10740	11110	10555	10987	10493
10750	11125	10563	11000	10500
10760	11140	10570	11013	10507
10770	11155	10578	11127	10513
10780	11170	10585	11040	10520
10790	11185	10593	11053	10527
10800	11200	10600	11067	10533
10810	11215	10608	11080	10540
10820	11230	10615	11093	10547
10830	11245	10623	11107	10553
10840	11260	10630	11120	10560
10850	11275	10638	11133	10567
10860	11290	10645	11147	10573
10870	11305	10653	11160	10580
10880	11320	10660	11173	10587
10890	11335	10668	11187	10593
10900	11350	10675	11120	10600
10910	11365	10683	11213	10607
10920	11380	10690	11227	10613
10930	11395	10698	11240	10620
10940	11410	10705	11253	10627
10950	11425	10713	11267	10633

PARTI-GYLE ESTIMATION–°P

TOTAL BATCH	1/3 • 2/3 SPLIT		1/2 • 1/2 SPLIT	
	1/3	2/3	1/2–#1	1/2–#2
12	18	9.0	16.9	7.1
12.2	18.3	9.2	17.2	7.2
12.4	18.6	9.3	17.5	7.3
12.6	18.9	9.4	17.8	7.4
12.8	19.2	9.6	18.0	7.6
13	19.5	9.7	18.3	7.7
13.2	19.8	9.9	18.6	7.8
13.4	20.1	10.1	18.9	7.9
13.6	20.4	10.2	19.2	8.0
13.8	20.7	10.3	19.5	8.1
14	21	10.5	19.7	8.3
14.2	21.3	10.6	20.0	8.4
14.4	21.6	10.8	20.3	8.5
14.6	21.9	10.9	20.6	8.6
14.8	22.2	11.1	20.9	8.7
15	22.5	11.2	21.1	8.8
15.2	22.8	11.4	21.4	9.0
15.4	23.1	11.5	21.7	9.1
15.6	23.4	11.7	22.0	9.2
15.8	23.7	11.8	22.3	9.3
16	24	12.0	22.6	9.4
16.2	24.3	12.1	22.8	9.6
16.4	24.6	12.3	23.1	9.7
16.6	24.9	12.4	23.4	9.8
16.8	25.2	12.6	23.7	9.9
17	25.5	12.8	24.0	10.0
17.2	25.8	12.9	24.3	10.1
17.4	26.1	13.1	24.5	10.3
17.6	26.4	13.2	24.8	10.5
17.8	26.7	13.4	25.1	10.6
18	27	13.5	25.4	10.7
18.2	27.3	13.7	25.7	10.9
18.4	27.6	13.8	25.9	11.0
18.6	27.9	14.0	26.2	11.1
18.8	28.2	14.1	26.5	11.2
19	28.5	14.3	26.8	11.3

little more difficult than with entire brews. The whole batch is made up to a certain gravity, shown in the left-hand column. The resulting fractions can be read in the columns to the right.

If you wish to mix runnings to achieve a certain gravity, you will need to use the concept of degree-gallons. This is simply the wort gravity, in Plato or OG, multiplied by the number of gallons. Thus, 5 gallons x (1)090 = 450 degree-gallons. The second two-thirds contains the same amount of extract, 10 gallons x (1)045 = 450 degree-gallons. To do a swap between these beers, let's take

2 gallons of wort from the first runnings and add them to the second runnings: 2 x 90 = 180 degree-gallons. Replace this with 2 gallons of second runnings: 2 x 45 = 90, added to the 270 = 360. Divide this by the number of gallons and you get (1)072 OG for the first runnings. The second batch, with the addition of 2 gallons of 1090 wort, or 180 degree-gallons +360 = 540. Divide by 10 = (1)054 OG.

Estimate color with the chart below. Find batch color, then look up individual brew color on the table below.

PARTI-GYLE COLOR ESTIMATION

TOTAL BATCH	1/3 • 2/3 SPLIT		1/2 • 1/2 SPLIT	
	1/3	2/3	1/2–#1	1/2–#2
3	4.5	2.3	4.2	1.7
4	6	3	5.6	2.4
5	7.5	3.8	7	2.9
6	9	4.5	8.5	3.5
7	10.5	5.3	9.9	4.1
8	12	6	11.3	4.7
9	13.5	6.8	12.7	5.3
10	15	7.5	14.1	5.9
11	16.5	8.3	15.5	6.5
12	18	9	16.9	7.1
14	21	10.5	19.7	8.2
16	24	12	22.6	9.4
18	27	13.5	25.4	10.6
20	30	15	28.2	11.8
22	33	16.5	31	12.9
24	36	18	33.8	14.1
26	49	19.5	36.7	15.3
28	42	21	39.5	16.5
30	45	22.5	42.3	17.6
35	52.5	26.3	49.4	20.6
40	60	30	56.4	23.5
45	67.5	33.8	63.5	26.5
50	75	37.5	70.5	29.4
55	82.5	41.3	77.6	32.3
60	90	45	84.6	35.3
65	97.5	48.8	91.7	38.2
70	105	52.5	98.7	41.2
75	112.5	56.3	105.8	44.1
80	120	60	112.8	47
85	127.5	63.8	119.9	50
90	135	67.5	126.9	52.9
95	142.5	71.3	134	55.9
100	150	75	141	59
110	165	82.5	155.1	64.7
120	180	90	169.2	70.6
130	195	77.3	183.3	76.4

NAME

BEER TYPE

DESCRIPTION

BATCH SIZE

QTY	GRAVITY	INGREDIENT		COLOR
		◀ TOTAL	◀ ÷ GAL =HCU ◀	

QTY	HOP VARIETY		A ACID	TIME	UNITS
		◀ HOP UNITS ◀		

NOTES

NAME

BEER TYPE

DESCRIPTION

BATCH SIZE

QTY	GRAVITY	INGREDIENT		COLOR
		◀ TOTAL	◀ ÷ GAL =HCU ◀	

QTY	HOP VARIETY		A ACID	TIME	UNITS
		◀ HOP UNITS ◀		

NOTES

NAME

BEER TYPE

DESCRIPTION

BATCH SIZE

QTY	GRAVITY	INGREDIENT		COLOR
		◀ TOTAL	◀ ÷ GAL =HCU ◀	

QTY	HOP VARIETY		A ACID	TIME	UNITS
		◀ HOP UNITS ◀		

NOTES

NAME

BEER TYPE

DESCRIPTION

BATCH SIZE

QTY	GRAVITY	INGREDIENT		COLOR
		◀ TOTAL	◀ ÷ GAL =HCU ◀	

QTY	HOP VARIETY		A ACID	TIME	UNITS
		◀ HOP UNITS ◀		

NOTES

NAME

BEER TYPE

DESCRIPTION

BATCH SIZE

QTY	GRAVITY	INGREDIENT		COLOR
		◀ TOTAL	◀ ÷ GAL =HCU ◀	

QTY	HOP VARIETY		A ACID	TIME	UNITS
			◀ HOP UNITS ◀		

NOTES

NAME

BEER TYPE

DESCRIPTION

BATCH SIZE

QTY	GRAVITY	INGREDIENT		COLOR
		◀ TOTAL	◀ ÷ GAL =HCU ◀	

QTY	HOP VARIETY		A ACID	TIME	UNITS
			◀ HOP UNITS ◀		

NOTES

NAME

BEER TYPE

DESCRIPTION

BATCH SIZE

QTY	GRAVITY	INGREDIENT		COLOR
		◀ TOTAL	◀ ÷ GAL =HCU ◀	

QTY	HOP VARIETY		A ACID	TIME	UNITS
			◀ HOP UNITS ◀		

NOTES

NAME

BEER TYPE

DESCRIPTION

BATCH SIZE

QTY	GRAVITY	INGREDIENT		COLOR
		◀ TOTAL	◀ ÷ GAL =HCU ◀	

QTY	HOP VARIETY		A ACID	TIME	UNITS
			◀ HOP UNITS ◀		

NOTES

Form 1

NAME

BEER TYPE

DESCRIPTION

ORIGINAL GRAVITY   BATCH SIZE

COLOR (HCU)   BITTERNESS (IBU)

WATER

MASH TYPE

MASH CHART

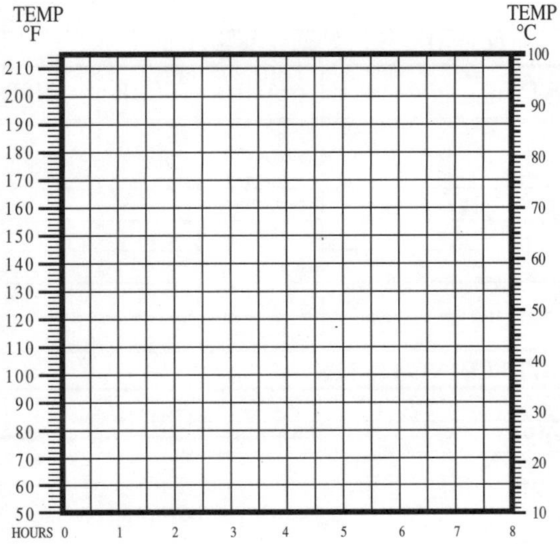 TEMP °F			TEMP °C

HOURS 0 1 2 3 4 5 6 7 8

QTY	GRAVITY	INGREDIENT	COLOR

TOTAL ÷ No gals = HCU

QTY	HOP VARIETY	α ACID	TIME	UNITS

HOP BITTERING UNITS

YEAST

FERMENT TEMP – PRI   SEC

CARBONATION

NOTES

Form 2

NAME

BEER TYPE

DESCRIPTION

ORIGINAL GRAVITY   BATCH SIZE

COLOR (HCU)   BITTERNESS (IBU)

WATER

MASH TYPE

MASH CHART

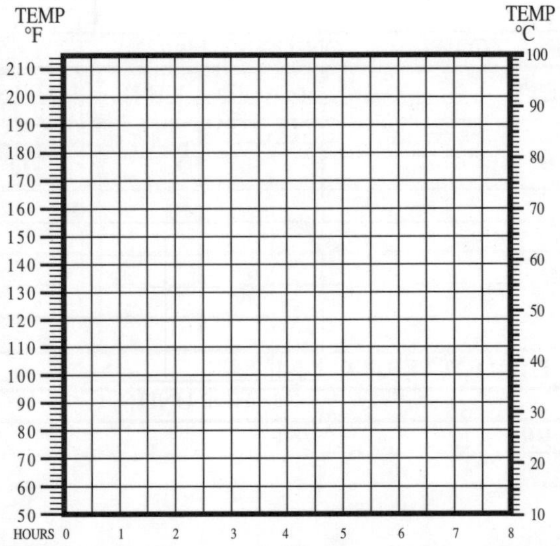 TEMP °F			TEMP °C

HOURS 0 1 2 3 4 5 6 7 8

QTY	GRAVITY	INGREDIENT	COLOR

TOTAL ÷ No gals = HCU

QTY	HOP VARIETY	α ACID	TIME	UNITS

HOP BITTERING UNITS

YEAST

FERMENT TEMP – PRI   SEC

CARBONATION

NOTES

NAME

BEER TYPE

DESCRIPTION

ORIGINAL GRAVITY   BATCH SIZE

COLOR (HCU)   BITTERNESS (IBU)

WATER

MASH TYPE

MASH CHART

QTY	GRAVITY	INGREDIENT	COLOR

TOTAL   ÷ No gals = HCU

QTY	HOP VARIETY	α ACID	TIME	UNITS

HOP BITTERING UNITS

YEAST

FERMENT TEMP—PRI   SEC

CARBONATION

NOTES

NAME

BEER TYPE

DESCRIPTION

ORIGINAL GRAVITY   BATCH SIZE

COLOR (HCU)   BITTERNESS (IBU)

WATER

MASH TYPE

MASH CHART

QTY	GRAVITY	INGREDIENT	COLOR

TOTAL   ÷ No gals = HCU

QTY	HOP VARIETY	α ACID	TIME	UNITS

HOP BITTERING UNITS

YEAST

FERMENT TEMP—PRI   SEC

CARBONATION

NOTES

BATCH NUMBER	
BEER A	
BEER B	
BEER C	

MASH CHART

QTY	GRAVITY	@%	INGREDIENT	@ CLR	C U
		TOTAL	⇨ ÷ No gals HCU ⇨		

MASTER OG　　MASTER COLOR (HCU)
TOTAL GAL　　WATER
NOTES:

A BEER / TYPE

BATCH SIZE	(GAL)
GRAVITY OG	°P
COLOR	(HCU)
BITTERNESS	(IBU)
BOIL LENGTH	(HRS)
YEAST	
NOTES	

QTY	OZ GM	HOP VARIETY	α ACID %	P L	BOIL TIME	UTIL RATE	IBU

TOTAL ESTIMATED IBU ⇥

B BEER / TYPE

BATCH SIZE	(GAL)
GRAVITY OG	°P
COLOR	(HCU)
BITTERNESS	(IBU)
BOIL LENGTH	(HRS)
YEAST	
NOTES	

QTY	OZ GM	HOP VARIETY	α ACID %	P L	BOIL TIME	UTIL RATE	IBU

TOTAL ESTIMATED IBU ⇥

BATCH NUMBER						
BEER A						
BEER B						
BEER C						

QTY	GRAVITY	@%	INGREDIENT	@ CLR	C U
	TOTAL	⇒ ÷ No gals HCU ⇒			

MASH CHART

MASTER OG   MASTER COLOR (HCU)
TOTAL GAL   WATER
NOTES:

A

BEER								
TYPE								
BATCH SIZE (GAL)								
GRAVITY OG °P								
COLOR (HCU)								
BITTERNESS (IBU)								
BOIL LENGTH (HRS)								
YEAST								
NOTES								

QTY	OZ GM	HOP VARIETY	α ACID %	P L	BOIL TIME	UTIL RATE	IBU
				TOTAL ESTIMATED IBU ↦			

B

BEER								
TYPE								
BATCH SIZE (GAL)								
GRAVITY OG °P								
COLOR (HCU)								
BITTERNESS (IBU)								
BOIL LENGTH (HRS)								
YEAST								
NOTES								

QTY	OZ GM	HOP VARIETY	α ACID %	P L	BOIL TIME	UTIL RATE	IBU
				TOTAL ESTIMATED IBU ↦			

Each of the charts in this section deals with a different brewing stage. Symptoms, problems, corrective actions, and what to do for the next batch are included for each stage.

PROBLEMS

14

SYMPTOM	POSSIBLE CAUSE	CORRECTIVE ACTION	NEXT BATCH ACTION
POOR YIELD OF MASH. Normally, expect a yield between 75 and 90 percent of estimated figures.	Incorrect grinding (too coarse) makes it difficult for starch in malt to be accessible to enzymes, resulting in a lack of converted sugars.	Beer will be weaker than expected, but otherwise just fine. Extract may be added to bring gravity up to desired strength.	Try to achieve better mix of particle sizes at grinding (see Section **6-3, Grain Crushing**). Most common mistake is grinding too coarsely.
	Improper temperatures during mashing keep enzymes from working properly.		Make sure correct time and temperature profile is followed during mashing. Check thermometer. Check starch conversion with iodine test.
	Beta glucan trouble (see **Set Mash**).		
	Estimate figures off, for some reason.		Revise estimate figures for the specific ingredient that was used.
	Sparge runnings not boiled down to correct volume for recipe (and estimate figures).		Make sure boiled-down wort is correct for the estimated yield figures. Boil down to correct volume.
SET MASH (Excessively slow draining during sparging.)	Grain ground poorly or too finely.	Cover grain with sparge water. Stir to about half the depth of the grain, and allow to settle. Fine flour will settle on top as a sticky paste. Remove and proceed as usual. (Goo sticks well to the back of a spoon.) Repeat if necessary.	Make sure husks are mostly intact. Proper grind is 1/3 husks, 1/3 grits, 1/3 flour.
	Husks chopped up too much. (Should be as intact as possible.)		
	Mash too cold (below 165°F/74°C).		Maintain 165°–175°F/74°–75°C mash temperature during sparge.
	Beta glucan trouble (jelly-like mash).	Or, add hot water to bottom and refloat mash. Allow to settle and slowly begin runoff.	Use 90°F/32°C dough-in when mashing large % of Munich malt.
	High wheat or unmalted grain content.	Wait. Wait some more.	Use six-row malt when mashing with unmalted grains or wheat.
	Bed of grain to be sparged too thick (over 12 inches).	Be patient. Try techniques listed above.	Don't mash as much grain with sparging setup, or do it in two batches. Get a larger or additional sparger for these big batches.

SYMPTOM	POSSIBLE CAUSE	CORRECTIVE ACTION	NEXT BATCH ACTION
YEAST NOT STARTING WITHIN 24–48 HOURS	Bad or old yeast. Check date, freshness of yeast.	Repitch with fresher batch of yeast.	Use only fresh yeast. Prepare starter.
	Dry yeast not rehydrated first.	Rehydrate dry yeast before using.	Always rehydrate dry yeast.
	Yeast pitched at too high a temperature (above 100°F/30°C).	Repitch with new yeast when cool.	Start only when wort is properly cool.
	Yeast shocked by too low a temperature (ale yeast below 60°F/16°C).	Move to warmer location. Ale yeast at 60°–70°F/16°–21°C.	Have a strong yeast starter ready at temperature of wort. Do not start below 60°F/16°C.
	Insufficient yeast nutrients. Causes trouble in worts under 1040 OG. May be too many adjuncts, which add no nitrogen to wort. Lack of protein rest during mash means less nitrogenous material.	Add yeast nutrient mix. Try repitching, also.	Use smaller proportion of adjuncts, such as rice and corn, and/or malt with higher %N, such as six-row. Allow for a protein rest during mashing. Change extract brand.
	Inadequate aeration of wort may result in a lack of oxygen available to the yeast.	Use sterilized spoon to vigorously stir unfermented wort. Wait. If no action after 24 hours, try repitching.	Allow wort to splash into primary. Use aquarium pump and stone to pump air into chilled wort.
	Residue from chlorine sterilizer may inhibit yeast growth.	Wait a day or two. Try repitching.	Always rinse three times with water after using chlorine sterilizer.
STUCK FERMENTATION Yeast activity seems to suddenly stop.	Temperature too cool, or temperature dropped too quickly.	Move to a warmer location. See above.	Start in a warmer spot next time. Avoid sudden temperature drops.
	Inadequate aeration of wort may result in a lack of oxygen available to the yeast. Especially important in high-gravity beers.	Use sterilized spoon to vigorously stir unfermented wort. Add more of the same yeast if you have it.	Allow wort to splash into primary. (This is the only time beer should be allowed to splash).
	Alcohol level too high. Over 8 percent or so may cause problems for beer yeast, especially ale yeast.	Add champagne yeast, or possibly lager yeast.	Start with lager or champagne yeast. Or add one to the secondary at racking.

SYMPTOM	POSSIBLE CAUSE	CORRECTIVE ACTION	NEXT BATCH ACTION
STUCK FERMENTATION Yeast activity seems to suddenly stop.	End-point of fermentation may have been reached. Quite possible if below 1025, or 25 percent of OG.	No problem. Go ahead and bottle it.	No problem. Krausening may create a more vigorous secondary fermentation, but is difficult for the homebrewer to do correctly.
	Inadequate aeration of wort may result in a lack of oxygen for the yeast.	Use sterilized spoon to vigorously stir unfermented wort.	Vigorously aerate chilled wort prior to pitching yeast.
ENDLESS FERMENTATION	Probable wild yeast infection. They have an enzyme that breaks down dextrins.	None possible. Problem will get worse.	Make sure wort is well aerated, and that enough yeast (lots!) is pitched.
"SWEAT SOCKS," "GOATY" OR CAPRYLLIC AROMAS	Probable Lactobacillus/Pediococcus infection.	Hold your nose when you drink it. Probably will taste good in chili.	Thoroughly sanitize all fermentation equipment.
DMS OR "COOKED CORN" AROMAS	Soured mash, if longer than 10 hours.		Shorter mash.
	May be produced by slow wort cooling.		Use a wort chiller.
DIACETYL, "BUTTERY" AROMAS At inappropriate levels:	If severe, a result of bacterial contamination.	Butteriness usually fades with time.	Be relentless about sanitation. Use a wort chiller. Try a different malt.
ALES—Some butteriness OK. ALT, KÖLSCH—Usually a defect if tastable. LAGER—A definite defect if tastable.	If mild, emphasized by certain yeast strains.	Allow lagers to warm up for a few days, then cool back down.	Try a different yeast variety.
	Mutated yeast due to high alcohol levels.	Wait. Diacetyl may be reabsorbed over time.	Use an alcohol-tolerant yeast or add champagne yeast to secondary.
	Lagering without "diacetyl rest."	Allow lagers to warm up for a few days to 60°–65°F at the end of lagering, then cool back down.	Allow lagers to warm up for a few days to 60–65°F at the end of lagering, then cool back down.
"CABBAGE," "GREEN BEANS," "CELERY," VEGETAL AROMAS	Bacterial contamination during wort cooling.	None. Add it to your next batch of chili.	Use a wort chiller; be careful about sanitation. Pitch adequate quantity of actively fermenting yeast.

SYMPTOM	POSSIBLE CAUSE	CORRECTIVE ACTION	NEXT BATCH ACTION
"BANANA," "BUBBLEGUM," "PINEAPPLE" AROMAS	Yeast contaminated with bacteria.	None. Hawaiian night special!	Switch yeast brands. Try liquid yeast.
	Fermentation temperature too high.	None possible.	Ferment below 68°F.
	Batch contaminated with bacteria.	None possible.	Watch sanitation. Pitch lots of yeast.
"SOAPY" FLAVORS	Beer sat in primary too long, picking up flavors from dead or autolyzed yeast.	None possible.	Use two-stage fermentation. Get beer off yeast after a week or so.
"BALLPOINT PEN" OXIDIZED AROMA	Probably old extract syrup. Some brands are worse than others.	None possible. Make it a spiced beer. A drop of vanilla may smooth it out.	Use fresher extract, or dry extract that doesn't change with age.
"METALLIC" AROMAS AND FLAVORS	Iron. Either present in water, or contact from brewing vessels.	None possible.	Use iron-free water source. Limit contact with iron in brewing process.
PHENOLIC "BAND-AID" AROMAS (Not the same as the clove character in weizens.)	Probable wild yeast infection. Giveaway is a fermentation that seems to never stop.	None possible. Problem will get worse. Bottles may burst. RUN!	Pitch an adequate quantity of active yeast into well-oxygenated yeast.
	Chlorine residue from bleach or sterilizer.	None possible.	Rinse equipment well before using. Don't make solution too strong.
EXCESSIVE BITTERNESS OR OVERLY HARSH HOP BITTERNESS	Hop rate too high.	Wait a while before drinking. Bitterness will lessen over time.	Check the hop rate and type. Make sure that it is appropriate for the beer. Determine alpha content of hops used. Watch out for high-alpha hops.
	Hop variety too harsh for style.		
	Carbonate water emphasizes harsh, bitter qualities of hops.	Mix with a less bitter beer at bottling if you discover the problem early enough. The beer may mellow eventually. Use it as a test of manhood.	If you have carbonate water, follow boiling instructions described in the water treatment section. Add sulfates.
SOURNESS	Symptomatic of a wide range of problems. Check for other problems—aromas, flavors, fermentation problems.	Repair unlikely, but depends on specific problem. Use it as a base for a fruit beer.	Usually helped by proper yeast handling and sanitation problems. Check for more specific problem.

SYMPTOM	POSSIBLE CAUSE	CORRECTIVE ACTION	NEXT BATCH ACTION
"CIDERYNESS"	Typically a symptom of beer made with a large proportion (over 20%) of sugar.	None possible, but you may want to add fruit.	Limit use of sugar. Make sure yeast is clean.
ASTRINGENT "HUSKY" FLAVORS	Too much tannin extracted from malt husks. Probable if husks were boiled, or if sparging was carried on too long. (Last runnings below 1005).	Husky flavor will lessen over time, but usually not much. Serve it to people you dislike. Herbs/spices (especially vanilla) may mask taste.	Make sure sparge temperature is not over 180°F/82°C. Do not use last runnings below 1005.
STALE "CARDBOARDY" FLAVORS	Oxidation. Always exists to some extent with homebrew, but shouldn't be noticeable unless beer was unduly splashed at racking, or bottles have too much headspace. Also, if beer is excessively old.	Drink it up as soon as you can. It will only get worse.	Minimize splashing at racking and bottling. Keep headspace in bottles to between 1/2" and 1". Ascorbic acid may be added as an antioxidant, but it doesn't do much.
RUBBERY, "SKUNKY" AROMAS	Overexposure to light. Even a short exposure can cause this problem. Clear or even green bottles are suspect. Fluorescent lights are very bad in this regard.	Nothing to do but drink it anyway. Make sure remaining bottles are protected from light.	Always keep bottles away from sunlight and fluorescent tubes. Be wary of clear and green glass bottles. Brown bottles are good protection.
OVERPRIMING Gushing, excess foaming.	Bacterial or fungal contamination. May not be detectable to the taste.	Just drink the stuff if it doesn't taste bad. The sooner the better, probably. If not severe, drink chilled.	Sterilize, sterilize, sterilize. Minimize headspace in bottles, as contaminating microbe is might be aerobic.
	Too much priming sugar for beer type or gravity. Check recipe or priming tables. Bottled too soon, possibly.	If beer gushes when chilled, loosen caps, and allow beer to release pressure. Recap.	Prime next batch more lightly, especially with fruit and strong beers.
	Residual sugars slowly fermenting may build up excess pressure. A problem only with fruit beers or very strong beers.	Really severe gushing may require that the caps be removed, and the beer be allowed to gush out until it stops, resulting in a loss of beer. Recap and allow to clear out before drinking.	Allow beer to sit in secondary for a longer time before bottling. Wait for beer to clear and bubbling to stop.
	Contamination by wild yeast that ferments sugars brewing yeast cannot.		Make sure adequate quantity of yeast is pitched into well-aerated wort.

SYMPTOM	POSSIBLE CAUSE	CORRECTIVE ACTION	NEXT BATCH ACTION
OVERPRIMING Gushing, excess foaming.	If gushing occurs only in a few bottles, it is probably caused by crud in the bottles.	Watch out. Don't drink the gushers. Chill before opening.	Scrub out bottles thoroughly before bottling. Better yet, soak them in chlorine cleaner or hot diluted caustic.
UNDERPRIMING Flatness, lack of carbonation.	Too little priming sugar. Check charts.	Wait a month or so. If beer is still not primed, open bottles and add up to 1/2 tsp. sugar (for really flat beer) per bottle. If that fails, use for cooking.	Follow priming instructions carefully.
	Insufficient yeast. Sometimes happens with beer that has gotten very clear from sitting in the secondary for a long time.	Wait a month or so. If still no action, open each bottle and add a few grains of yeast. Recap.	Stir up just a little bit of yeast off the bottom of the carboy. Or, add a packet of yeast when bottling. Rehydrate dry yeast first.
	Too cold. Ale yeast should be above 60°F/16°C. It may be shocked by a sudden temperature drop.	Move to a warmer location and wait a couple of weeks.	Don't ferment ale yeast below 60°F/16°C unless strain is known to be cold-tolerant.
	Yeast slowed by high alcohol content. Ale yeast more likely to do this than lager.	Wait a month or more. If still flat, open each bottle and add a few grains of champagne yeast.	Add champagne yeast to secondary, with high-alcohol beers. Use an alcohol-tolerant yeast.
HAZE When beer is warm as well as when chilled.	Unconverted starch. Sparge temperature that is too high has leached out residual starch from mash, or, improper mash temperature has left unconverted starch.	Diastase enzymes may be added to the secondary to break down starch. Turn it into a witbier (or just add the word "hefe" to the name.	Always sparge with water at less than 180°F/82°C. Follow mash time and temperature instructions carefully. Check thermometer.
	Wild or powdery yeast that will not settle has contaminated the batch.	If taste is OK, prime the beer with gelatin or isinglass. Bottle as usual.	Sterilize, sterilize, sterilize. Use adequate quantity of active yeast.
CHILL-HAZE Only hazy when beer is chilled.	Some haze is to be expected with all homebrew beers served at low temperatures. All-malt beers are worse in this regard. Lack of a protein rest at mashing contributes severely to the problem. Six-row malt is worse than two-row.	Haze will not affect taste. If beer is already bottled, keep in the refrigerator for a couple of weeks. Haze will settle out and stay there if beer is not warmed again. Chill beer for two weeks before bottling.	If beer is to be drunk chilled, use protein rest when mashing, especially when using lager or six-row malt. Avoid repeated cycles of warming and chilling during storage of beer.

SYMPTOM	POSSIBLE CAUSE	CORRECTIVE ACTION	NEXT BATCH ACTION
CHILL-HAZE	Contamination by iron, tin, or aluminum.	Try the technique described above. No remedy available.	Avoid contact with these metals (especially of solder) at any stage. Iron in water should be <.5ppm.
POOR HEAD RETENTION	Lack of sufficient head-forming proteins as a result of too little nitrogen in the mash. Usually caused by too large a portion of corn or rice adjuncts. May also be a result of inadequate breakdown of protein at mashing, which could be caused by lack of a protein rest, especially with poorly modified malt.	Heading agents available for beers like this. Make sure glassware is free from grease, oil, or traces of detergents.	Use smaller percentage of adjuncts in recipe. Use a higher-N malt. A small amount (5 percent) of wheat or unmalted barley can contribute to a better head.
	Oils from orange peel may collapse head.		Avoid orange peel. Try Curaçao.
	Contamination of beer (or even the beer glass) with oil or detergent.		Avoid the use of detergents on your equipment, except to remove oil. When you do use it, rinse incredibly well.

15   HOMEBREW EQUIPMENT

A detailed description of the items necessary and useful for brewing. Also, a discussion of construction materials, and instructions for making a wort chiller.

HOMEBREW EQUIPMENT

15

BREWERY MATERIALS

Brew-friendly materials are often user hostile. The ingredients that give stainless steel its incredible durability make it resistant to efforts to shape and join it. And what works for one material is often a disaster for another. The right tools and methods can make the difference between a shiny new brewhouse and a stack of expensive twisted wreckage on the basement floor.

In general, always get the best tools you can, and try to do the job right. Remember, with dangerous chemicals and large quantities of boiling liquids around, shoddy equipment can endanger your well-being. ALWAYS observe sensible workshop precautions when working with tools, especially where your eyes are concerned. You could poke your eyes out with some of this stuff, and they do not grow back. Wear safety-rated goggles whenever there is the slightest danger.

Stainless Steel

Stainless steel is the best material for almost everything. It is good for every stage of the brewing process, from mashing to lagering. Stainless steel is resistant to all chemicals used in brewing and cleaning, with the caution that extended contact with chlorine-based cleaners will cause corrosion. Poor heat conduction is its only drawback, but it is adequate for most brewing purposes.

Unfortunately, stainless steel is very expensive when new, and it is often difficult to obtain exactly what you're looking for, especially at salvage prices. This requires some ingenuity and perseverance on your part, but it's out there if you know where to look. (And for a buck a pound, it seldom hurts to buy whatever you find at a junkyard that you think there is even a remote possibility of using. You can always trade for something you really do need.)

Stainless steel is very hard stuff. And when it gets hot, it gets even harder. This why you might have encountered smoking drill bits and melting saber saw blades when you tried to cut or drill the stuff.

For drilling holes in stainless steel, the secret weapon is a cobalt drill bit. Cobalt bits cost more, but they're virtually indestructible. Any large hardware store should have them. Hard as they are, most tungsten carbide bits don't have the proper sharpness or geometry to drill stainless steel. However, a tungsten carbide rotary file or burr is a useful tool to chuck into your drill to clean up rough-edged holes and saw cuts.

If you're tapping (threading) stainless steel, get the most expensive taps you can find—high-speed steel, at least—and be very careful. It's very easy to break off a small tap when trying to thread a hole. A good lubricant is essential. It's also important to back the tap out frequently, to keep the hole clear of chips. If you're doing a lot of tapping, it might be worth seeking out taps specially made to cope with stainless steel, but you won't find them at the

THE F.C. DECKEBACH SONS CO. ESTABLISHED 1840. MANUFACTURERS OF BREWER'S FIRE & STEAM KETTLES, COPPER COILS, COPPER FALSE BOTTOMS. STEAM COPPER AND BRASS WORKS. PATENT ENCLOSED AERATED BEER COOLERS. Copper Attemperators for Fermenting Tubes. BREWER'S BRASSWORK A SPECIALTY. 123·125·127·129·W·COURT 916·918·ELM·ST. CINCINNATI O.

hardware store. Try an industrial or machine tool supply house.

Most pieces of stainless steel sheet metal you need to work with are too tough to cut with tin snips, so must be cut with a hacksaw or saber saw. Of course, this is true of scrapped-out beer kegs, as well. Use a bimetal blade, which has very hard cutting edges. A variable-speed saber or reciprocal saw is the best choice. Watch the speed carefully, because the blade can get red-hot trying to chew through the stuff, and will dull (or melt) rapidly. Carbide grit blades work very well, too, and are the blade of choice with a single-speed saw.

Some people use a spray bottle filled with water to cool down the metal in front of the cut. This works well, but observe the normal precautions that apply whenever electricity and water are in danger of mixing.

Stainless steel requires an exotic and expensive welding process. TIG (Tungsten in Gas) welding uses an inert gas, usually argon, to prevent oxidation of the weld. Before you take your job to the welder, make sure he has TIG capability. If the fitting to be welded is for a fermenter, make sure the welder has adequate knowledge of sanitary welding and fabrication techniques, or you could end up with welds that cannot be effectively cleaned. Do not be tempted to cut corners on fermenter materials or construction.

Brazing uses special copper alloys as a kind of high-temperature solder, but is not as strong and corrosion-resistant as welding. It is suitable for affixing a pipe fitting to the bottom of your boiling kettle, which is the thing you'll be most likely to need. Be sure the brazing material is compatible with food and drink, and doesn't contain any heavy metals—especially cadmium. Silver brazing wire is expensive, but is the best material to use.

There are two types of stainless steel commonly used for industrial process equipment, 304 and 316. The latter is the higher-grade material, with extra manganese for better resistance to corrosion. Either type is perfectly fine for any imaginable homebrew purpose.

Copper

The traditional material for boiling kettle construction is copper because of its excellent ability to conduct heat. Copper is highly resistant to acids, but easily damaged by contact with alkaline materials, such as chlorine cleaner and lye. Copper is suitable for anything on the hot side of the brewery, but is less serviceable for fermentation and cooling because it reacts with the common materials used in cleaning and sterilizing.

Copper is very easy to work with and with the proper material, can be brazed together. (Do not use solder; it is harmful to yeast.) Copper is a material that is "sticky," that is, it grabs onto certain types of cutting tools, such as taps. If you do need to tap it, use lubricant and back the tap out of the hole frequently to clear the chips.

Because of its extremely good heat conduction, copper is a perfect material for heat exchangers and heat sinks. A thick strip attached to an electric element, such as a BruHeat, can dissipate the heat and greatly reduce the amount of charring of mash that occurs with the bare element.

Brass and Bronze

These similar materials are alloys of copper—brass with zinc and bronze with tin or other materials. They are most often encountered as pipe and tube fittings, valves. All the precautions about the corrodibility of copper apply to these metals, too. Brass and bronze are both very easy to work with and require no special tools. Ordinary bronze window screen from the local hardware store is an acceptable brewery material, useful for screening the hops out of wort and, with proper support, for the false bottom of a lauter tun. Some brass contains lead, which is added to make machining easier, so bronze is generally a more preferable material to have in contact with wort.

Aluminum

Aluminum is cheap, available, and an excellent conductor of heat. Possibly passable as a boiling kettle material, aluminum corrodes violently on contact with such alkalis as chlorine cleaner and lye, but is resistant to acids. Aluminum is OK for heating water (for strike and sparge) and possibly acceptable for boiling kettles.

Solder

Solder is a mix of tin and lead, both of which are toxic to yeast and are powerful haze-formers, as well. Don't use solder for anything that comes in contact with either wort or beer. The lead-free solder you can get is less toxic, but it is mostly tin, which can be leached out by the acidic wort or beer. So-called "silver" solder is mostly tin, too. Avoid solder if you can.

Iron/Steel

Iron and steel are sources of bad flavor and significant haze-formers. Don't allow either to come in contact with wort or beer. Enamel canning kettles are steel underneath, so if they're chipped, they're capable of contaminating your beer. It's probably best to relegate steel to burner stands and other supporting roles in the brewery.

Glass

Glass is inert and inexpensive and in many respects is an ideal material for fermentation vessels, such as carboys. Glass is resistant to all cleaning and sterilizing materials you would ever use. The one caution is that long contact with strong solutions of caustic (lye) will etch the glass, so it's best to limit the soaking time when you're using that cleaning material. Thermal sensitivity makes boiling vessels out of the question. The

SAFETY NOTE

There are safety concerns with glass, due to its brittleness and sensitivity to thermal shock, so limit its use to situations where that won't be a problem.

exception is laboratory glassware, which is made from borosilicate glass (for example, Pyrex and Kimax). This special glass is highly resistant to thermal shock and therefore suitable for contact with open flame; it is the kind used for laboratory vessels and cookware.

Its extreme brittleness makes glass difficult to cut and drill. You can get special tungsten carbide drill bits should you have some mysterious reason for needing a hole in a carboy or other glass item.

Polyethylene and Other Plastics

Polyethylene is inexpensive and abundant. Of course, it is not at all heat-resistant, but it's fine for water treatment and storage, mashing, sparging, and wort collection vessels. High-density or linear is the premium grade—it's harder, tougher and stands up to heat better than the garden variety. Often used for primary fermenters (never age your beer in this), polyethylene is highly resistant to all common cleaning and sterilizing materials. But after some use it will develop minute scratches, which can be a haven for contaminating microbes. White kitchen trash bags, fresh from the box, are relatively sterile and can be used as liners for primary fermenters.

Another useful plastic is acrylic (Plexiglas, etc.), which is good for fabricating many brewery items. Acrylic is stiff, somewhat brittle, easily cut, and can be glued together with special cement.  Metal-cutting blades in a saber saw cut it well; to avoid cracking, use special drill bits. Acrylic is best for equipment racks, control panels and other items that will not come into contact with heat or beer.

Nylon is often used in industrial applications, as it is stiff, tough, machinable, safe for food, and impervious to most solvents and cleaners. It comes in sheets of various thicknesses. Note that nylon does not glue well.

Flexible tubing is an essential brewery material. Most is PVC (polyvinyl chloride). It is very important that the PVC be of food-grade material, which is more expensive and sometimes more difficult to find, but lower grades can leach toxic vinyl chloride into your beer, a very hazardous situation. If it is not specified as food-grade, it probably isn't. Silcone and polyethylene tubing are useful as well, and are sometimes available at industrial surplus stores.

Epoxy is useful, but not suitable for contact with beer or other foodstuffs.

Pure silicone sealant, the kind used for bathtub caulking, is a good material to use for certain kinds of sealing. It is safe for contact with wort.

Insulation

Foil-faced foam building sheathing is inexpensive and easy to work with. It is useful for insulating mash and lauter tuns, it can be cut with any sharp knife, and taped together with duct tape. For round vessels, cut a series of v-shaped grooves vertically, cutting halfway through the material. It will then bend easily, forming "barrel staves." The insulating shells can be held on the vessel with nylon webbing and buckles or strips of velcro. The tan stuff, polyisocyanurate, is a lot less messy to work with than the white styrofoam.

And don't forget about duct tape, the substance that allowed man to reach the moon. I don't know how you can brew without it. It is especially useful for assembling and finishing the edges of things made from insulation board.

PIPE AND FITTINGS

Most homebrewing connections can be made with 1/4" or 3/8" tubing or pipe. The quantities of liquid or gas involved in brewing don't really justify anything larger. The important thing is to pick one size of fittings and stick with it. This makes hooking everything together much simpler.

There are several different systems in use:

• NPT—The standard American rigid plumbing pipe and fittings. The threads are tapered so that as they are screwed into one another, they tighten. The size of these pipes and fittings are measured by the inside diameter of the pipe.

Iron and sometimes brass NPT pipe and fittings are available at hardware and plumbing supply

NPT PIPE SIZES		
NPT Size	Inside dia	Outside dia
1/8"	1/8"	3/8"
1/4"	1/4"	1/2"
3/8"	3/8"	5/8"
1/2"	1/2"	3/4"
3/4"	3/4"	1"

shops. The iron ones are suitable only for tap water supplies, as the more acidic wort, or even treated water, will leach away the iron and give your beer a metallic taste and possibly some haze. Brass fittings are quite acceptable, as copper and zinc in small quantities are actually valuable yeast nutrients, as well as being acid-tolerant metals. Stainless steel NPT fittings are available from industrial sources, at five to ten times the cost of the brass variety! Or, from your local junkyard, if you can find what you need, for a buck a pound.

Most of the commonly available valves have NPT fittings, which makes NPT the valve of choice for the majority of homebrew tasks.

But because of the deep (and therefore uncleanable) threads on NPT fittings, they are not suitable for use on fermenting vessels or anything that comes in contact with chilled wort or fermenting beer.

• Compression fittings and a tube have certain advantages over the NPT system. The fittings have a threaded nut that tightens over a tapered ring, which fits snugly over the tube, squeezing it tight and making a watertight seal as the nut is tightened. They are much more practical for fittings that must be changed frequently, such as pump inputs and outputs, as they tighten down with just a fraction of a turn past finger-tight. Compression fittings are measured by the outside diameter of the tubing they connect.

Two formats are available: the garden-variety brass fittings available from your local hardware store, and the heavier-duty industrial ones from the usual expensive industrial sources or surplus outlets. Unfortunately, the two systems are not interchangeable. The industrial variety is available in stainless as well as brass. Because of the lack of internal threads, compression fittings are more suitable for items that may contact chilled wort or fermenting beer.

Flexible copper tubing works well with these fittings, as does stainless steel. Choose according to need and availability.

Fittings are available that go from compression to NPT to compression, so you can use NPT valves with compression fittings.

• Quick-disconnect fittings are very useful for brewing setups and are available in several sizes and types. One of the most useful is the kind designed for garden hoses. These fittings make it simple to hook up your wort chillers and carboy washers to the water supply. The smaller-diameter fittings, normally used for compressed air, also work well for transferring hot fluids from water tank to lauter tun, and other similar purposes. The type made for CO_2 systems makes it easy to hook up the gas to your draft system.

Standardizing your brewing system with the same size and type of fittings makes it easy to move hoses from vessel to vessel to pump to whatever, and also to accommodate future changes and improvements to your brewery. I think 3/8" compression fittings are the way to go, but if you stumble onto a motherlode of surplus stainless goodies of a different type, go for it.

Valves & Stuff

Valves come in many varieties. The best all-around type to use is a ball valve. The ball valve has a ball in the middle, which has a hole drilled through it, to which the valve-handle is connected. When the hole lines up with the pipe, liquid flows. When it doesn't, the flow stops. Just a quarter of a turn opens it all the way, making it very convenient to use. Hardware stores sell nice brass ones in a variety of sizes. Often they're nickel plated, so they may look like stainless at first. The ball inside is usually stainless. Regular faucet-type

valves work fine for most purposes, but are just a little less convenient than ball valves.

Hose barbs let you connect tubing to pipe fittings. Hose barbs come in brass and plastic, to fit various pipe and tubing sizes. With compression fittings, you don't need hose barbs, as the plastic hose can simply be clamped right over the copper or stainless tubing to serve that purpose.

INDUSTRIAL EXOTICA

A homebrewery may be thought of as a tiny factory, so parts used in big factories often work well for our purposes. You can find many useful things out there in surplus sources. Filters, solenoid valves, float switches, flow meters, pumps, thermoregulators, heating elements, pressure regulators and more can often be had for a few cents on the dollar. You don't need to be an engineer to use this kind of stuff, either; most of it works in a simple, logical manner.

BREWERY EQUIPMENT

Fermenting Vessels

It is essential that fermenting vessels be containers that can be adequately sanitized. The best choice is the standard five-gallon glass carboy. Being able to see what's going on inside is a real bonus. You'll probably end up owning several. Even brewers who brew larger batches like the convenience of dealing with five-gallon lots. Anything larger is very unwieldy to move about, and even a five-gallon one weighs around 45 pounds, and they can get slippery. Make sure they (and your hands) are dry when lifting. Even an empty carboy dropped on your foot can be catastrophic. Some brewers recommend a wooden or plastic "safety cage" around the keg to ease handling and minimize chances of breakage. I like to use a little plywood cart to roll them around from room to room rather than carrying or dragging them.

Plastic carboys are OK for storing and treating water, but they are not recommended for beer. If you can find them, 6½-gallon industrial chemical carboys are excellent, provided you are comfortable with their former contents (usually acid), from a safety point of view. The larger size makes a perfect closed primary fermenter for a five-gallon batch. Many brewers use plastic first-stage fermenters, especially when starting out. These work OK, but can harbor bacteria after they become old and scratched up, so you'll probably want to change to glass eventually.

A few stratospheric brew "goo-roos" ferment in stainless steel vessels, but you should know that in practice this is very hard to do, as these vessels can be very difficult to clean without a source of steam, and being opaque, it is difficult to even tell when they are clean. Also, vessels suitable for fermenting require specialized fittings and welding techniques. A properly constructed stainless steel home fermenter could cost as much as $1,000.

Brewpot/Boiling Kettle

The traditional material in breweries is copper, giving its name to the brewer's "copper." Stainless steel is a more realistic choice for the homebrewer because of its availability, but there are several options.

You can start with one 22-quart canning kettle for extract brewing, then add a second to give you lots of room to handle a mash. You will need about 1¼ times your batch size (for all-grain mashing), at least. A large stainless steel restaurant stockpot is perfect, but expensive. A six-gallon container is the absolute minimum for boiling five gallons of wort. Be aware that the enamel canning kettles sometimes chip, and when they do, they're unusable due to the potential for iron contamination.

Some homebrewers use two smaller kettles instead of one large one. This arrangement boils faster, having two burners heating instead of only

BASIC BREWING EQUIPMENT Mash or Non-mash	ADDITIONAL EQUIPMENT For Mashing (5-gallon batch size)
• 5-gallon glass carboy • 7- to 10-gallon plastic food-grade container, or better, a 6½-gallon glass carboy • Stoppers to fit carboy, with 3/8" hole drilled to accept a fermentation lock • Fermentation locks—at least 2 • 4 feet of 3/8" I.D. food-grade vinyl tubing • Racking tube • Bottle-filling tube • Bottle capper • Long-handled stainless steel spoon • 3-gallon kettle, or bigger • Hydrometer with jar • Hose shut-off clip	• 1 additional 3-gallon pot, or one 6-gallon vessel • Mashing/sparging vessel to hold 5 gallons • Sturdy wooden spoon or paddle • Accurate thermometer, 80°–212°F/27°–100°C • 1 additional 5-gallon tub to sparge into • Scale, with a 1- to 5-pound capacity • Grain grinder **For yeast starters** • 200 and 1,000 ml heat-resistant lab flasks • Inoculation loop • Propane torch (for flaming flask necks) **Generally desirable** • Wort chiller • Hop strainer for boiling kettle • Water filter or purifier • Jet-Spray bottle washer

one. Using two kettles makes the transition from extract beers simpler, too. When you're ready to start mashing, just buy another kettle the same as you're already using instead of a more expensive larger one.

Anything bigger than five or six gallons should have a stainless steel pipe fitting welded on the bottom. When you start dealing with hot liquid in quantities larger than that, it's just too hot and heavy to lift 'n'pour. Also, when using a counterflow wort chiller, a spigot at the bottom supplies the pressure needed to push the wort through the considerable length of tubing.

You will need a fair amount of headspace for your boiling kettle, about half again as large as the finished beer volume. Evaporation and boilover drives this dimension. If you need five gallons of boiled wort, seven and a half gallons is about the right size.

You can make a very good boiling kettle from a decommissioned stainless steel beer keg. Cut the top off, or cut a large hole in the top itself. If you do it just right, you can use the edge of the cut-off top to make a hop strainer for the kettle. This ring of metal cut from the keg top just fits inside the keg. Cut a bronze or stainless steel screen in a circle and fit it to the metal to make a strainer.

Put the screen into the kettle before the unboiled wort is added, and leave it in throughout the boil.

The keg should also have a stainless steel pipe fitting welded to it. A half-inch NPT (U.S. standard) pipe fitting, called a half-coupling, is a good choice, because lots of valves, etc. are available to hook up to it, but there's nothing magic about that size. Put the fitting on the side, as close to the bottom as you can.

Some brewers have a three-inch pipe fitting welded to their mash tun. They then use a large brass pipe cap, with a hole drilled in the center, tapped to accept a more normal size valve. With the cap on, the valve can be used normally; when the mash is finished, the cap is removed and the mash is allowed to glorp out the large hole into a bucket for disposal.

Do remember that the beer kegs you may be tempted to slice into, fresh from the recent kegger, cost the brewer about 200 clams apiece. The $10 deposit is not the purchase price, so please be kind to your local brewer and go to a junkyard, where junked-out kegs, no less useful as brewing vessels, may be had for scrap value.

If you need welding done, take it to a place that can do TIG or other specialized welding suited to stainless steel. Best is a place that specializes in food and process equipment.

Mash Tun

The mash tun should be about the same size as your brew kettle. Indeed, many professional and amateur brewers use their boiling kettles as their mash tuns. The boiling kettle can be put directly on a heat source to raise the temperature of the mash, although care must be taken to prevent the mash from scorching. Constant stirring is needed, and a loose mash helps. Electric elements may be used, but the same precautions about scorching apply. Use a thermostat to regulate the temperature. For a really slick setup, add a stirring motor to keep the mash moving. It is a good idea to insulate the mash tun in some way, to pre-

vent the temperature from dropping too quickly. The smaller the vessel, the more important this is. If nothing else, throw a blanket or a sleeping bag over the whole thing.

Lauter Tun

The lauter tun is an insulated vessel with some kind of a false bottom to hold back the crushed grain, while allowing the clear wort to drain through. One popular setup is two five-gallon plastic buckets, one inside the other. The bottom one has a spigot for draining off the wort, while the top one has the bottom cut out and replaced with a coarse screen. You can drill holes rather than using a screen, but this operation is exceedingly tedious, and having done it once, I cannot recommend it to anyone. Stainless steel is ideal, but bronze window-screen works fine. I have found it best to cut out large sections of the bottom, leaving a crosswise pattern of bucket-bottom in place to support the weight of the grain. Other variations that use cloth grain buckets or custom-made false bottoms in a single bucket are available commercially. With all false bottoms, it is important to not have too fine a screen or it will become clogged with fine flour and cease to drain. Screen openings or drill holes should be a minimum of 1/16"; slightly larger— up to 1/8"—is probably better.

Many homebrewers make their lauter tun from a picnic cooler, so the insulation is built right in. A conventional false bottom may be used, or more commonly, a tree-like network of 1/2" copper pipe hooked up to the outlet. The main pipes have a number of slots cut into them about every 1/2" or so, through which the mash can drain.

You can make a mini-mash tun by dropping a vegetable steamer—the kind with the little fold-up wings—into a one- or two-gallon picnic cooler with a spigot. This is great for doing mini-mashes to enhance extract brews.

It is helpful to have a valve on the outlet of the lauter tun to control the rate of outflow when sparging. When first drawing off the wort, don't let it drain too fast, or the grain bed will compact. Commercial breweries have a hydrostatic gauge attached to the underside of the lauter tun to show the negative pressure when the mash is draining. A short-scale vacuum gauge can do the job in a home version.

Heat Sources

The kitchen stove works fine for five gallons or less. If you have a choice, gas is preferable. With an electric stove, you just have to be a bit more patient and more careful about not scorching the mash. Many people build special brew stoves from old gas water heater burner rings. These are inexpensive and readily available, but you have to have some know-how to put one together. I know of a brewer who has two 500,000 BTU burners in his backyard brewery. Outrageous, even for the 60-gallon brewpots, which will come shrieking to a boil in less than a half an hour. Be warned that large burners consume large amounts of oxygen and can output large amounts of carbon monoxide and other unwholesome gases. These large burners are best used outside, or with a very large exhaust fan and a reliable source of fresh air. Commercially available burners—Brinkman Small-Fry and Cajun Cooker are two common ones—are typically set up for operation on LP gas, but they might be modifiable to natural gas if you know what you're doing. Selling for $60–$75, you can find them in or order from sporting, hunting, and fishing shops, as well as many homebrew suppliers. Single-burner stoves can also be found at restaurant supply houses.

Electric-element brewkettles, such as the BruHeat, are serviceable, but you have to be careful when doing step mashes, as the element can

cause the mash to stick and scorch. A thick copper slab attached to the element as a heat sink may ease this somewhat. Electric kettles are best for heating water for treatment and mashing, as they may be put on a timer and a thermostat, and so do not require the kind of attention that gas burners do. I like to set my mash kettle to switch on at about 5:00 A.M. and heat to my desired strike temperature, then hold until I have a cup of coffee in my hand at a more civilized hour.

Small heaters—under 50 watts—work well for fermenting or yeast culturing. An aquarium heater installed under an aluminum plate makes a good incubator or carboy warmer. Good results have also been had using a lightbulb as a heat source to keep carboys warm enough for ale fermentation during arctic midwestern winters. If you're trying to heat a whole carboy, having it well insulated makes it easier to maintain an even temperature.

Hose

The homebrew standard is 3/8" vinyl tubing. You'll be siphoning and transferring both beer and water with it, so use food-grade variety because ordinary tubing can release toxic vinyl chloride. Remember, choosing one tubing size and matching all connectors to it simplifies life in the brewery.

Siphon Tube

The standard bent 3/8" plastic version works OK, but it gets soft and bends in hot wort. It has a little tip on the end that keeps the tube from sucking up the yeast from the bottom.

You can have a deluxe version made for you at a hydraulics repair shop. Tell them you want "a two-foot length of their least expensive 3/8" O.D. stainless steel tubing, with a 90° bend of unspecified radius, 2" from one end." They'll know what you mean. It should cost around $15—it will last forever, is easy to sterilize, and won't sag when used to transfer very hot liquid. Put the plastic tip from the end of your plastic tube on it, or plug the end and drill a 1/8" hole, one-quarter inch from the tube end.

Scale

You need a scale to weigh hops, grain, and priming sugar (or any other ingredients). The range should be 1/4 ounce to 1 pound, at least. Either, metric or non, as you like, and it should have a pan or something to hold malt or hops.

Hydrometer

This device measures specific gravity. The triple scale (OG, °Balling, % Alcohol Potential) models are inexpensive and work quite well. The professional varieties I've seen are calibrated in °Plato, and you need three different ones to cover the range encountered in homebrewing. Units that have a thermometer inside make readings on hot wort easier. A jar that will hold the hydrometer when taking readings is essential. Be careful that the fit is not too tight, or your readings will be off.

Thermometer

Your thermometer must be accurate to within one degree or so. Glass laboratory thermometers are accurate and not too expensive, but fragile. Dial type photo thermometers work well, providing they cover the range needed. Watch out for those floating thermometers; they're often inaccurate. At mashing temperatures, just a few degrees error can have an effect on the mash. You need to cover the range from freezing to boiling, Fahrenheit or Celsius, as you please. Digital units are great, but the cheap ones may be off by several degrees, so be wary. A high temperature thermometer (up to 500°F) is great to calibrate your oven for grain roasting.

SAFETY NOTE

The mercury in glass thermometers is highly toxic. If you break one in a mash or wort, you must throw the batch away. Alcohol-filled models are much safer.

Bottle Filler

This is a handy device that attaches to your siphon hose. At the tip there is a small spring-loaded valve. When the filler is inserted in a bottle and pushed down on the bottom, beer begins to flow; when lifted, the flow stops. I can't imagine bottling any other way. The standard plastic jobs work OK, but improved versions are available for just a little more money.

Hose Shut-off Clip

Simply a small plastic or metal clamp that shuts off the flow through your siphon hose by squeezing the plastic shut. You only need one.

Jet-Spray Bottle Washer

This is a simple unit that attaches to your faucet. It is a J-shaped piece of brass tubing that has a built-in valve that is opened by pushing a beer bottle down over it. You push the bottle down, you get a spray inside. It's a miracle. It saves lots of time when bottling and is worth every bit of its $12 price tag.

Fermentation Locks

These little gizmos come in a variety of styles and materials. Which one you decide on is strictly a matter of preference. You'll need at least four to start, more if you are doing big batches or yeast culturing.

Stoppers

Get a bunch of them—to fit every vessel you might be fermenting in. A 3/8"-diameter hole drilled through is the standard.

Spoon

A long-handled stainless steel spoon is best for stirring hops into wort. Wooden ones are fine for the mash, but stainless is better for boiling because it can be sterilized. You can cut a mash paddle or rake out of a piece of hardwood, such as oak or maple.

Bottle Capper

There are numerous varieties, but all work by crimping the flare of the crown caps around the necks of the bottles. Hammer cappers are cheap, but are awkward and perhaps even dangerous. Two-handled lever cappers work fine, but sometimes have problems with nonstandard containers, such as champagne bottles. Try before you buy, if this is important to you.

The old-fashioned bench cappers are the best, but they are quite expensive to purchase new. Flea markets are a good bet for this item, at least in the East and Midwest, and they can be usually had for under $10. Use a wire brush to get off any rust, and then give them a couple of coats of spray paint—literally better than new.

Wort Chiller

This is a device that uses cold water to chill the boiled wort. There are various configurations, but they all do the same thing. Benefits include a much shorter period of vulnerability for the unfermented wort, and a cold break, removing unwanted protein goo. Plus, there is less oxidation and DMS formation when the wort is chilled quickly.

One type, counterflow, is a coil of copper tubing inside a jacket of plastic hose through which water flows. This type cools faster, but can be difficult to clean, as the wort deposits a stubborn protein film inside the tubing. The other, an immersion chiller, is simply a coil of bare copper tubing that you put into your wort at the end of boiling. The hot wort sterilizes it. Tap water flows through the tubing and cools the wort right in the pot. Immersion chillers are easier to use, but cool more slowly, giving a less-pronounced cold break. Both types are available from homebrew sources, but are very easy to make. A trip to any hardware store should get you everything you need. People in water-rationed areas make use of closed systems where the water is pumped through an ice bath, then through the chiller, and back to the ice bath. The water so used can even be used for the next batch.

To build an immersion chiller, all you need is 20 to 30 feet of 3/8"-diameter copper tubing, and a 20-foot garden hose. Wrap the copper tubing around something round to form an open coil a little more than half the diameter of your brew-kettle. Bring one end up to the top so both ends of the tubing are on the same end of the coil. Cut the hose in half, and use hose clamps to attach it

to the coil. Hook it up so that the water enters the coil at the top and exits after it has traveled to the bottom. If you want to get really fancy, bend the ends of the tubing down horizontally, and use compression fittings to attach hose fittings to the ends of the tubing so the hoses can be disconnected more easily.

To use it, simply hook up the hoses, and set the coil in your boiling wort, about 15 minutes before the end of the boil. This will sanitize it.

A counterflow chiller is a little more complicated. You need 20 feet of 3/8" O.D. copper tube, plus 22 feet of 3/4"-diameter I.D. vinyl tubing, which need not be food grade. You also need two 3/4" x 3/4" plastic T-fittings, two garden hose fittings that will fit 3/4" tubing, and a few inches of tubing that will build up the copper tube so that it fits snugly into the T-connectors.

Start by straightening out the copper tube and inserting it into the plastic tubing. At one end, slip the buildup tubing over the end of the copper tube, then slip the T-fitting straight over, leaving about 2 inches of copper tube hanging out. The tube should fit very snugly into the T.

Make sure the buildup tube goes no farther than one end of the T, or it will block things up. Use one of the hose clamps to tighten the connection securely. Smooth off the end of the copper tube, using a file or a small knife. Making sure the open end of the T is pointed to the outside, bend the concentric tubes into about a 1-foot-diameter coil. Cut the vinyl tube off so it is 4 inches shorter than the copper tube. Repeat the T-connection at this end. To the open end of the T-fittings, attach 6-inch stubs of the vinyl tube, using hose clamps. To the ends of these, attach the garden hose fittings. Be sure to smooth off the other end of the copper tube. If desired, you can use plastic cable ties or brass wire to bind the coil into a tight coil to keep it from flopping around.

Before you use it, sanitize the inside of the copper tube by squirting a mild chlorine solution through it, followed by a rinse of cold water. Then connect the bottom end to a source of cool water, the top end to a drain which is secured so it can't fall out of the sink. The top end of the copper tube should be connected to your brewkettle, the bottom end to a hose going to the fermenter. It is best to let the wort drip or even spray into the carboy to help aerate it before fermentation. When finished, rinse the inside of the tube immediately. At some point, you may need to clean out the tube with TSP and/or a commercially available diary equipment phosphoric acid rinse. *Note:* It can be difficult to get the wort to flow well using a siphon from your brewkettle. A bottom-mounted spigot on your brewkettle will help, although some people report satisfactory results with a siphon.

Water Treatment Systems

There are several ways to purify water: filtering, reverse osmosis, and distillation. For normal, clean tap water, the most important thing to filter out is chlorine. The quantities present in tap water have a noticeable effect on the flavor of beer. A carbon filter (activated charcoal) is effective in removing chlorine, as well as small amounts of organic chemicals that may be present in the water, which is especially likely if the water source is a river. Filters don't last forever, and they can develop bacterial contamination problems, especially if they sit around unused most of the time. But filters are much less expensive than the other types of water purification, and for most water types are sufficient.

Reverse-osmosis devices force water through a thin membrane with molecule-sized holes, which strips out everything but the water. These devices are expensive, but are reliable and long-lasting. However, unless you have really crummy water or brew a lot of Czech pilsners, they're probably unnecessary,

Distillation is overkill, unless you have really bad water, or insist on making nothing but authentic Czechoslovakian pilsners.

Normal water softeners remove hardness minerals such as carbonates. Check the manufacturer's information about exactly what minerals they remove and add.

Draft Systems

Draft systems are expensive, but relieve you of the considerable tedium of bottling. The system consists of a tank of carbon dioxide gas hooked up to a pressure regulator. The gas is hooked up to a standard soda fountain syrup can. These "Cornelius" kegs come in a couple of sizes, but the five-gallon ones are by far the most common. Out of the keg, a hose takes beer to the tap. Quick-disconnect fittings allow you to easily switch kegs. Draft systems are low maintenance, high wonderfulness, especially if you hate to bottle. For more information, see **Section 12–3, Draft Beer Basics**.

Heating and Cooling

Various systems can be used to maintain even fermentation temperatures. What is needed varies according to what your needs are—and those vary from season. Small heaters can be made from lightbulbs; refrigerators can be enlarged with plywood and insulation. Breweries typically use chilled glycol systems that circulate coolant through jackets on tanks. Even this complex can be emulated by a homebrewer with a small pump, a refrigerator, and a length of copper tubing. Experiment with parts and materials you can find; you'll be amazed what you can put together.

16   GLOSSARY

This is a complete lexicon of the brewing terms used throughout this book, as well as in the brewing industry.

GLOSSARY

16

A

AAU (Alpha Acid Unit) Alternate, and probably more sensible, name for Homebrew Bitterness Units. Ounces x Alpha % ÷ gallons. *See also* alpha acid.

acetaldehyde Chemical present in beer that has a "green apple" aroma.

acrospire The shoot of the barley grain, which develops during malting.

adjunct Any grain added to barley malt for beer-making, especially rice, corn, and roasted malt and barley.

adsorption Physical process involving adherence of particles to one another, at the microscopic level. Important in fining and other processes.

albumin An important group of proteins that remain in beer, affecting head retention and long-term stability.

alcohol A type of simple organic compound containing one or more oxygen atoms per molecule. Ethanol is the type found in fermented beverages. Other types occur in beer and other fermented products, but in small quantities. *See also* fusel alcohol, oils; and "Alcohol" in **Section 17–2.**

ale Any beer produced with top-fermenting yeast. In the old days, a strong unhopped beer.

aldehyde Group of important flavor chemicals found in beer and other foodstuffs.

alkalinity A measure water hardness, expressed as ppm of calcium carbonate.

alpha acid (α acid) Complex of substances that are the bitter component of hop flavor. Analyses of hops are given in percentage of alpha acid, which may be used to estimate the bitterness for a particular beer.

alt or altbier German type of beer made from top-fermenting yeast. Includes a wide variety of particular styles, including Kolsch and Dusseldorfer.

amino acids A group of complex organic chemicals that form the building blocks of protein. Important in yeast nutrition.

amylase (alpha and beta) Primary starch-converting enzymes present in barley and malt. They both break the long chains of starch molecules into shorter, fermentable, sugars.

ASBC American Society of Brewing Chemists. Standards-setting organization for beer analysis in North America.

ascorbic acid Vitamin C, sometimes added sparingly to beer in later stages as an antioxidant. Of questionable usefulness.

attenuation The degree to which residual sugars have been fermented out of a finished beer. *See also* "Attenuation" in **Section 17–2.**

autolysis Self-digestion and disintegration of yeast cells. This can give rise to "soapy" off-flavors if beer is not racked off dead yeast after primary fermentation.

B

°Balling European measurement of specific gravity based on the percentage of pure sugar in the wort. Measured in degrees. *See also* "°Balling" in **Section 17-2.**

barley Cereal grains, members of the genus *Hordeum*. When malted, the primary ingredient in beer.

barrel Standard unit in commercial brewing. U.S. barrel is 31.5 gallons; British barrel is 43.2 U.S. gallons.

Baume A specific gravity scale seldom used in brewing, but often found on hydrometer scales.

bead Bubbles in beer. Important qualities are fineness and persistence.

beer Broad term that correctly describes any fermented beverage made from barley malt or other cereal grains. Originally denoted products containing hops instead of other herbs.

beta glucans A group of gummy carbohydrates in malt. Some varieties have an excess, and can cause problems with runoff, and during fermentation, where they may precipitate as a sticky goo.

bittering units *See* IBU.

body A quality of beer, largely determined by the presence of colloidal protein complexes. Also partially due to the presence of unfermentable sugars (dextrins) in the finished beer.

break The sudden precipitation of proteins and resins in wort. The *hot break* occurs during the boil, and the *cold break* occurs during rapid chilling.

brewer's pounds British measurement of wort sugars expressed as pounds of dissolved sugars per barrel. One brewer's pound per barrel equals a gravity of 10036. *See also* "Brewer's Pounds" in **Section 17-2.**

bung Wooden plug for beer barrel.

Burton salts Mixture of minerals added to brewing water to approximate the water of Burton-on-Trent, England, famous for the production of pale ales.

Burtonize To treat with Burton salts.

Burton Union A fermentation system unique to Burton-on-Trent. Unbelievably complex system of numerous interconnected small barrels, now largely abandoned due to high cost of operation. Said to give a unique flavor to beers produced by this method.

C

Campden tablets Pellets of sodium metabisulphite used as infection-inhibiting agent. Not technically a sterilizer. Used more in wine, mead, and cider making than brewing.

caramel Sugar syrup, cooked until very dark, and used as a coloring and flavoring ingredient in commercial beers. Compared to roasted grains it is an inferior product, and finds little use in homebrew, except for its presence in canned malt extracts.

caramel malt *See* crystal malt.

Cara-Pils Tradename for a specially processed malt used to add body to pale beers. Similar to crystal but not roasted. Also called dextrine malt.

carbohydrates The class of chemicals including sugars and their polymers, including starch and dextrins.

carboy Large glass bottle used to ferment beer or wine. Available in 2-, 5-, 6.5-, and 7-gallon sizes.

carrageen Alternate name for Irish moss.

Celsius European thermometer scale, formerly called centigrade.

centigrade Same as Celsius.

cereal Broad term for a group of grass plant species cultivated as food grains.

chill-haze Cloudy residue of protein that precipitates when beer is chilled. Occurs when protein rest stage of the mash is inadequate, especially with high %N malt, such as six-row.

chit malt A type of malt sometimes used in Europe, which is malted for a very short time, and thus highly undermodified.

chocolate (malt) Medium-brown roasted malt.

cold break Rapid precipitation of proteins, which occurs when boiled wort is rapidly chilled.

colloid A state of matter involving very minute particles suspended in a liquid. Beer is a colloid, as is gelatin. Many reactions in beer involve the colloidal state, especially those affecting haze and stability.

conditioning The process of maturation of beer, whether in bottles or in kegs. During this phase, complex sugars are slowly fermented, CO_2 is dissolved, and yeast settles to the bottom.

cone The part of the hop plant used in brewing, consisting of the flowers.

conversion In the mash, of starch to sugar.

copper The brewing kettle, named for its traditional material of construction.

corn sugar Also called dextrose or glucose. A simple sugar sometimes used in beermaking, derived from corn.

crystal malt A specially processed type of malt that is used to add body and caramel color and flavor to amber and dark beers. It is heated to mashing temperatures while wet, causing starch to be converted to sugars while still in the husk. These sugars crystallize on cooling and contain large amounts of unfermentable sugars. Comes in several shades of color.

CWT Abbreviation for hundredweight. An English unit of weight equal to 112 pounds.

D

decoction Continental mashing technique that involves removing a portion of the mash, boiling it, then returning it to the mash to raise its temperature.

dextrin, dextrine A family of long-chain sugars not normally fermentable by yeast. Contributes to body in beer. Roughly the same caloric value as sugar.

dextrose Also called glucose or corn sugar. A simple sugar, easily fermented by yeast, sometimes used in beermaking.

diacetyl A powerful flavor chemical with the aroma of butterscotch; created during fermentation.

diastase An enzyme complex present in barley and malt that is responsible for the conversion of starch into sugars.

diastatic activity An analytical measure expressed in degrees Lintner of the power of malt or other grains to convert starches to sugars in the mash.

diatomaceous earth (DE) Microfine fossil single-cell creatures of almost pure silica, used in the filtering of beer in preparation to bottling.

disaccharide Sugars formed by the combination of two simple sugar units. Maltose is an example.

DMS Dimethyl sulfide, a powerful flavor chemical found in beer, with the aroma of cooked corn.

dough-in The process of mixing the crushed malt with water in the beginning of the mash operation.

draft, draught Beer from a cask or a keg, as opposed to bottled beer. Generally unpasteurized.

dry-hopping A method of adding hops directly to the secondary, to increase hop aroma without adding bitterness.

dunkel German word for "dark," as in dark beer. Usually refers to Munich dark style.

E

EBC European Brewing Convention. Continental standards-setting organization for brewing. *See also* "°EBC" in **Section 17–2.**

endosperm The starchy middle of a cereal grain that serves as the food reserve for the young plant. It is the source of fermentable material for brewing.

entire Old term meaning to combine the first, middle, and last runnings into one batch of beer. This was begun in the large mechanized porter breweries in London during the 1700s, and is accepted common practice today.

enzyme Proteins that act as catalysts for most reactions crucial to brewing, including starch conversion, proteolysis, and yeast metabolism. Highly dependent upon conditions such as temperature, time, and pH.

Epsom salts Magnesium sulphate. A common mineral found in water, sometimes added to brewing water.

esters Large class of compounds formed from the oxidation of various alcohols, including many flavor components commonly found in fruits. Created in beer as a by-product of yeast metabolism. Especially noticeable in top-fermented beers.

ethanol The alcohol found in beer; its intoxicating component.

extract Term used to refer to sugars derived from malt. Also, the commercially prepared syrups or dried products.

F

FAN (free amino nitrogen) Type of protein breakdown products in the wort. Amino acids and smaller molecules are included. Indicates yeast nutrition potential

formol nitrogen *See* FAN.

fructose A hexose monosaccharide found abundantly in fruits and elsewhere in nature, but totally unimportant in beer. Present in honey.

fusel alcohol, oils Higher (more complex) alclohols, found in all fermented beverages.

G

galactose A type of hexose sugar occuring in small quantities in beer, which is very slowly fermentable by brewer's yeast.

gelatin Used in beermaking as a fining agent.

gelatinization The cooking of corn or other unmalted cereals to break down the cell walls of the starch granules. The resulting starch is in a colloidal state, making it accessible for enzymatic conversion into sugars. Occurs at 140°F/60°C.

globulin An important protein group present in barley and in beer. It is the prime component in chill-haze, so its breakdown and elimination during mashing is critical.

glucose Corn sugar or dextrose. A simple sugar sometimes used in brewing.

glutelin A protein group found in beer.

goods The stuff being mashed.

gravity *See* original gravity; and "Gravity" in **Section 17–2.**

grits Ground degermedcorn or rice used in brewing.

gruit Medieval herb mixture used in beer.

gueuze A Belgian ale, uniquely fermented with wild yeasts. Final product is made by blending old and young beers.

gyle A single batch of beer.

gypsum Calcium sulphate—$CaSO_4$. Very common in water. Often added, especially in the production of pale ales.

H

hardness A common measurement of water mineral levels, especially sulphates and carbonates. Expressed as parts-per-million of calcium carbonate.

Homebrew Bittering Unit (HBU) Measure of amount of hop bitterness added to beer. Alpha acids x ounces ÷ gallons. *See also* "Homebrew Bittering Units" in **Section 17-2.**

head Foam on the surface of beer or fermenting wort.

helles German word for "light," denoting a pale Munich syle, as opposed to the older *dunkel*, or dark beer.

hexose A category of simple sugars containing six oxygen atoms per molecule. Dextrose is an example.

hop A climbing vine of the *Cannibicinae* family, whose flower cones are used to give beer its bitterness and characteristic aroma.

hop back A strainer tank used in commercial brewing to filter hops and trub from boiled wort before it is chilled.

hordein One of the two principal protein groups of barley. It is largely broken down into amino acids during mashing.

hot break The rapid coagulation of proteins and resins, assisted by the hops, which occurs after a sustained period of boiling.

humulene One of the most plentiful of the many chemicals which give hops their characteristic aroma.

husk The outer covering of barley or other grains. May impart a rough, bitter taste to beer if sparging is carried out incorrectly.

hydrolysis The enzyme reaction of the breakdown of proteins and carbohydrates.

hydrometer Glass instrument used in brewing to measure the specific gravity of beer and wort.

I

IBU (International Bittering Unit) The accepted method of expressing hop bitterness in beer. Ppm of dissolved iso-alpha acids present in beer. *See also* "International Bittering Units" in **Section 17–2.**

infusion Mash technique of the simplest type used to make all kinds of English ales and stouts. Features a single temperature rest, rather than a series of gradually increasing steps common in other mashing styles.

iodine test Used to determine if a mash in progress has reached starch conversion. An iodine solution turns dark blue or black in the presence of unconverted starch.

ion An electrically charged component of a molecule, which may be one atom, or a combination of atoms. When calcium sulphate, $CaSO_4$, is dissolved in water, it breaks into the ions Ca^{++}, and SO_4.

Irish moss A marine algae, *Chrondus crispus*, that is used during wort boiling to enhance the hot break. Also called carrageen.

isinglass A type of gelatin obtained from the swim bladder of certain types of fish (usually sturgeon), used as a fining agent in ales.

isomerization In brewing, the structural chemical change that takes place in hop bittering resin which allows them to become soluble in wort. Boiling is the agent of this change.

K

kettle Boiling vessel, also known as a copper.

Kieselguhr Diatomaceous earth, a powder of microscopic fossils, used to filter beer.

kilning The process of heating grains to dry them out, or to roast it to varying degrees of darkness. Also applied to the drying of hops.

Kölsch A style of ale made in the city of Köln (Cologne).

Kraeusen The thick foamy head on fermenting beer.

Kraeusening The practice of adding vigorously fermenting young beer to beer in the secondary.

kriek Belgian cherry ale, made from lambic.

L

lactic acid An organic acid sometimes used to assist the acidification of the mash. Also, a by-product of *Lactobacillus*, responsible for the tart flavor of Berliner weisse and some Belgian ales.

Lactobacillus Large class of aerobic bacteria. May be either a spoilage organism, or a consciously added fermenting agent in such products as yogurt, Kolsch, or Berliner weisse.

lactose Milk sugar. Unfermentable by yeast, it is used as a sweetener in milk stout.

lager Beers made with bottom-fermenting yeast and aged at near-freezing temperatures.

lambic A highly distinctive wheat ale made in Belgium. Fermented with wild yeast, it has a sharp, tart taste, and a bright gold color.

lauter tun A great term for a sparging vessel.

light-struck An off-flavor in beer that develops from exposure to short-wavelength (blue) light. Even a short exposure to sunlight can cause this "skunky" odor to develop. Often occurs to beer in green bottles sold from lighted cooler cases. Brown bottles are excellent protection.

°Lintner The commonly used European standard measurement of diastatic activity.

lock Small water-filled device used on a carboy to let CO_2 gas to escape, without allowing air to enter.

°Lovibond Beer and grain color measurement, now superseded by the newer SRM method. *See also* "°Lovibond" in **Section 17–2.**

lupulin The resiny substance in hops containing all the resins and aromatic oils.

M

Maillard browning The caramelization reaction, also known as nonenzymic browning. Responsible for all the roasted color and flavor in beer.

malt Barley or other grain that has been allowed to sprout, then dried or roasted.

malt extract Concentrated commercial preparations of wort. Available as syrup or powder, in a wide range of colors, hopped or unhopped.

malto-dextrin Purified long-chain sugar (dextrin) that is unfermentable by yeast. Used as an additive in extract beers, to add body and richness; 6 to 8 ounces per 5 gallons is typical.

maltose A simple sugar that is by far the predominant fermentable material in wort.

maltotetraose Type of sugar molecule consisting of four molecules of glucose hooked together.

maltotriose Type of sugar molecule consisting of three molecules of glucose hooked together.

Märzen Type of German lager brewed in March for consumption during Oktoberfest. Slightly darker and stronger than standard pale lager.

mash The cooking procedure central to beer-making which converts starch into sugars. Various enzyme reactions occur between 110°–175°F/43°–74°C).

mash tun Vessel in which mashing is carried out. Has a perforated false bottom to allow liquid to drain through.

mead Wine made from honey, sometimes with the addition of malt, fruit, spices, etc.

melanoidins Group of complex color compounds formed by heating sugars and starches in the presence of proteins. Created in brewing during grain roasting and wort boiling.

milling Term for grain grinding or crushing.

millival Measurement of chemicals or minerals expressed relative to actual numbers of molecules rather than weight. This allows calculations of equivalent amounts involved in reactions, which can then be converted back to actual weight.

modification The degree to which malting has been allowed to progress. More modification means less nitrogen, and more accessible starch.

monosaccharide Simple sugars, such as glucose, having only one sugar unit.

mouthfeel Sensory qualities of a beverage other than flavor, such as body and carbonation.

N

nitrogen Element used as a measure of protein level in malt. Important in a free amino state as a yeast nutrient. Also used to pressurize stout.

O

oast house Facility where hops are dried and processed.

oligosaccharides Sugars that contain a few molecules of a monosaccharide, joined.

original gravity (OG) Specific gravity of wort before fermentation as an indicator of potential strength. The decimal point is dropped. *See also* "Original Gravity" in **Section 17–2.**

oxidation Chemical reaction that occurs between oxygen and various components in beer. In homebrewing, air trapped in the bottle is the culprit, and the resulting off-flavor resembles the smell of wet paper or cardboard.

oxygen Element important in yeast metabolism, especially during startup. Also may cause problems in long-term storage. *See also* oxidation.

P

parti-gyle Antiquated brewhouse practice in England. First and strongest runnings become strong ale, second runnings become ordinary beer, and the last and weakest runnings become small beer. Useful technique for homebrewers.

pasteurization The process of sterilizing by heat. Used in almost all canned or bottled commercial beer.

pellicle A film that forms on the surface of liquids being fermented with certain wild yeast and bacteria. A sign of infection in beer, but technically speaking, top-fermenting yeast has a pellicle, too.

pentosans Polymers of pentose, a five-sided sugar, found in barley as gums.

pentose A group of simple sugars having five carbon molecules. Less common in beer than hexose. Includes arabinose and xylose.

peptidase An enzyme that breaks apart proteins during the early stages of the mash. Most effective around 122°F/50°C.

peptide Short fragment of a protein. Also the bond holding amino acids into chains of protein.

peptonization Alternate name for proteolysis.

pH (percent hydrion) Logarithmic scale used to express the level of acidity and alkalinity in a solution. 7 = neutral; 1 = most acid; 14 = most alkaline. Each step on the scale represents a tenfold change from the previous one.

pin mill Type of grinding mill used in grain and coffee mills. Only occasionally used in commercial brewing, usually to grind green malt.

pitching The act of adding yeast to wort to start fermentation.

°Plato European and American scale of gravity based on a percentage of pure sugar in the wort. A newer, more accurate version of the Balling scale. *See also* "°Plato" in **Section 17–2.**

polishing Final ultrafiltration prior to bottling in commercial brewing. Renders beer sparkling clear, but unfortunately polishing is not too practical for the homebrewer.

Polyclar The tradename for a material used to clear beer. Consists of microscopic plastic beads that remove chill-haze by adsorbtion.

polymer Chemical molecule made of the repetition of smaller basic units. In brewing, they are common as polysaccharides and polypeptides.

polypeptide Chain of amino acids. Includes proteins and other related molecules.

polyphenol Tannins, important in beer in connection with protein coagulation and chill-haze.

polysaccharide Polymers of simple sugars. Includes a range from complex sugars through dextrins, up to starches.

ppb Parts per billion. 1 microgram per liter.

ppm Parts per million. 1 milligram per liter.

precipitation A chemical process, involving a material coming out of solution.

primary fermentation Initial rapid stage of yeast activity when maltose and other simple sugars are metabolized. Lasts about a week.

priming The process of adding sugar to beer before bottling or racking to kegs. Restarts fermentation, pressurizing with CO_2 gas.

protein Complex nitrogenous organic molecules important in all living matter. In beer, involved in enzyme activity, yeast nutrition, head retention, and colloidal stability. During mashing, boiling, and cooling, they may be broken apart, and/or precipitated.

proteinase Enzyme complex that breaks proteins apart into smaller, more soluble units. Most active at 122°F/50°C.

protein rest During mashing, a 120°–125°F/26°–52°C temperature rest for 20 minutes or more to eliminate proteins which cause chill-haze.

proteolysis The breaking up or digestion of proteins by enzymes that occurs in the mash around 122°F/50°C.

proteolytic enzymes Enzymes naturally present in barley and malt that have the power to break up proteins in the mash.

Q

quarter An English measure of malt equal to 336 pounds; of barley, 448 pounds. Only the Queen knows why.

R

racking Transferring the fermenting beer from one vessel to another to avoid tainting by off-flavors that result from autolysis.

raffinose A simple sugar, important in a test to differentiate ale and lager yeast, as only lager yeast can ferment it completely.

Rauchbier A dark lager beer made in Germany from smoked malts.

Reinheitsgebot German beer purity law, enacted in 1516, which limits beer ingredients to malt, water, hops and yeast. Wheat beers are also permitted.

rocky Term used to describe the texture of head on beer, especially during primary fermentation.

roller mill The preferred malt grinding device. Crushes the starchy middle of malt between rollers without pulverizing the husks. For the homebrewer, only available in homemade form.

ropiness Spoilage condition causing beer to be thick and slimy. Certain bacteria produce gums, which cause this condition.

runnings Wort that is drained from the mash during sparging.

runoff The draining of wort from the mash during sparging.

S

Saccharomyces Scientific genus name of yeast used in brewing. Except for the wild yeasts of Belgium, only two species are used—*Saccharomyces cerevesiae*, which is top fermenting, and *Saccharomyces carlsbergensis*, which is bottom fermenting, or lager yeast.

saccharification The conversion of starch to sugars in the mash through enzyme activity.

salt Minerals present in water that have various effects on the brewing process.

secondary fermentation Slow phase of yeast activity during which complex sugars are metabolized. May take weeks or months.

set mash Condition that sometimes develops during sparging which makes runoff difficult. Too much fine flour as a result of improper grinding is often the culprit. Mashes with a high percentage of un-malted grains often have this problem.

six-row A type of barley most often grown in the United States and used in the production of American-style beers. High diastatic activity makes it ideal for the mashing of corn or rice adjuncts, which have no starch-converting power of their own.

skunky Faint "rubbery" aroma caused by overexposure of beer to light. *See also* light-struck.

sparge Process of rinsing mashed grains with hot water to recover all available wort sugars.

specific gravity A measurement of density, expressed relative to the density of water. Used in brewing to follow the course of fermentation.

SRM (Standard Reference Method) Measurement of beer color, expressed as 10 times the optical density (absorbance) of beer, as measured at 346 nm in a spectrophotometer. Nearly the same as the older Lovibond color series, measured with a set of specially colored glass samples. *See also* "SRM" in **Section 17–2.**

starch Complex carbohydrates, long polymers of sugars, which are converted into sugars during mashing.

starch haze Cloudiness in beer due to suspended starch particles. Usually caused by: (1) Incorrect mash temperature resulting in incomplete saccharification, or (2) Sparging temperatures over 180°F/82°C, which can dissolve residual starch from the mash.

starter Small amount of fermenting beer, prepared in advance, then added to the main batch. Allows for a quicker beginning of fermentation.

steely A quality of raw or undermodified malt in which portions of the grains are hard and "flinty." These hard ends resist milling and saccharification.

steep The process of soaking barley or wheat in water to begin malting.

steinbier Type of beer brewed in Germany, using hot stones to boil the wort.

step mash Mashing technique using controlled temperature steps.

strike The addition of hot water to the crushed malt to raise the temperature and begin mashing.

sucrose Cane sugar, a disaccharide consisting of one unit of dextrose, and one unit of fructose. Passable, but not particularly well suited to brewing.

T

tannin Polyphenols, complex organic materials with a characteristic astringent flavor, extracted from hops and the husks of barley. Most noticeable in the last runnings.

teig Gray sludgy protein material that settles on top of the mash during sparging.

terpenes Group of flavor chemicals forming the main component of hop oils.

tetrasaccharide Sugar type containing four molecules of a simple sugar linked together.

torrefication Process of rapidly heating grain so it puffs up like popcorn. Commonly applied to barley and wheat. Often used in British pale ales.

trisaccharide Sugar molecule consisting of three simple sugars linked together.

trub Coagulated protein and hop resin sludge which precipitates out of wort during boiling and again at chilling.

two-row The most common type of barley for brewing everywhere in the world except America. Has a lower protein content than six-row. Generally considered to have a better flavor than six-row.

U

underback In commercial breweries, a receiving tub for wort drained from the mash.

underlet The addition of water to a mash-in-progress from below so the grains float a bit. Encourages quicker and more thorough mixing.

undermodified Applies to malt that has not been allowed to malt to an advanced stage.

W

weiss Term applied to German wheat ales of the Bavarian, or Suddeutsch, style.

weisse German word meaning "white," applied to the tart wheat beers of the Berliner style.

weizen German word for "wheat." Synonymous with weiss.

whirlpool Device used to separate hops and trub from wort after boiling. Wort is stirred in a circular motion and and collects in the center of the whirlpool. Clear wort is drained from the edge.

wind malt A type of very pale malt dried in the sun or by exposure to the air, without kilning. Once used in the production of witbier.

witte Belgian word for "white," a type of wheat beer brewed in the north, around Louvain. Often spiced with coriander and Curaçao.

wort Unfermented beer, the sugar-laden liquid obtained from the mash.

wort chiller Heat exchanger used to rapidly cool wort from near boiling to pitching temperature.

X–Y–Z

xylose A pentose sugar present in small quantities in wort. Relatively unimportant in brewing.

yeast Large class of microscopic fungi, several species of which are used in brewing.

Yorkshire (stone) **square** English system of fermentation using shallow, square, traditionally slate vessels for fermentation. Still in use by the Samuel Smith Brewery in Tadcaster, Yorkshire.

zymurgy The science of fermentation, used as the name of the magazine of the American Homebrew Association. The last, and coolest, word in the English dictionary.

A label is your beer's birth certificate. Computer programs such as FreeHand and Adobe Photoshop let you create professional-looking designs.

Homebrew labels courtesty of Liberty Malt Supply Company.

REFERENCES
& RESOURCES

17

FAHRENHEIT TO CELSIUS

°F	°C
212	100
210	
	95
200	
	90
190	85
180	80
170	75
160	70
150	65
140	60
130	55
	50
120	45
110	40
100	35
90	30
80	25
70	20
60	15
50	10
40	5
32	0

ORIGINAL GRAV TO °PLATO

O.G.	°P
1100	24
1095	23
1090	22
	21
1085	20
1080	19
1075	18
1070	17
1065	16
1060	15
1055	14
1050	13
1045	12
1040	11
1035	10
1030	9
1025	8
1020	7
1015	6
1010	5
1005	4
1000	3
	2
	1
	0

OG TO ALCOHOL POTENTIAL

O.G.	% Vol.
1100	
1095	13.0
1090	12.0
1085	11.0
1080	
1075	10.0
1070	9.0
1065	
1060	8.0
1055	7.0
1050	
1045	6.0
1040	5.0
1035	
1030	4.0
1025	3.0
1020	
1015	2.0
1010	1.0
1005	
1000	0.0

*POTENTIAL

GRAMS TO OUNCES

Gm.	Oz.
200	7.0
190	6.5
180	6.0
170	
160	5.5
150	5.0
140	4.5
130	
120	4.0
110	3.5
100	
90	3.0
80	2.5
70	
60	2.0
50	1.5
40	1.0
30	
20	0.5
10	0
0	

LITERS TO GALLONS

Ltr.	Gal.
100	26
95	25
90	24
	23
85	22
80	21
75	20
	19
70	18
65	17
60	16
	15
55	14
50	13
45	12
	11
40	10
35	9
30	8
	7
25	6
20	5
15	4
	3
10	2
5	1
0	0

ALC % VOL TO ALC % WT

% Vol.	% Wt.
9.0	7.0
8.0	6.0
7.0	5.0
6.0	4.0
5.0	3.0
4.0	
3.0	2.0
2.0	
1.0	1.0
0.0	0.0

Use these scales for a quick translation between various commonly-used measurements. Just find the number you wish to convert, and read across the scale to the other measurement.

ALCOHOL

The percentage of alcohol in beer may be expressed two ways: percentage by volume or percentage by weight. Since alcohol is less dense than water, % volume is a higher number than % weight, for any given concentration. % weight x 1.267 = % volume. % volume is the European and Canadian measurement. % weight is the traditional American scale, but the new labels will be in % volume.

ATTENUATION

This is a measure of the thoroughness of mashing and fermentation, determined by the amount of sugars and dextrins left in the beer when fermentation is complete.

Apparent Attenuation—The measure of the difference between the original gravity and the terminal gravity, expressed as a percentage of the original gravity. It is not a totally accurate description because the lower density of alcohol makes terminal gravities lower than they would be by elimination of sugars only, resulting in attenuation figures that are erroneously high. A rule-of-thumb is to multiply apparent attenuation by 0.816 to get real attenuation. This is not totally accurate—the real calculation is much more complicated—but it will get you as close as you need to be for homebrewing purposes.

Real Attenuation—Usually used by breweries, this is a more accurate measurement of attenuation in beer. Real attenuation is measured by heating a sample of finished beer until all the alcohol is boiled off. Water is then added to make the sample back to the original volume, and its specific gravity is measured.

Real attenuation is usually expressed as the difference, in °Plato, between the original and terminal gravities. Percent of real attenuation is more useful for comparing different beer types, and may be figured by dividing the original gravity by the difference between original and terminal gravities.

GRAVITY

The measure of the sugars present in wort before it is fermented. There are many systems in use.

°Plato—The system used everywhere except Great Britain and Belgium. The numbers of the scale represent the percentage of sugar in the liquid. This is the same scale that the winemakers use, but call Brix.

°Balling—An earlier, less accurate scale, similar to the more accurate Plato system.

OG (original gravity)—The British system of measuring wort gravity, expressed as the specific gravity with the decimal point removed. When doing calculations with OG, be sure to remove the "1" at the front, or the numbers won't work out.

Belgian Degrees—System of gravity measurement traditionally used in Belgium. Expressed as a shortened form of original gravity, wherein 1070 becomes 7.0°Belgian, 1050 = 5.0, etc.

Brewer's Pounds—Gravity measurement based on the number of pounds of extract per (British) barrel of wort. A British barrel equals 43.2 U.S. gallons.

BITTERNESS

Homebrew Bittering Units—This is a simple way of expressing the bittering power of a beer recipe. It is simply the weight, in ounces of the hops used, times their alpha acid content divided by the number of gallons in the batch being brewed. As hop utilization decreases with shorter boiling times, you must assign an arbitrary cutoff point, and any hops added for less than 20 minutes are assumed to contribute no bitterness (even though that's not actually true).

This HBU number is commonly used in other homebrew texts, but not in this book. Following HBUs out the window may cause you to seriously over- or underestimate the bitterness of your beers. And generally, it will lead you to use far fewer hops towards the end of the boil than you really might want.

International Bittering Units—The number used commercially to describe the bitterness of any given beer. It is expressed as the parts-per-million of isomerized alpha acids present in beer as determined by laboratory analysis.

IBUs can be roughly estimated by applying a conversion factor to Homebrew Bittering Units. Although different people use different numbers for homebrew purposes, I have settled on a constant of 17, which assumes a utilization of 23 percent, which seems to produce bittering taste levels in homebrews that are in accord with their commercial counterparts. This holds true for hops boiled for an hour or more in normal gravity worts. But there are many factors that affect the bitterness of beer and you may want to estimate up or down from this, according to the type of beer you're brewing. For more accurate prediction, use the **Hop Utilization charts, 8–4** and **8–5**.

COLOR

Measuring beer color is a complex subject and predicting it is even more vexing. The difficulty is that beer does not obey Beer's Law: Beer does not become uniformly darker as more dark stuff is added. The large molecules that give beer its color tend to clump together at higher concentrations, diminishing their coloring power.

°Lovibond—An old scale of measurement of malt and beer color based on a series of tinted glass filters that were used as a visually determined standard of wort, beer, and grain color. The name lives on in the color applied to malt and grain, although beer color is no longer measured visually.

°SRM—The new American standard of color measurement, which roughly corresponds to the old Lovibond scale. °SRM is expressed as 10 times the optical density of the sample at 430 nanometers measured in a 1/2" thick cell. A spectrophotometer is used to do the measurement. The 430 nm wavelength corresponds to a deep blue color, the range at which beers are most different from one another.

Grain color is measured by the same technique, but the wort is extracted in a laboratory mashing process called the Congress mash.

°EBC—The European measurement system for describing the color of malt and beer. Various formulas have been given for translating between EBC and SRM, but all are rather flawed. Nevertheless, here they are:

EBC color = 2.65 x SRM - 1.2

SRM color = 0.375 x EBC + 0.46

This formula is accurate to about 10, but then goes haywire at the dark end of the color scale. 500°Lovibond black malt calculates to 1325, but is actually 1150° EBC. If you need only a rough measure, Lovibond/SRM is about half of EBC.

Homebrew Color Units—A very rough measure of beer color created by multiplying the SRM color by the total number of pounds of grain, then dividing by the total number of gallons. This is a useful, if inaccurate, technique. At low colors the scale corresponds very roughly to °SRM. By 50 HCU, you get numbers that are twice as dark as the beer would measure. At 300 HCU, the beer would really measure at 100, only one-third of its calculated value. See the scale at the bottom of **Section 3–1, Beer Color & Gravity**.

CONGRESS TEST MASH PROCEDURE

1. 50 grams of finely crushed malt are added to 200 ml distilled water at 45°–46°C (113°–115°F). This is stirred for 30 minutes and maintained at 45°C (113°F).

2. The temperature is raised 1°C per minute (over 25 minutes) to 70°C (158°F). 100 ml distilled water at 70°C (178°F) is added. The temperature is maintained for 1 hour. Any measurement of time to conversion begins at this time.

3. At the end of the hour, the total weight in the mash container is increased to 450 grams.

4. The mash is put into a funnel with filter paper and filtered. The first, cloudy portion is run back through.

5. The mash is then ready for analysis.

Note: For color determinations, diatomaceous earth (0.1–0.2 percent) may be added to the wort, which is then filtered again to remove any haze that might distort the color readings. Centrifuging the turbid wort accomplishes the same thing. HOMEBREW COMPARISON: 50 grams of malt plus 400 ml water is equivalent to 5.23 pounds of malt per 5-gallon batch, or 1.046 pounds per gallon (1 pound + 0.74 ounce).

Even with all this inaccuracy, I would argue that this method is worth using. Because the SRM scale is logarithmic, an error of 20 percent isn't as bad as it sounds. Whether it's 10 or 12, your pale ale is still pale; at 27 or 37, your porter's still porter-y.

HECTOLITER (100 Liters)	26.418 U.S. gallons 0.387 U.S. barrels 21.998 British gallons 0.611 British barrels
LITER	0.01 hectoliter 1000 milliliters 1 kilogram of water 33.815 U.S. fluid ounces 1.057 U.S. quart 0.2642 U.S. gallons 35.196 British fluid ounces 0.8799 British quart 0.2199 British gallons
KILOGRAM (1000 grams)	2.20462 pounds 35.274 ounces
GRAM	0.0022 pounds 0.03527 ounces 15.432 grains
U.S. BARREL	31.5 U.S. gallons 1.924 hectoliters 0.7291 British barrels
U.S. GALLON	128 ounces 3.7853 liters 0.8327 British gallons 8.345 pounds of water
U.S. QUART	32 U.S. ounces 0.9463 liters 946.3 milliliters 0.8327 British quarts
FLUID OUNCE	0.03125 US quart 0.025 British quart 0.02957 liters 29.57 milliliters
BRITISH BARREL	36 British gallons 43.2 U.S. gallons 1.6365 hectoliters 2 kilderkins/4 firkins
BRITISH GALLON	160 British fluid ounces 1.201 U.S. gallons 4.546 liters
BRITISH QUART	1.201 U.S. quart 1.365 liters
BARRELS:	1 butt = 2 hogsheads = 3 British barrels
POUND	0.45359 kilogram 453.59 grams 256 drams 7000 grains 0.1198 gallons of water

HUNDRED-WEIGHT (CWT)	(U.S.) 100 pounds (British) 112 pounds	
OUNCE (Avdp)	0.0625 pound 28.35 grams	
GRAIN	64.80 milligrams	
CUBIC FOOT	7.481 U.S. gallons 6.229 British gallons 28.317 liters	

1 ATMOSPHERE OF PRESSURE
14.70 pounds per square inch

1 POUND PER SQUARE INCH
0.068 atmospheres of pressure

BRITISH BARRELS (water) PER QUARTER (malt)	0.386 U.S. quart per pound 0.321 British quart per pound	
BUSHEL	U.S. malt U.S. barley U.K. malt U.K. barley	34 pounds 48 pounds 40 pounds 50 pounds
QUARTER	Malt 336. pounds Barley 448 pounds	
ALCOHOL % VOLUME	1.267 x % weight	
ALCOHOL % WEIGHT	0.789 x % volume	
DENSITY OF WATER	1.000 (specific gravity)	
DENSITY OF ETHYL ALCOHOL	0.789 (specific gravity)	
ALCOHOL BOILING POINT	173°F/78.5°C	
°F to °C	Subtract 32, then multiply by 5/9	
°C to °F	Multiply by 9/5, then add 32	

TEMPERATURE

| 35°F/1.7°C | 40°F/4.4°C | 50°F/10°C | 60°F/15.5°C | 70°F/21°C | 80°F/26.5°C | 90°F/32°C | 100°F/37.5°C | 110°F/43°C | 120°F/1.7°C | 130°F/54°C | 140°F/60°C |

ACTUAL   G R A V I T Y   OBSERVED

HOW TO USE THIS CHART

This chart compensates for the fact that the density of liquid changes with temperature, giving erroneous readings at temperatures other than those for which the instrument is calibrated. Liquid expands when hot, lowering its density, causing low readings. Liquid is denser when cool, giving high readings.

To Use: (1) Measure the gravity and jot it down. (2) Take the temperature of the wort or beer tested. (3) Find the vertical line on the chart closest to the measurement temperature. (4) Find the observed gravity on the right side of the chart. Follow the gray curve to where your vertical (temperature) line is. (5) Trace across horizontally

(ignore the curves now) to the scale at the far left of the scale. The number on the left-hand scale is your actual gravity, corrected for temperature errors.

This chart is for hydrometers calibrated at 60°F/15.5°C. With others, you must make some changes. Write in the new calibration temperature under the heavy vertical line at 60° F. Then, renumber the other vertical lines 10°F apart, starting with your calibration temperature. If your hydrometer's stated temperature is 68°F, the heavy vertical line becomes 68° F. The line immediately to its right becomes 78° F, the next 88° F, and so on. To the left, subtract 10° F: 58° F, 48° F, etc.

YELLOW PAGES HEADINGS

There are lots of great sources for useful home-brew items, especially if you live in a big city. Check the Business-to-Business section in your trusty yellow pages for places in your locality.

Restaurant Supply Shops

A good source for many useful items, including plastic tubs, long-handled spoons, and other fascinating and even useful items. Every modestly sized city has one, and they'll usually sell to anybody, not just commercial accounts.

Wire Cloth

Screen wire is available in a bewildering variety of sizes and materials, such as stainless steel and bronze. You can buy small pieces, but be warned, the stuff isn't cheap.

Scrap Metal

Look for one that specifically lists stainless steel (or other exotics). Usually for a buck or two a pound, you can find some truly useful things—sheets, tubes, rods and other stranger stuff.

Hardware Stores

Valves, fittings, hoses and other useful brewing items can be had at the trusty neighborhood hardware stores. Many of the best items are hidden away in drawers—stainless steel nuts and bolts, for example. Check out the ball-valves and hose barbs.

Industrial Surplus

A gold mine if you can find one. If it's used in industry, it will eventually show up in one of these places. Chicago has a wonderful one, with an entertaining catalogue:

American Science & Surplus
601 Linden Place
Evanston, IL 60202

Flea Markets

All kinds of stuff, but totally unpredictable. A good bet for bottle cappers, scales, and carboys of various types. If you get lucky, you might find a barrel, tapping equipment, breweriana, a grain grinder. I even found a nice microscope at one. You need to keep going to them to really find what you need.

Beverage Dispensing Equipment

Soda Fountain Equipment

These places can usually get you set up for home kegging operations. Used stuff is common.

Police Auctions

A good place to pick up a laboratory gram balance for a great price. Strange, but it makes sense if you think about it.

Health Food Stores

Good source for exotic grains—rice, bulgur, barley, wheat, oats, millet, buckwheat, and so on. Don't overdo it with specialty grains. Quantities over 20 percent can cause mash conversion problems and very slow sparging.

Home Wine- and Beermaking Shops

Homebrew shops should be the first place you look for all your regular brewing needs. In addition to supplies, these shops can be great sources for information and contact with other home-brewers in your area.

Maltsters, Malting Companies

Although accustomed to selling malt by train-car loads, some maltsters will now sell smaller quantities. Fifty-pound bags are the standard, usually loaded 500 or 1,000 pounds to a skid. Most companies will ship this amount and some will even mix various types on a skid. If you're fortunate enough to be able to drive to a malting company, you might even be able to buy individual bags. Get the club together because you can save 50 to 75 percent off the retail price. Your local homebrew merchant might even order this way, if you guarantee a certain amount of sales.

Libraries

Your local public library is the first place to look, but unless you live in a big city, there may not be much on the shelves relevant to brewing. University and commercial libraries are other places to check. Most books, however exotic, can be obtained by an interlibrary loan program.

Note: Books marked with an asterisk* are suitable for beginning brewers or those just interested in beer and should be available from your bookseller or homebrew supplier, although you may have to special-order some of them.

Anderson, Will. *Beer U.S.A.* Dobbs Ferry, NY: Morgan & Morgan. ISBN 0-87100-247-7.*

—*From Beer to Eternity.* Lexington, MA: The Stephen Greene Press. ISBN 0-8289-0555-X.*

Arnold, John P. *Origin and History of Beer and Brewing.* Chicago: Alumni Association of the Wahl-Henius Institute, 1911.

Aspinall, Gerald. *Polysaccharides.* Oxford: Pergamon Press, 1970.

Bickerdyke, John. *The Curiosities of Ale and Beer.* London: Spring House, reprinted in 1965 from the original 1889 edition.

Clerck, Jean de. *A Textbook of Brewing.* Translated by Kathleen Barton-Wright. London: Chapman & Hall Ltd., 1987.

Corran, H.S. *A History of Brewing.* London: David & Charles Ltd. ISBN 0-7153-6735-8.

Downard, William L. *Dictionary of the History of the American Brewing and Distilling Industries.* Westport, CT: Greenwood Press, 1980. ISBN 0-313-21330-5.

Eckhardt, Fred. *A Treatise on Lager Beers.* Portland, OR: Hobby Winemaker. ISBN 0-9606302-3-6.*

—*Essentials of Beer Style.* Portland, OR: Fred Eckhardt Associates, 1989. ISBN 0-9606302-7-9.*

Finch, Christopher. *Beer: A Connoisseur's Guide to the World's Best.* New York: Abbeville Press, 1989. ISBN 0-89659-913-2.*

Findlay, W.P.K., Editor. *Modern Brewing Technology.*

Glover, Brian. *CAMRA Dictionary of Beer.* London: Longman Group, Ltd., 1985. ISBN 0-582-89261-9.*

Guinard, Jean Xavier. *Lambic (Classic Beer Styles Series).* Boulder, CO: Brewers Publications, 1990. ISBN 0-937381-22-5.

Heath, Henry B. & Gary Reineccius. *Flavor Chemistry and Technology.* Westport, CN: AVI Publishing, 1986. ISBN 0-87055-517-0.

Hind, H. Lloyd. *Brewing, Science & Practise.* London: Chapman & Hall Ltd.

Hough, J.S. *The Biotechnology of Malting and Brewing.* Cambridge: Cambridge University Press, 1972. ISBN 0-521-25672-0.

Hough, J.S., Briggs, R. Stevens. *Malting & Brewing Science.* London: Chapman & Hall Ltd.

Hudson, J.R. *Development of Brewing Analysis.* London: The Institute of Brewing, 1960.

Jackson, Michael. *Beer Companion.* Philadelphia, PA: Running Press. 1993. ISBN 1-56138-288-4.*

—*The Great Beers of Belgium.* Antwerp, Belgium: CODA, 1992. ISBN 90-5373-005-2.*

—*The Simon and Schuster Pocket Guide to Beer.* New York: Simon & Schuster. ISBN 0-671-72915-2.*

—*The New World Guide to Beer.* Philadelphia, PA: Running Press, 1988. ISBN 0-89471-884-3.*

Jefferies, E.J. *Brewing: Theory and Practice.*

Luers, Heinrich. *Die Wiessenschaftlichen Grund Lagen von Malzerei und Brauerei.* 1950.

Line, Dave. *The Big Book of Brewing.* Andover, Hants, U.K: Standard Press (Andover) Ltd., 1974.*

—*Brewing Beers Like Those You Buy.* Andover, Hants, U.K: Standard Press Ltd., 1977.*

Lohr, E.W. and S.K. Love. *The Industrial Utility of Public Water Supplies in the United States, 1952.* Washington, DC: U.S. Government Printing Office.

Margalith, Pinhas Z. *Flavor Microbiology.* Springfield, IL: Charles C. Thomas.

Master Brewers Association of the Americas. *The Practical Brewer.* Madison, WI: MBAA, 1977.

Miller, Dave. *The Complete Handbook of Home Brewing.* Pownal, VT: Graden Way Publishing. 1988. ISBN 0-88266-517-0.

Noonan, Gregory J. *Brewing Lager Beer.* Boulder, CO: Brewers Publications. ISBN 0-937381-01-2.

Noonan, Gregory J. *Scotch Ale.* Boulder, CO: Brewers Publications.

Papazian, Charlie. *The New Complete Joy of Homebrewing.* New York: Avon Books, 1991.*

Protz, Roger. *The European Beer Almanac.* Moffat, Scotland: Lochar Publishing, 1991. ISBN 0-948403-28-4.

—*The Real Ale Drinker's Almanac.* Moffat, Scotland: Lochar Publishing, 1989. ISBN 0-948403-18-7.

Rajotte, Pierre. *Belgian Ale (Classic Beer Styles Series).* Boulder, CO: Brewers Publications, 1992.

Robertson, James D. *The Connoisseur's Guide to Beer.* Ottawa, IL: Jameson Books. ISBN 0-915463-05-9-1.*

Ross-Mackenzie, John. *A Standard Manual of Brewing and Malting.* New York: Van Nostrand.

Steiner, S.S. Co. *Steiner's Guide to American Hops.* S.S. Steiner, 1973, 1986. ISBN 73-81457.

Sykes, Walter J. & Arthur R. Ling. *The Principles & Practice of Brewing.* 1907.

Thausing, Julius E. *The Theory & Practice of the Preparation of Malt and the Fabrication of Beer.* Vienna, 1882.

van Remoortere, Julien. *Belgisch Bier.* Aartselaar, Belgium: Keyser, 1895. ISBN 90-6798-012-9.

Wahl, Robert & Max Henius. *A Handy Book of Brewing.* Chicago: Wahl-Henius Institute, 1901.

Yenne, Bill. *Beers of North America.* New York: Gallery Books. ISBN 0-8317-0725-9.*

—*Beer Labels of the World.* Secaucus, NJ: Chartwell Books. 1993. ISBN 1-55521-857-1.

VIDEOS

Beer & Ale. Seattle: St. Clair Production Company. 1994. ISBN 1-882949-06-4.*

The Beer Hunter. Michael Jackson. Three-volume set. The Discovery Channel. 1989.*

Beer Brewed at Yorkshire's Oldest Brewery. Seattle: Alephenalia Publications.

PERIODICALS

Alephenalia Beer News. Lively broadsheet published by Merchant du Vin, 140 Lakeside Avenue, Suite 300, Seattle, WA 98122-6538.

Ale Street News. Bulging tabloid newspaper serving the whole East Coast. P.O. Box 5339, Bergenfield, NJ 07621.

All About Beer. General wide-world-of-beer magazine, published six times a year by Chautauqua, Inc., 1627 Marion Avenue, Durham, NC 27705.

American Brewer. Published by Bill Owens of Buffalo Bill's Brewpub. Very hip, good technical info. 1080 B Street, Hayward, CA 94541.

Barley Corn. The first East Coast brewspaper. P.O. Box 2328, Falls Church, VA 22042.

Beer, The Magazine. Bimonthly glossy magazine of general beer interest. Published by Bill Owens. 1080 B Street, Hayward, CA 94541.

The Brewers Bulletin. Weekly beer industry newspaper, with the latest quotes on boxcar-loads of grain. P.O. Box 906, Woodstock, IL 60098.

Brewers Digest. Big-beer industry bible. Published monthly, affiliated with Siebel. Send inquiries to *Brewers Digest*, 4049 W Peterson Avenue, Chicago, IL 60646.

Brewing Techniques. High-quality magazine dedicated to serious amateurs and microbrewers alike. New Wine Press, P.O. Box, 3222, Eugene, OR 97403.

Celebrator. West Coast brewspaper, published bimonthly. Write: 4747 Hopyard Road, Suite 100, Pleasanton, CA 94566.

Hoppenings. Fat beer and brewing newsletter, published more-or-less bimonthly by the Chicago Beer Society, P.O. Box 1057, LaGrange Park, IL 60525.

Jobson's Beer Industry Marketing. Just what it sounds like. Useful if you are thinking about starting a mid- to large-size brewery. 352 Park Avenue South, New York, NY 10010.

Liberty Malt News. Illustrated newspaper and catalog featuring the best in malt hops, hardware and books on beer. Liberty Malt Supply Company, 140 Lakeside Avenue, Suite 300, Seattle, WA 98122-6538.

Midwest Beer Notes. Upper Midwest brewspaper, published bimonthly by Mike Urseth. 6227 Third Avenue South, Richfield MN 55423.

Healthy Drinking. Incisive anti-neo-prohibitionist journal published by Gene Ford. 4714 NE 50th Street, Seattle, WA 98105-2908.

The Northwest Beer Journal. Bimonthly microbrew beer newspaper. 2677 Fircrest Drive SE, Port Orchard, WA 98366.

The New Brewer. Microbrewery trade magazine, published by the Association of Brewers. Technical material that's not too heavy for advanced homebrewers. P.O. Box 287, Boulder, CO 80306.

The Pint Post. Quarterly newsletter from the Microbrew Appreciation Society. Cadillac Pins, 12345 Lake City Way NE, Suite 159, Seattle, WA 98125.

Southern Draft Brew News. Beer tabloid, southern style. P.O. Box 180425, Casselberry, FL 32718-0425.

Southwest Brewing News. Free monthly newspaper. 11405 Evening Star Drive, Austin, TX 78739.

World Beer Review. Bimonthly beer newsletter, focusing on high-quality beers. P.O. Box 71, Clemson, SC 29633.

Yankee Brew News. Free quarterly beer newspaper serving—you guessed it—New England. Brasseur Publications, P.O. Box 8053, JFK Station, Boston, MA 02114.

Zymurgy. Homebrewing-oriented magazine, published five times a year by the American Homebrewers Association, P.O. Box 1679, Boulder, CO 80306.

ASSOCIATIONS

American Homebrewers Association. Part of the Association of Brewers, this is the only significant national organization for homebrewers. Publishers of *Zymurgy*. P.O. Box 1679, Boulder, CO 80306.

American Breweriana Association. Brewery collectibles club. P.O. Box 11157, Pueblo, CO 81001.

American Society of Brewing Chemists. 3340 Pilot Knob Road, St. Paul, MN 55121.

Association of Brewers. Microbrewery trade association. P.O. Box 1670, Boulder, CO 80306.

Beer Can Collectors of America. Brewery collectibles not strictly limited to cans. 747 Merus Court, Fenton, MO 63026.

Beer Drinkers of America. Broad-based beer interest club. 150 Paularino Avenue, Suite 190, Costa Mesa, CA 92626. (Tel: 1-800-441-BEER.)

The Beer Institute. Beer industry lobbying group. Focused on the big guys. 1225 I Street NW, Suite 825, Washington, DC 20005.

Beer Judge Certification Program (BJCP). Administers homebrew judges in a tested, ranked system. Contact BJCP Administrator, American Homebrew Association, P.O. Box 1679, Boulder, CO 80306-1679.

Campaign for Real Ale (CAMRA). British ale devotee group. Good newsletter, *What's Brewing*. 34 Alma Road, St. Albans, Hertfordshire AL1 3BW, UK.

Home Wine & Beer Trade Association. Homebrew suppliers organization, cosponsors of the Beer Judge Certification Program.

Institute of Brewing. Venerable brewing institute and publishers. 33 Clarges Street, London W1Y BEE, UK.

Master Brewers Association of the Americas. Professional technical society, publishes *MBAA Technical Quarterly*. 4513 Vernon Blvd., Suite 202, Madison, WI 53705.

The Microbrew Appreciation Society. Microbrew-interest organization in the Pacific Northwest. Publishes *The Pint Post*, c/o Pink Cadillac Pins, 12345 Lake City Way NE, Suite 159, Seattle, WA 98125.

SCHOOLS

American School for Malting & Brewing Science & Technology, University of California, Davis. A variety of short and long sessions focusing on all aspects of brewing practice and theory. Some sessions are appropriate for homebrewers. Contact the Registration Office, University Extension, University of California, Davis, CA 95616-8727.

The Siebel Institute of Technology. Comprehensive program of brewing education. Short and long classes, as well as shorter seminars. Some classes suitable for advanced homebrewers. Also offers brewing analytical lab services. 4055 West Peterson Avenue, Chicago, IL 60646.

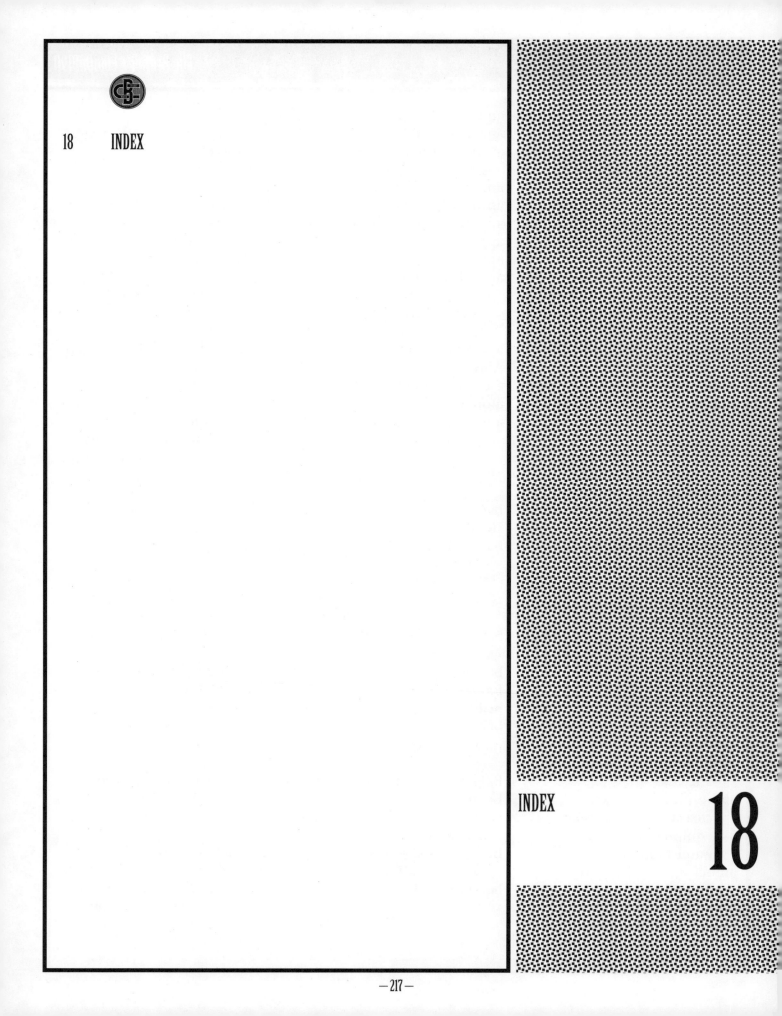

18   INDEX

INDEX

18

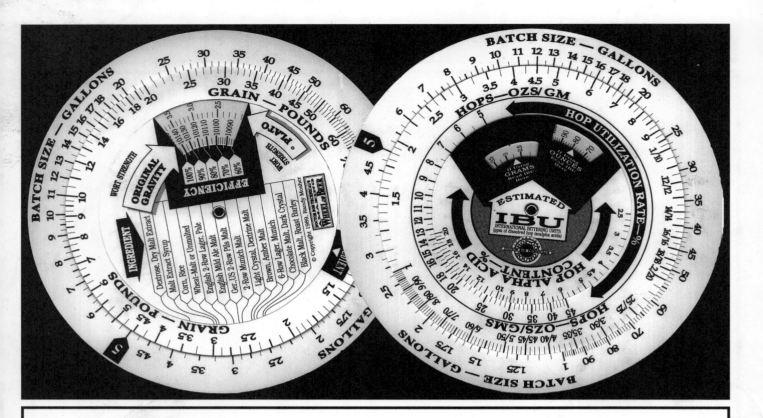

These two useful additions to *The Brewer's Companion* were created by homebrewer, artist and writer, Randy Mosher, H.B. A graphic designer and beer consultant, Randy writes for *Brewing Techniques, Zymurgy,* and *Beer, The Magazine,* and other beer publications.

AMAZING WHEEL OF BEER——Wort Gravity Calculator

The Wheel of Beer is an easy-to-use slide rule-type calculator that allows you to accurately predict the amount of gravity you'll get from 20 different malts, grains, and extracts. Works from 1 to 100 gallons, from 1 to 100 pounds. Takes into account the efficiency at which you are mashing. Indispensable for all grain brewers, highly useful for extract brewers, as well. Just line up pounds with gallons, select the grain, and read the gravity. Who needs computers! Instructions are on the back. Wortproof, beergeek-resistant construction.

HOP-GO-ROUND——Hop IBU Calculator

The Hop-Go-Round simplifies the sometimes-difficult task of estimating the bitterness of hops. Unlike other methods, it takes into account the utilization rate, a critical factor ignored by simpler calculations, such as Homebrew Bittering Units. The back contains a chart to determine utilization of whole or pellet hops at various boil times and gravities. Once utilization has been determined, you line it up with hop alpha acid content on the front. Then, line up ounces or grams against gallons, and read the estimated IBUs (International Bittering Units). Or, work backward from a desired IBU figure. Much simpler than a pocket calculator. Equally useful for extract and all-grain brewers. The same high-quality laminated plastic construction as the Wheel of Beer.

For more information please write:
Alephenalia Publications
140 Lakeside Avenue • Suite 300
Seattle, Washington 98122-6538.

You can order these
and other fine Alephenalia
products and publications by
calling (206) 322-5022.